ELITE ACADEMY COACHING

The Secrets Behind the Development Program for Pep Guardiola's Methodology

**Written by
Darren Bowman**

Published by

ELITE ACADEMY COACHING

The Secrets Behind the Development Program for Pep Guardiola's Methodology

First Published October 2023 by SoccerTutor.com

info@soccertutor.com | www.SoccerTutor.com

UK: 0208 1234 007 | **US:** (305) 767 4443 | **ROTW:** +44 208 1234 007
ISBN: 978-1-910491-65-2

Copyright: SoccerTutor.com Limited © 2023. All Rights Reserved.

All rights reserved. No part of this publication may be reproduced, stored in a retrieval system, or transmitted in any form or by any means, electronic, mechanical, photocopy, recording or otherwise, without prior written permission of the copyright owner. Nor can it be circulated in any form of binding or cover other than that in which it is published and without similar condition including this condition being imposed on a subsequent purchaser.

Written by
Darren Bowman

Edited by
Alex Fitzgerald - SoccerTutor.com

Diagrams
Diagram designs by SoccerTutor.com. All the diagrams in this book have been created using SoccerTutor.com Tactics Manager Software available from www.SoccerTutor.com

Note: While every effort has been made to ensure the technical accuracy of the content of this book, neither the author nor publishers can accept any responsibility for any injury or loss sustained as a result of the use of this material.

Contents

Coach Profile and Experience 7
Meet the Author: Darren Bowman 8
Introduction by Darren Bowman 9
High Profile Players Developed in the Manchester City Academy 11
Other Notable Players Coached in the Manchester City Academy 12
Coaching Testimonials 13

The Manchester City Academy Program 14
Key Aspects of Why the Manchester City Academy is So Successful 15
The Role of Lead Youth Development Phase Coach 16
A Player Centred Philosophy at Manchester City Academy 17
Creating a Winning Culture 18
Professionalism and Performance Targets 19
Key Influences on Elite Player Development 20
Team/Player Management 21
Preparation for Competitive Matches 23
The Psychological Aspect 24
Working with Rodolfo Borrell (Pep Guardiola's Assistant Manager) 25
Junior Academy Program & St Bede's School Program 26

The Manchester City Game Model 27
Manchester City's 4-3-3 Formation 28
Diagram Key and Practice Format 29
The City Way Methodology from the Academy to the First Team 30
Game Principles at the Foundation of the City Way Methodology 31
Manchester City's 3 Build-up Phases 32
Manchester City's Attacking Tactics 33
Manchester City's Defending Tactics 35
Manchester City's Transition Phase Tactics 38

Manchester City Academy Training Process and Structure 39
Training Sessions Process 40
Training Session Content to Deliver the Right Process and Outcome 41
Manchester City Academy Training Session Structure 43

Building the Training Program 44
How Was Training Structured for Individuals and for the Collective? 45

6 Week Training Methodology (Tactical Periodization Curriculum) 46
Manchester City Academy U15 Team Physical Loading Program 47
How the 6 Week Training Methodology Works Alongside the 4 Week Physical Loading Program . 51

City Academy Session 1: Build-up Phase 1 - Short Build-up from the GK (1) 52

1. Angles of Support and Playing Through the Thirds in a 4-Line Passing Drill with Multiple Combinations 53
2. Play Inside and Outside to Break the Line in a 3v3 (+2) Directional Possession Game 54
3. End to End Game Related Attacking Overloads Wave Game (1v1 to 6v5) with Small Goals 55
4. Create 3v2 Attacking Overloads in a Back to Back Goals 5v5 (+GKs) Small Sided Game 56

City Academy Session 2: Build-up Phase 1 - Short Build-up from the GK (2) 57

1. One-Touch Technical Passing Triangle Drill with Third Man Run 58
2. Possession Play & Fast Transitions in Dual Directions in a Game Related 6v6 Transition Game ... 59
3. Game Related Attacking Organisation and Overload for 3v2 Finish in a 2 Zone 3-Team SSG 60
4. Continuous Game Related 2v2 Duels in Pairs Wave Game with Large Goals + GKs 61

City Academy Session 3: Build-up Phase 1 + 2 - Short Build-up from GK + Midfield Combination Play (1) 62

1. "Figure of 8" Technical Passing Diamond Drill with Free Decision Making 63
2. Side and Central Diamond Patterns in a 7v7 (+1) Directional Possession Game with End Goal Zones 64
3. Game Principles and Side Diamond Patterns of Play in a 10v8 (+GKs) Functional Practice 65
4. Break Lines and Create Attacking Overloads in a Position Specific 7v7 (+1) +GKs 3-Zone SSG .. 66

City Academy Session 4: Build-up Phase 1 + 2 - Short Build-up from GK + Midfield Combination Play (2) 67

1a. Side Diamond Pattern to Play Through the Thirds in a Technical Pass and Move Circuit 68
1b. Technical Side Diamond Pattern Box to Box Pass and Move Circuit 69
2. Side and Central Diamond Patterns in a 7v7 (+1) Directional Possession Game with End Goal Zones 70
3. Break Lines and Create Attacking Overloads in a Position Specific 7v7 (+GKs) 2-Zone SSG 71
4. Break the Lines and Create Attacking Overloads in a Position Specific 7v7 (+1) +GKs 3-Zone SSG 72

City Academy Session 5: Build-up Phase 3 - Finishing the Attack (Final Third) ... 73

1a. Break Past Opponent and Play Final Pass in a Technical Triangle Drill with Finish 74
1b. Open Up and Switch Play with Diagonal Pass in a Technical Triangle Drill with Finish 75
1c. One-Two, Set, and Final Pass in a Technical Triangle Drill with Finish 76
1d. One-Two, Set, and Give & Go in a Technical Triangle Drill with Finish 77
2. Side Diamond Pattern of Play to Receive in Between Lines, Set + Through Pass and Finish 78
3. Game Principles for Switching Play in a Corners End Zones Possession Game 79
4. Possession Play and Transitions in a 4-Goal Conditioned Small Sided Game with Variations 80

City Academy Session 6: Build-up Phase 2 + 3 - Midfield Combination Play + Finishing the Attack (1) 81
1. Technical Attacking Combination Play and Finishing Circuit 82
2. Midfield Combinations + Crossing in Functional 6v5 (+GK) Attacking Overloads 83
3a. Game Related 3v2 (+GK) Attacking Overload Duels............................. 84
3b. Game Related 4v3 (+GK) Attacking Overload Duels 85
4. Attacking Overloads in a Dynamic 2-Zone 5v5 (+GKs) Small Sided Game 86

City Academy Session 7: Build-up Phase 2 + 3 - Midfield Combination Play + Finishing the Attack (2) 87
1. One-Touch Technical Passing Triangle Drill with Set Through Combination 88
2. Central Diamond Pattern of Play, Crossing, and Finishing vs 2 Box Defenders 89
3. Game Related Attacking Organisation and Overload for 3v2 Finish in a 5v2 (+GKs) SSG 90
4. Attacking Organisation and Overloads in a Position Specific 7v7 (+GKs) 2-Zone SSG.......... 91

City Academy Session 8: Build-up Phase 2 + 3 - Midfield Combination Play + Finishing the Attack (3) 92
1a. One-Touch Technical Passing Triangle Drill with Overlapping Runs to Receive 93
1b. One-Touch Technical Passing Triangle Drill with Quick One-Two Combinations 94
2. Central Diamond Pattern of Play with Wing Play, Crossing, and Finishing 95
3. Game Related 3v2 to 4v3 Attacking Overload Duels 96
4. Game Principles and Patterns of Play in an 8v8 (+GKs) Small Sided Game 97

City Academy Session 9: Build-up Phase 1, 2 + 3 - Short Build-up, Midfield Combinations + Finishing the Attack (1) 98
1a. Switching Play and Attacking Combination in the Final Third Pattern with Crossing & Finishing.. 99
1b. Combination Play in the Final Third Pattern with Winger Receiving Inside + Overlapping Full Back...100
2. Break the Line in a Game Related Directional 4v4 End Zone Possession Game 101
3. Game Related Position Specific Attacking Overloads in a Functional Practice with Channels ... 102
4. Attacking Overloads in a Dynamic 2-Zone 5v5 (+GKs) Small Sided Game 103

City Academy Session 10: Build-up Phase 1, 2 + 3 - Short Build-up, Midfield Combinations + Finishing the Attack (2) 104
1. Support Play and Attacking Combination in the Final Third Pattern with Crossing & Finishing..105
2. Runs from Deep in Behind the Defensive Line + Crossing and Finishing Functional Practice ...106
3. Game Principles and Side Diamond Patterns of Play in a 10v8 (+GKs) Functional Practice......107
4. Create 3v2 Attacking Overloads in a Back to Back Goals 5v5 (+GKs) Small Sided Game 108

City Academy Session 11: Pressing from the Front (1) 109
1a. Side Diamond Pattern when Forward Pass is Blocked & Full Back Plays into Forward (Left) ... 110
1b. Side Diamond Pattern when Forward Pass is Blocked & Full Back Plays into Forward (Right)...111

2. Defensive Organisation and Pressing in a 4v4 (+3) Directional Possession Game 112
3. Pressing from the Front to "Set the Trap" in a Dynamic 6v8 (+GK) Phase of Play 113
4. Defensive Organisation and Pressing in Midfield in a 5v5 (+1) 4-Goal Small Sided Game 114

City Academy Session 12: Pressing from the Front (2) 115
1. Side Diamond Pattern of Play to Receive in Between Lines, Set + Overlapping Full Back Cross . 116
2. Pressing with a Numerical Disadvantage in a Game Related 2-Zone 5v5 Transition Game 117
3. Pressing from the Front to "Set the Trap" in a Full Man for Man Pressing Game (10v10 +GK) ... 118
4. Defensive Organisation and Pressing from the Front in a Rotational 3-Team 6v6 (+GKs) SSG .. 119

City Academy Session 13: Defending in Midfield 120
1. Winger Comes Inside to Set Att. Midfielder's Pass for Forward to Open Up and Finish
Pattern of Play 121
2. Pressing with Numerical Disadvantage in a Game Related 2-Zone 6v6 Transition Game 122
3. Continuous Overloads in Game Related Situations (2v1, 3v2, 4v3, 5v4, 6v5) 123
4. Defending Potential 3v2 Overloads in a Back to Back Goals 6v6 (+GKs) Small Sided Game 124

City Academy Session 14: Pressing from the Front + Defending in Midfield (1) .. 125
1. Midfield & Forward Units Attacking Combination Play in Final Third with Free Decision
Making 126
2. Possession Play and Pressing in a 3-Team Transition Game 127
3. Pressing from the Front with Diamond Midfield Shape in a 9v9 (+GKs) Tactical Game 128
4. Pressing from the Front & Defending Through the Thirds in a Multi-Zone End to End Game ... 129

City Academy Session 15: Pressing from the Front + Defending in Midfield (2) . 130
1. Angles of Support and Playing Through the Thirds in a Technical 4-Line Passing Drill 131
2. Defensive Organisation and Pressing in a 4v4 (+3) Directional Possession Game 132
3. Pressing from the Front with Diamond Midfield Shape in a Functional 8v9 (+GK) Practice 133
4. Pressing from the Front to "Set the Trap" in a Full Man for Man Pressing Game (10v10 +GK) ... 134

City Academy Session 16: Defending Around the Box (1) 135
1. Defending Around the Box and Development of the Defensive Unit Arc when the Ball is
Played Wide 136
2. 8v4 Attacking Overload Non-directional Possession Game with 3 Phases 138
3. Game Related Back 4 Defending Around the Box in a 6v4 (+GK) Phase of Play 139
4. Defending Around the Box with Game Principles in an 8v6 (+GK) Position Specific Phase
of Play 140

City Academy Session 17: Defending Around the Box (2) 141
1. Defending First and Second Phase Long Passes and Crosses Around the Box 142
2. Game Principles for Defending Around the Box in an 8v8 (+GK) Phase of Play 143
3. Defending the Box from Crosses in a Functional Practice 144
4. Position Specific Game Related Practice for Zonal 2v3 Defensive Organisation 145

ELITE ACADEMY COACHING

Coach Profile and Experience

Coach Profile and Experience

Meet the Author: Darren Bowman

Darren Bowman

Former **Manchester City Academy Coach**

Credentials (Coaching & Academic):

- **UEFA A Coaching Licence**
- **Sport, Fitness & Coaching BSc (Hons)** The Open University
- **Foundation Degree in Coach Development for Elite Coaches**, Hult International Business School
- Studied best practice techniques at **FC Barcelona, Real Madrid, Atlético Madrid, Rayo Vallecano, Málaga,** & **Atalanta** academies
- **Professional playing career** at West Bromwich Albion, Grantham Town, Ramsbottom United, Rossendale United & Stalybridge Celtic

Coaching History:

- **Manchester City U13 Head Coach** (2011-2012)
- **Manchester City U14/U15 Head Coach** (2012-2015)
- **Manchester City Head of Junior Academy & Schools Program** (2009-11)
- **Manchester City Part-time Academy Coach** (2006-2009)
- **Lee Man FC Academy Director** (2022-present)
- **Technical Advisor** for Fans Owned Club (FOC) and International Advisory Council
- **Founder** of @DB7K, a football consultancy business in Hong Kong and Shanghai (2019-present)
- **Head of Football** at Wellington International College, Shanghai (2020-2022)

Key Achievements:

- Implemented St Bede's program, Manchester City's first full time bespoke education and football program for U14-U15 players
- 2012 and 2013 Premier League Academy National Champions

Coach Profile and Experience

Introduction by Darren Bowman

My goal is for this book to enable others to further their ambitions. I've been fortunate in my career evolution in that, along with a bit of luck, I've been guided and mentored by many great individuals, both inside and outside of my profession. I welcome the chance to try to "pay that forward" for others.

The **knowledge shared in this book has been instrumental to my success** and has proven rewarding in terms of the **development of some of the top players in today's professional game**. These players are regularly performing at the highest levels in the United Kingdom and across Europe, competing in the best league competitions in world football and representing their countries on the international stage.

For those that think that this may be too difficult, I'd like them to understand that coaching effectively is not beyond their capacity. Success at this level is possible if the individual remains committed to imagining, and to creating.

We all learn from experts in their field, and I embrace this opportunity to share my expertise with others, to make a direct impact, to inspire, and motivate.

I honour the opportunity to make additional connections, and to allow those who are interested to expand their network.

It is exciting that this book will expose me to areas I have not yet uncovered in the world of football, sport, and business.

I hope to enhance my reputation as a "go-to" person for advice or ideas. I want to be seen as the sort of **professional who encourages others**, as well as myself, to think creatively, to **think outside the box**.

It is my goal that, by publishing this book and declaring these intentions, my competence in the field of international football consultancy will be further proved so that I may continue to have an impact for years to come.

The information and content in this book are my true accounts and they will no doubt benefit others.

In 2006, Paul Power gave me the opportunity to **join the academy coaching team at Manchester City Football Club**, a position that is the holy grail for the majority of young people when they set out on their coaching journey.

The 9 seasons that followed gave me the opportunity to pay it forward to the global coaching fraternity. During that period of my career, **I was at the forefront of elite player development**. I was able to develop as a professional coach at a place that would grow into what is now known as **one of the leading academies in the global game**.

In this book, coaches will be presented with a very specific and detailed method of coaching. The content ranges from the development of a game model to the execution of the sort of methodology that is highly valued and analysed in the game today.

Coach Profile and Experience

During my time at the **Manchester City academy**, I was fortunate to have the opportunities to hold a **variety of positions**:

- Talent Identification
- Player Recruitment
- Junior Academy Programs
- Foundation / Development Phase Roles
- Lead Development Coach

During my time as lead development coach, I coached many of the best potential professional footballer prospects playing in Europe on a daily basis. I coached the players that you see performing at the highest levels of the game today.

In addition to the fantastic training content, this book provides an insight into both my personal philosophy and the philosophy of the Manchester City academy at the time. I outline and explain how we performed our important role in elite player development at one of the most successful football clubs in the world.

Over the years, I have hosted many speaking events and webinars, and I have delivered hundreds of training sessions to other coaches. However, writing this book has afforded me the opportunity to appreciate the language I have been using in a way I never have before. I have been allowed to hone my own voice and tone, to fine tune the language I have been using the majority of my life to connect with sport. It is exciting that others will connect with it and grow from it. It is exciting that there are those who, perhaps at this very moment, are working towards the same goals I have been working towards since the beginning of my journey in sport and coaching.

I acknowledge the privilege afforded to me in that my personal truth, what I know in my head and what I believe in my heart, will now be used to encourage coaches around the world to search, to research, to go beyond whatever restrictions they might think they have, and to further explore what they have yet to learn. It is a privilege that my experiences will be able to help them grow.

With this book, I hope to accomplish something that many do not attain. Over the last few years, I've created many new goals for myself. I've aimed to learn outside of my comfort zone, to see challenges and roadblocks as potential opportunities for unexpected growth and success. By starting an international business, by learning the ins and outs of trademarks and branding, for example, or by immersing myself in the worlds of technology and marketing, I have proved to myself that I can accomplish what it is I set my mind to.

Writing this book has been a welcome challenge. It has required me to think deeply and to think critically, has been an important step on the road to self-discovery, and helped me to recognise that every one of us is walking around with more knowledge and experience than we realise. This writing, for me, has been therapeutic. From organising my thoughts to focusing on the details of a session planned, I have grown.

It is my hope that, as others read this book, they will find the same.

Coach Profile and Experience

High Profile Players Developed in the Manchester City Academy

Phil Foden

- Coached for 3 years in the St Bede's Program, which Darren Bowman implemented
- UEFA Champions League Winner
- 5 x Premier League Winner
- FA Cup Winner + 4 x EFL Cup Winner
- 61 Goals & 46 Assists in 226 total club appearances
- 27 England International Caps (4 Goals)

Jadon Sancho

- Coached by Darren Bowman at U14 & U15 level
- Joined Borussia Dortmund for €20m in 2017
- DFB-Pokal Winner 2021 & DFL-Supercup Winner 2019
- Joined Manchester United for €85m in 2021
- EFL Cup Winner 2023
- 62 Goals & 70 Assists in 219 total club appearances
- 22 England International Caps (3 Goals)

Brahim Diaz

- Coached by Darren Bowman at U14 level
- Manchester City First team debut in 2016
- Premier League, FA Cup & 2 x EFL Cup Winner
- Joined Real Madrid in 2019 for €17m (loaned to Milan)
- La Liga & Serie A Winner
- 22 Goals & 18 Assists in 165 total club appearances
- 22 England International Caps (3 Goals)

Coach Profile and Experience

Other Notable Players Coached in the Manchester City Academy

Cole Palmer
- Recruited as part of Junior Academy Program / Coached at U7-U9 level
- Manchester City First team debut in 2020 (41 total appearances)
- UEFA Champions League, Premier League & FA Cup Winner
- Joined Chelsea for £42.5m in 2023
- 6 Goals & 2 Assists in 44 total club appearances

David Brooks
- Coached by Darren Bowman at U13 & U14 level
- Developed at Manchester City Academy
- Joined AFC Bournemouth for £10m in 2018
- 23 Goals & 21 Assists in 145 total club appearances
- 21 International Caps for Wales

Jeremie Frimpong
- Coached by Darren Bowman at U14 & U15 level
- Developed at Manchester City Academy
- Joined Celtic for £380k in 2019
- Joined Bayer Leverkusen for €11m in 2021
- 16 Goals & 31 Assists in 153 total club appearances

Lukas Nmecha
- Coached by Darren Bowman at U14 & U15 level
- Manchester City First team debut in 2017
- Joined VfL Wolfsburg for €8m in 2021
- 39 Goals & 13 Assists in 160 total club appearances

Coach Profile and Experience

Coaching Testimonials

Brian Marwood
Managing Director of Global Football for City Football Group

"Darren worked for Manchester City Football Club in a variety of football and recruiting roles working with players ranging between ages 5 to 16. He was the first student and graduate of the Elite Coaches Apprenticeship Scheme (ECAS) administered by the Premier League. Darren grasped this opportunity whilst continuing with the expectations of leading and coaching a talented group of academy players. Darren achieved this, maintaining high standards of behaviour and conduct, creating a winning culture evident in the team's results."

Tony Carr MBE
Premier League Coaching Adviser and former West Ham United Director of Youth Development

"I first crossed paths with Darren when he was enrolled on a diploma course run by the English Premier League which I attended. Darren showed how important is to constantly look for self-improvement and gain knowledge that would make him a better coach. I recommended Darren to a Chinese company (Football Talents) who were looking for a football coach to run a grassroots football programme in Shanghai.

His approach was first class, immersing himself in the culture and set about building a team of English coaches to take football to the children of Shanghai. At one time he had over 20 English coaches taking football to dozens of schools. It was a very successful project.

I have no hesitation in recommending Darren to any football coaching programme that he may wish to apply for."

ELITE ACADEMY COACHING

The Manchester City Academy Program

The Manchester City Academy Program

Key Aspects of Why the Manchester City Academy is So Successful

1 ETHOS
- Strong foundations underpinned by an ethos that runs through club.
- "The 4 Ps": **Passion**, **Patience**, **Perseverance**, **Professionalism**.
- Football-focused ethos = *"We train to develop and play to win."*

2 MISSION
- Attract, develop, motivate and retain the best natural talent.
- Provide the greatest possible experience for all.
- All academy players to **fulfil their potential and achieve greatness**.

3 VISION
- Academy of choice delivering an **optimum development program**.
- Players recruited locally, nationally and internationally.
- Ethos that addresses both the football and the footballer.

4 DEVELOP
- Training drives development, and matches provide the experiences.
- Develop strong minded, independent and balanced individuals.
- Develop a **loyalty/affinity** to the club, **resilience**, and **positivity**.

5 SUPPORT
- Administration, coaching, medical, sports science, and operations.
- Education, parents, player care/welfare, and facilities.
- Communications, scouting, recruitment, and performance analysis.

6 EDUCATION
- Deliver a comprehensive education with **excellence at every level**.
- High standards of conduct from players and staff + communication.
- Tailored age-specific program with **clear targets and outcomes**.

7 FAMILY
- **Every player was a potential professional** and member of our family.
- Every player felt special and valued, creating great people.
- One team with **one goal**, player development was everything.

The Manchester City Academy Program

The Role of Lead Youth Development Phase Coach

The Role of Lead Youth Development Coach

- For 9 seasons, I was at the forefront of elite player development at one of the best and most successful academies in the world.
- You must describe in detail to players on and off the pitch the **HOW**, the **WHAT**, and perhaps most crucially, the **WHY**.
- Consistently work towards the goal day in & day out & work in a manner that inspires.

Multi-disciplinary Team

- Engage players and staff as part of a multi-disciplinary team.
- Release **potential**, inspire **growth**, remove fear, **empower** all to make own decisions.
- Foster a culture of responsibility and accountability.

The Elite Level & Learning

- Manchester City is coaching some of the **best young players in Europe** to go onto perform at the highest levels of game.
- Mistakes are OK and normalised → Be brave and grow → Shared **PURPOSE**.

Coaching Method

- **Development of a Game Model** (which is fully described later in the book).
- Complete control in **possession with purpose**, numerical advantages in all moments.
- Executing the methodology that is highly valued in the game today.

Transition to the Next Level

- Right level of engagement, emotional control, and intelligence.
- Prepare players for transition to next level (becoming first team players).
- **TRAIN HARD → PLAY EASY**.

The Manchester City Academy Program

A Player Centred Philosophy at Manchester City Academy

1

My Coaching Philosophy

- My coaching philosophy is based around a holistic approach for the whole development of both the team dynamic and the individual players.
- Produce technically gifted, independent, decision-making winners.
- View and treat each player as a person and as an individual, not just a football player.

2

A Player Centred Approach

- Winning is achieved by approaching the game holistically.
- The ability to create an environment of inspiration and dedication is key for coaches, and this can only be achieved by involving both the players and the parents.
- My aim was always to produce a culture of competition where the players always come first.

3

Focusing on Simplicity in a Complex Game

- A player-led environment should be created and upheld by a democratic style of communication.
- Player development should work in harmony with a climate of motivation and a distinct focus on task and process for all staff and players (not just ego and outcome).
- Rather than reward and status, the environment should value and foster teamwork, hard-work, and practice.

Creating a Winning Culture

To create a **winning culture**, we aimed to challenge the players at the right time in the right way whilst also providing the support they needed **technically, tactically, physically** and **psychologically** *(4 Corner Model)*.

By working in alignment with this model, we enabled the players to **reach peak performance on a consistent basis**, and this resulted in winning.

Simplicity in a Complex Game

- Rather than reward and status, the **training environment** should value and foster **teamwork, hard work, dedication, practice, passion,** and **enjoyment**.
- Players and coaches take steps together towards **growth and further success**.

Philosophy and Playing Style of the Club

- At Manchester City, we first needed to both understand and defend the philosophy and playing style of the club.
- High levels of focus and concentration in training (as demanding as matches).

Long-term Athletic Development (LTAD)

- To learn, **mistakes during training and game play must be allowed** to happen.
- This requires the coach to be brave and bold, and to operate with a **growth mind-set**.
- Develop the whole team, individually and collectively, towards a shared **PURPOSE**.

Intelligent Development

- Academy coaches need the right level of engagement, emotional control and intelligence to **prepare for the transition to next level**, to become first team players.
- Hard work alone won't be enough, so we have to **work smart**.

Professionalism and Performance Targets

Professionalism

To work at the elite level of academy football, it is essential that coaches pay close attention to their continued professional development.

Not only are you responsible for the development of the players under your remit, but you are also responsible for your own development as a coach and as an individual. This is a fundamental requirement, and fulfilling it will enable you to deliver your role more efficiently and effectively over time.

The following are examples of my own continued professional development during my time at Manchester City:

- **Performance Clock:** Identify specific areas for your personal development that will enhance your skill set in delivering your role.
- **Sports Psychology:** Understanding of the softer skills is key to improving the individual players and team's performance.
- **Formal Qualifications:** These are "must have" core qualifications that all coaches acquire when following the national association coach development pathway.
- **Pedagogy:** The art of teaching.
- **Growth Mind-set:** Essential to your development as a coach and a person.
- **Leadership and Management:** Coaches must know which style to use, at the time, in the moment, to achieve the outcome desired, depending on the audience.
- **Player Development:** This is everything.
- **Technical and Tactical Knowledge:** A never ending journey of a coach's development. We can always improve.
- **Communication Styles:** A variety of concepts make this a complex area that coaches must become consciously competent in.
- **Professional Experiences and Skills:** Be curious, build your body of work.
- **The Art of Recruitment (Staff and Players):** Recruit staff who are experts in their field and cover your blind spots. Players must have the skills to execute the way you want to play.

Performance Targets

Performance targets are long term objectives that are personal to you.

You must work towards these objectives while part of an elite academy, and ideally, these personal objectives will be aligned with the vision of the organisation:

- **Be a leader, not a follower**.
- **Become a world class communicator and presenter**.
- **Develop people skills**.
- **Be the best ideas coach you can be**.
- **Ability to impact performance and achieve flow in individuals/teams**.
- **Create positive learning environments**.

Key Influences on Elite Player Development

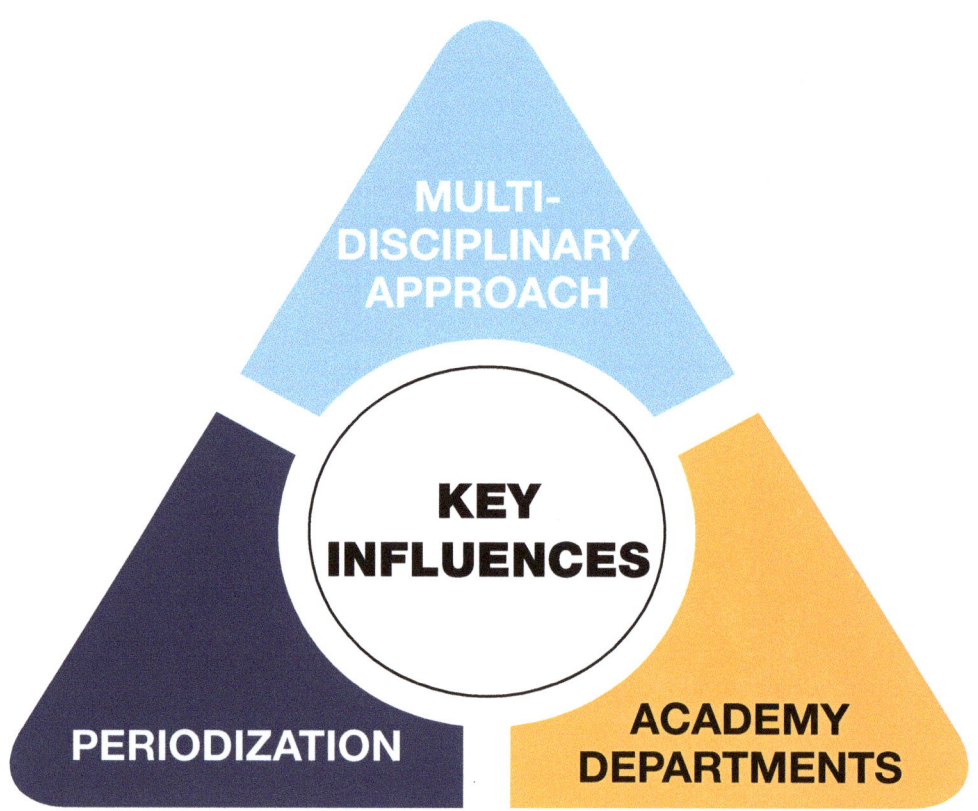

Multidisciplinary Approach

A multidisciplinary approach requires a specialist coaching cell in place to support all aspects of player development on and off the pitch, which resembles a player centred approach.

Periodization

Tactical and physical periodization must be planned carefully with attention to detail covering all aspects of the season, the methodology, and player development.

Academy Departments

Academy departments must work in synchronisation and with fluidity to enable operations, logistics, administration, player welfare and education to support the coaching, sports science and medical aspects of the academy. High performance organisations make sure all functions operate to their maximum to achieve peak performance and flow.

The Manchester City Academy Program

Team / Player Management

Preparing for Games

- Different levels of games organised for the players holistic development to provide each player with the opportunity to play their full quota of minutes for the season.
- Competitive and development game preparation should be different in environment, the expectations set, and the performances/results you expect to achieve.

Development and Competition

- Development games give the coach great flexibility and should be different to games when you are setting up the team to win playing a certain way.
- Every game was an opportunity for the players to work on their development.

Managing Game Time

- Responsibility and duty of care towards every player. You must be fair when **giving all players the opportunity to play**.
- Communication and trust are key factors to getting this right.

Developing Individuals within the Team

- **Your role in the academy is to develop players** rather than win games.
- The objective is to achieve both, but never at the expense of development.
- The team is the vehicle that high potential players require to reach the highest level.
- How you manage this as a coach will determine your success in terms of players produced, games won and performances achieved individually and collectively.

Roles and Responsibilities

- It is crucial that all people involved (staff and players) play their position and deliver their role to the highest possible standard on a daily basis.
- This is every individual's responsibility.

Conduct, Standards, and Preparation

▶ When part of an Elite Premier League Academy in a key position, you are a role model and **responsible for the image and reputation of that club**.

▶ The standards and expectations of you as a professional and also as a person are extremely high and rightly so. This is the **culture of high performing environments**.

The Art of Communication

▶ To work **at the highest level you must become a good communicator**.

▶ You must be aware of all the different audiences you will be exposed to, the type of communication (or noncommunication) required in all situations to get the outcomes, responses, performances, and results you want to achieve.

Long-term Athletic Development

▶ The key word is "Long" - **be fully prepared to be patient**.

▶ You must always persevere, have huge amounts of passion, and always be professional.

Preparation for Competitive Matches

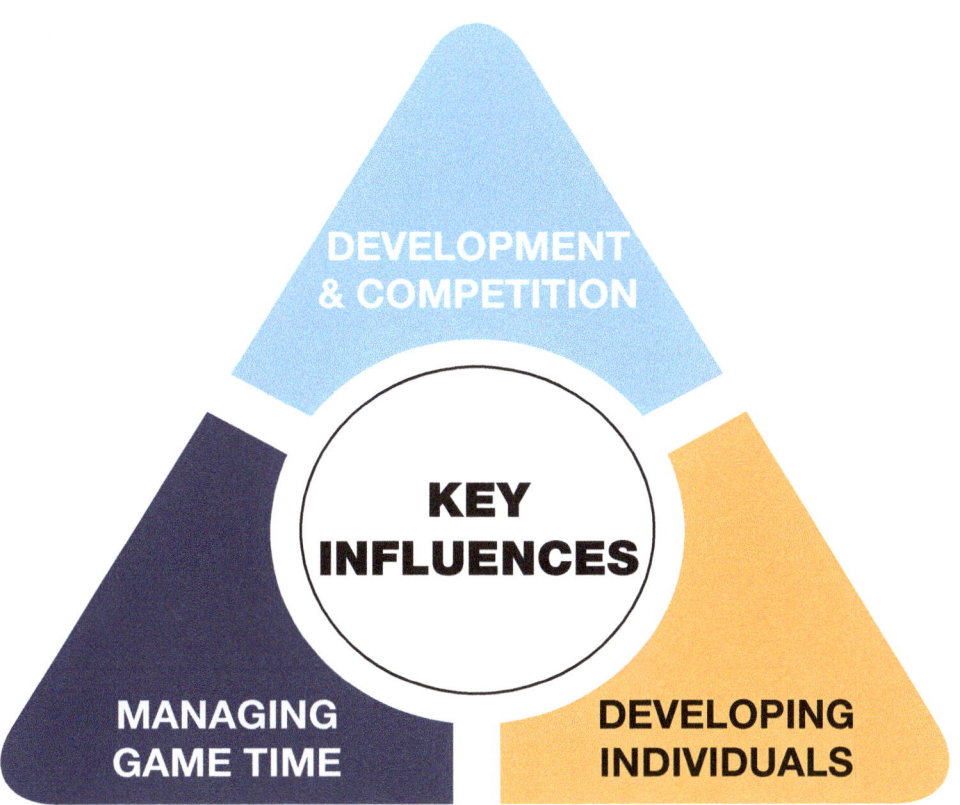

Development & Competition
- For development, we played players in a variety of positions for different reasons.
- Our strongest players played in marque Premier League fixtures and international competitions.

Managing Game Time:
- All coaches must be aware that this area needs to be fair and in line with the rules and regulations for the development of all players. We were required to comply with the Premier League criteria.

Developing Individuals:
- The team and squad is the catalyst for the individual player's development, both in training and in matches.
- Other aspects of player development are the responsibility of the individual, who must take ownership and responsibility whilst being guided by the coaches and staff.

The Manchester City Academy Program

The Psychological Aspect

How, what and why should always be applied in a variety of contexts. The question is in regard to the tactical concepts, yet we also applied this with individual development, unit development within the team dynamic, and the team as a whole. This is a key component when developing the correct learning and motivational environment.

HOW?
- **Execution of the action** in the moment at the time under pressure.

WHAT?
- **Action required** to gain an advantage or provide the solution to the situation in the different moments of the game.

WHY?
- To **play the way we wanted to play** and perform as individuals and a team.

The Manchester City Academy Program

Working with Rodolfo Borrell (Pep Guardiola's Assistant Manager)

Rodolfo Borrell (Assistant Manager to Pep Guardiola) was one of my head coaches during my time with Manchester City. I asked Rodolfo why he joined, and his reply was that Manchester City fit with his philosophy.

He believed (and I agree) that our beliefs are shaped by both our successes and failures we experience in our careers. Rodolfo came from a very strong and successful culture of alignment at FC Barcelona, a fantastic club with a very clearly defined style of play and identity.

What is Needed at an Elite Club

- My belief is that each club should first decide upon its style, which may be influenced or dictated to by the club's history and traditions.
- The club needs to choose a manager with the capacity to enforce and maintain this style, define the players to fit, and work side by side with the recruitment department to achieve this.
- Coaches and players must understand and then feel the need to defend the philosophy and football style (as was my own experience at Manchester City).
- To believe in what you do is crucial at any club.

What I Learned from Rodolfo

- Of course, it is important to win games and titles, but **most important is to develop and produce first team players**.
- To understand that the **TEAM was far more important than any individual** player.
- Players need to understand the **high levels of focus and concentration required**, particularly in training. It is not about what they do but how they do it.
- You must **train as you play** because training should be as demanding as the game.
- Player recruitment is crucial to the philosophy success and pushing in the same direction is essential.
- Choosing the appropriate players to play in each position is very important and getting it right in the centre of the pitch is key. You **must have players to dominate the game and give the team the necessary balance** in this area.
- Always try to **maintain triangles throughout the width and depth of the pitch**.
- The players should not lose their position on the pitch and always make sure balance is retained.

Junior Academy Program & St Bede's School Program

St Bede's School Program

At the time of its launch, the St Bede's program was seen as pioneering as the first full time player education program for selected Manchester City academy players. In line with the Premier League Elite Player Performance Plan (EPPP). This meant the academy could meet one of the key criteria to be awarded Category 1 status by the Premier League.

The club made a big investment in partnering with St Bede's, a well renowned independent school in Manchester, to cover the costs of the players' education for 4 years.

St Bede's is a **bespoke program that saw our players educated in the mornings and then transported to the academy to train in the afternoons and evenings**.

This program enabled the academy to have a **significant impact on the U12-16 development phase players on and off the pitch**.

Junior Academy Program

My time as Head Coach of the Junior Academy Program was my first introduction to the world of **player recruitment**. Geographically, the North West of England is a hot bed of potential talent. However, this also makes it fiercely competitive when tasked with recruiting the brand new U9 Manchester City Academy team.

The Junior academy program was a **full-time program and I managed a team of young coaches**, all of which still work for the City Football Group (CFG) today in various roles around the world.

This was another major investment made by the club to employ full time coaches to deliver Manchester City FC Schools sessions throughout the North West in all primary schools during the day and then delivering our coaching program for our selected 5-8 year old players in the evenings and weekends. This type of program really is 24/7 with many moving parts and various audiences to consider.

Recruitment

The Junior Academy team are hugely important ambassadors for the club and play a key role in enhancing reputations in the local community. They are also key in the recruitment process. Recruiting the best local potential for the U9 Academy team is a big responsibility which involves managing coaches, scouts and parents.

Communication and environment are the two key factors when recruiting. It is about the people and the experience in this type of role, not just the coaching.

I am very proud of what we achieved during my two years in the role, and it is a pleasure to see **Cole Palmer**, **Tommy Doyle**, **Taylor Harwood Bellis**, **CJ Riley**, and a few more **recruited at U7 who have made it all the way through to the professional ranks**. There are also players who attended our Junior Academy Program that we unfortunately weren't able to recruit, but also play professionally today.

ELITE ACADEMY COACHING

The Manchester City Game Model

The Manchester City Game Model

Manchester City's 4-3-3 Formation

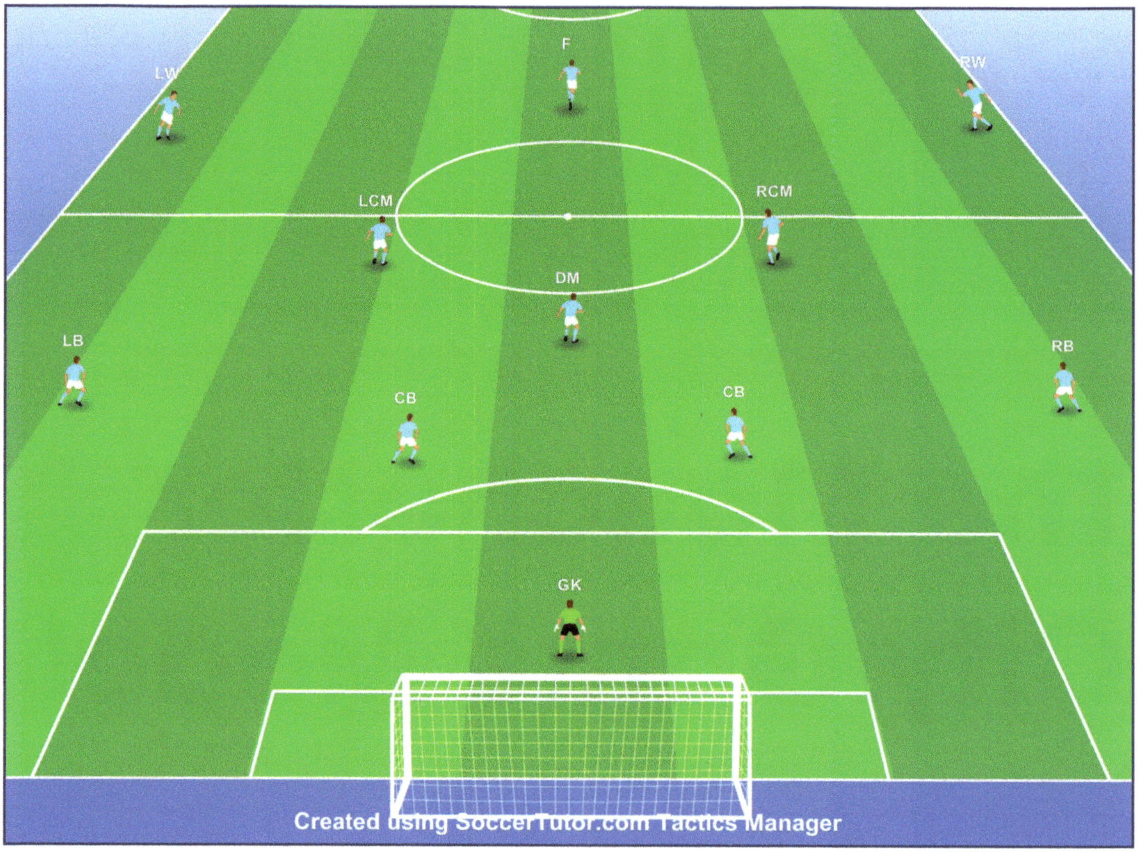

- **GK:** Goalkeeper
- **LCB:** Left Centre Back
- **RCB:** Right Centre Back
- **LB:** Left Back
- **RB:** Right Back
- **DM:** Defensive Midfielder
- **LCM:** Left Central Midfielder
- **RCM:** Right Central Midfielder
- **LW:** Left Winger
- **RW:** Right Winger
- **F:** Forward

The Manchester City Game Model

Diagram Key

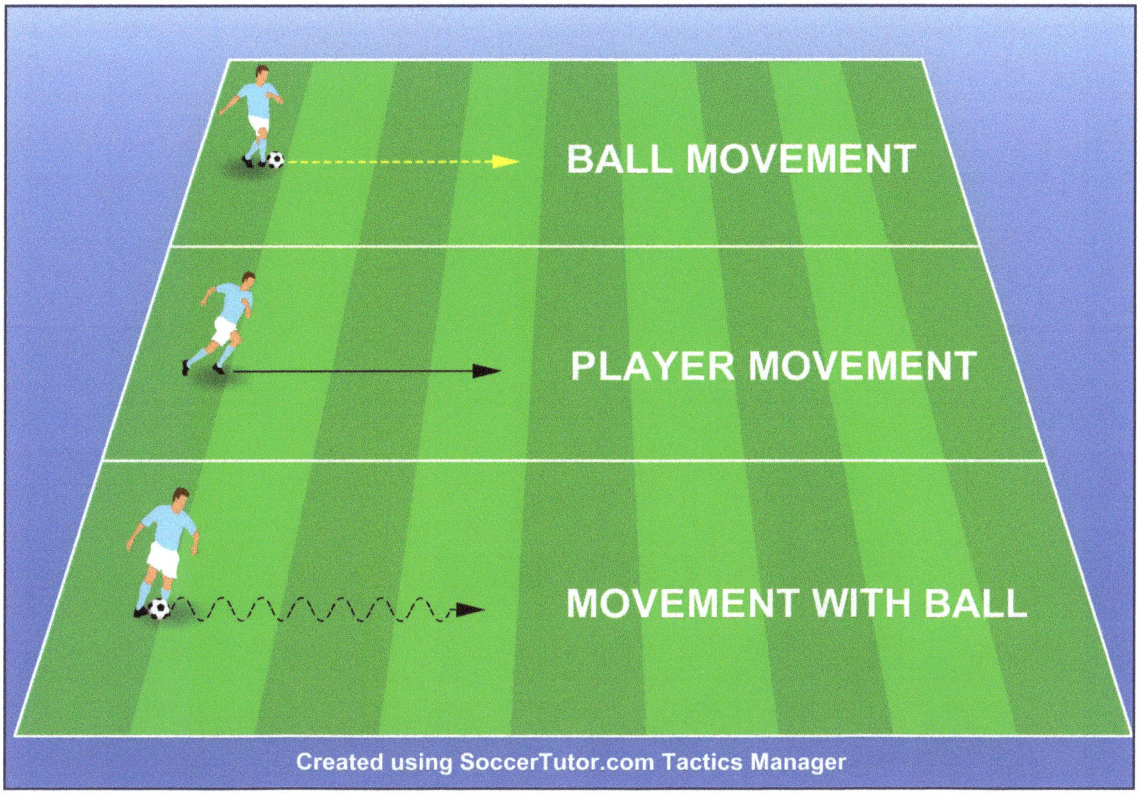

![Diagram key showing Ball Movement (yellow dashed arrow), Player Movement (black solid arrow), and Movement with Ball (black wavy arrow)]

Created using SoccerTutor.com Tactics Manager

Practice Format

- The practices in this book are direct from Darren Bowman's training sessions at the Manchester City Academy, Etihad Campus Training Ground, Manchester between 2011 and 2015.

- Each practice includes the practice topic/name and clear diagrams with a detailed description.

The City Way Methodology from the Academy to the First Team

Attacking Principles:

- Create numerical superiority in all moments of the game.
- Keep possession with a purpose.
- Control to create opportunities to score.

Defensive Principles:

- Protect the depth and keep the ball in front.
- Stop penetration in central areas.
- Create numerical advantages to win the ball back quickly and early.

Transition Principles:

- The beauty of the methodology is that the positioning of the players when in possession means they are in a position to press quickly on the transition.
- This is due to them being "in between," meaning 1 player can normally cover 2 opponents.

The Manchester City Game Model

Game Principles at the Foundation of the City Way Methodology

Be Ready to Attack, Ready to Defend
The Ball Comes to You, Don't Go to the Ball!

- Each players' positioning is key. When it is correct, the team can transition very quickly in and out of possession.
- This concept also means you are efficient in regard to the players' energy levels, which are a key consideration for performance.
- The ball is the quickest object on the pitch in any game, so make the ball do the work. By adopting this concept and players playing their position, the team can create space, time, and conserve energy.

Play Your Position
Play in Between and in Behind

- Players playing their position means the team have the correct shape and the player in possession will have a variety of options.
- Occupy spaces for penetrative passes to break lines.
- Create numerical advantages in the middle and final third.
- The timing of when players arrive in spaces is a key aspect.

Possession with a Purpose
Create Overloads + Break Lines

- Dependent on game situation and time.
- In each action, the purpose is to create an advantage to progress, to attack, to score, or to control.
- Create an advantage in possession with overloads (+ create defensive overloads).

Manchester City's 3 Build-up Phases

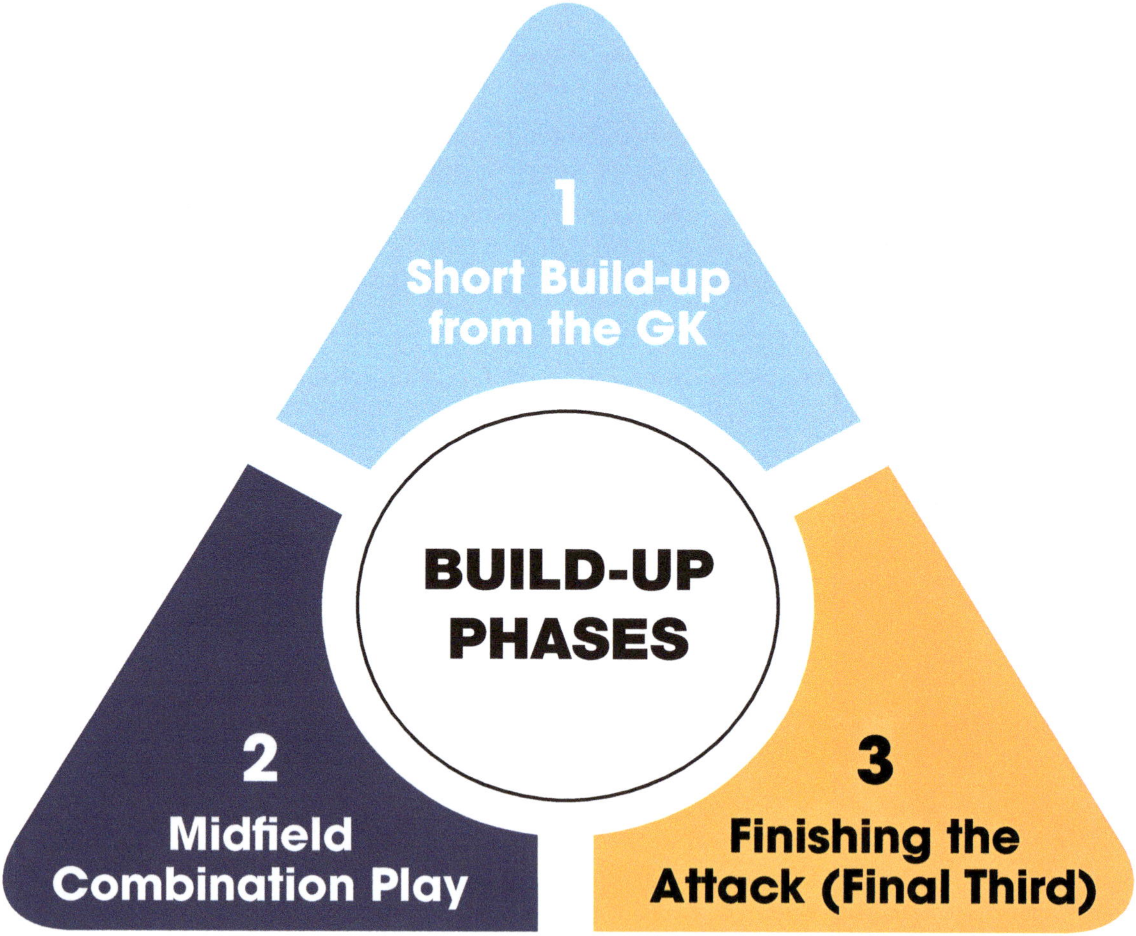

1. **Short Build-up from the GK**

BUILD-UP PHASES

2. **Midfield Combination Play**

3. **Finishing the Attack (Final Third)**

The Manchester City Game Model

Manchester City's Attacking Tactics

Build-up Play Phase 1

Short Build-up from the GK

- Centre backs split, full backs push up high, and the defensive midfielder drops as third option for the goalkeeper.
- Create numerical advantages through player rotations.
- Who, where and how can we create the spare player?
- All units must be involved to create the quickest route to the opposition's goal.

Long Pass = 2nd Option

- Target the forward, a winger, or a full back (positioned high and wide).

Build-up Play Phase 2

Midfielders Initiate the Combination Play (Rotations)

- Defensive midfielder + 2 central midfielders play their position.
- Central midfielders pick up the ball and turn.
- Control the centre of the pitch.
- Be ready to attack, ready to defend.

Full Backs Move Up

- Full backs provide width and attacking outlet on flanks.

Wingers Play Between the Lines

- Numerical advantage inside opposition's defensive formation and good movement/mobility between the lines.

The Manchester City Game Model

Build-up Play Phase 3

Inside Support Play (Centre) -> Penetration

- Play in between and in behind.
- Occupy the right spaces at the right times.
- Create overloads through combinations.
- Break lines and think about opposite movements.
- Coordinated movements e.g. Central midfielder comes short and forward runs in behind.
- Wide players = Inside diagonal runs.
- Attack space behind defenders (through passes).

Wide Support Play -> Crossing

- Width from full backs/wingers → Dynamic quick crosses.
- Receive wide to drag opponents out and open up space inside.

The Manchester City Game Model

Manchester City's Defending Tactics

Pressing from the Front

Aggressive High Press to Win Possession Quickly or Force Mistakes

- The players knew the different ways to press depending on the formation of the opposition, the way they wanted to play and the details regarding the opposition's weaknesses.
- Pressing from the front is all units working together.
- The first trigger activates a chain reaction from behind.

Initiate to Limit Opponents' Options

- Block positioning (high/middle) depends on tactical context and the defined team strategy.
- Show opponents outside (starts from the front players).
- Other players adjust → Shorten spaces.
- High defensive line = Keep a compact block.

The Manchester City Game Model

Defending in Midfield

Protect the Depth + Keep the Ball in Front

- Always be in a position to see the opposition player and the ball.
- Dictate the game without the ball.
- Force the ball where we want it to go, win it, and counter to score!

Create "Small Field" + Pressure On the Ball

- Narrow and compact = Reduced space between players.
- High density of players on ball side/area (leave opposite side empty).
- Always apply pressure on the ball → Solidarity!
- Show opponents outside.
- Stop forward passes and switches of play.

Other Principles

- Zonal Marking → Occupying good spaces (positioning).
- Leadership and communication.
- Aggressive on pressing to regain possession (duels + second balls).

The Manchester City Game Model

Defending Around the Box

Stop Penetrative Passes in Behind

- Always keep the ball in front.
- Positioning of the defensive unit is dependent on where the ball is.
- Press any cross or pass that is cut back or passed away from the goal.
- Central area "T-shape" - cover and depth to stop the ball in behind.
- Make sure the full back does not play the opposition's opposite winger onside.
- The defensive midfielder is key - defending in this way is an art with many details.

Coordination of the Back 4

- Narrow formation when the ball is in the central channel.
- Full backs are aggressive to stop crosses (+ keep opponent outside).
- Constantly covering teammates and marking opponents in the box.

Compactness and Balance

- Midfielders to fill in and protect the back 4.
- Provide cover for full backs.
- Control the space to prevent shots from edge of the box.
- Forwards are in touch whilst maintaining attacking balance.

Manchester City's Transition Phase Tactics

Transition from Attack to Defence

The Moment After Losing Possession

- Quick reactions and pressing to regain/delay any progression from opponents.
- Hold the midfield and defensive lines (do not drop back in the first moment).
- Be aware of the space behind the full backs, who are most likely positioned high.
- Recover to get behind the ball (reorganise into formation/shape).

Transition from Defence to Attack

The Moment After Winning Possession

- Quick reactions and instant progression towards the opposition's goal → Counter attack.
- Use players in front of the ball.
- Make runs beyond the ball.
- Second option when counter attack isn't possible = Retain possession.

ELITE ACADEMY COACHING

Manchester City Academy Training Process and Structure

Training Sessions Process

This is standard practice and coaches have their own habits and methods in this area. We always took pride and spent considerable time when planning and preparing sessions, with an attention to detail to ensure the delivery and presentation was always to the highest standard.

This process also means I have an extensive library of sessions in my portfolio today which I have shared later in this book that are unique and cannot be copied.

In my experience, many coaches execute the first two parts of the process very well. However, **it is the review that is the key to coach and player development**, which is sometimes forgotten.

There are different ways to deliver a session at academy level, but we had a **foundation of sessions which covered the key aspects of the methodology**. As a coach, you should have a bank of sessions (maybe 15-20) which you can deliver 200 different ways. This is the skill and the magic of coaching.

Manchester City Academy Training Process and Structure

Training Session Content to Deliver the Right Process and Outcome

Basic Movement Patterns

- We would develop a **variety of unopposed patterns** including all the concepts of our methodology to **create numerical advantages in all phases of play** in possession.
- This is done at the beginning of every training session, **teaching the players all the tactical details and the WHY**, under no pressure.

Directional Possession

- **Progressions** of the Basics Movement Patterns, which involve pressure and transition with a numerical advantage in possession and disadvantage out of possession.
- Directional possessions are **snapshots of the game**.

Non-directional Possession

- We would deliver this dependent on the loading cycle and fatigue of the players.
- This is a good way for **players to learn to rest with the ball and control the tempo**.

Position Specific Possession

- Sessions would be **done to an outcome** e.g. Finish or shot at goal under pressure.
- Jokers are placed strategically as part of the defensive, midfield and attacking units, so there is **always an advantage in possession**.
- The aim is to **deliver the tactical knowledge the players require in each unit** and show how everything is linked together.
- Coach organisation when building these practices is key to their success.

Game Related Even/Odd Numbers

- 1v1, 2v1, 2v2, 3v2, etc. (with and without the ball).
- **High intensity and competition**, while continuously changing numbers.
- **Easiest way to gain an advantage is 1v1 with players who can beat their opponent**.

Manchester City Academy Training Process and Structure

City Game Principles

▶ As part of the training session, we would either deliver game related even/odd numbers or game principles training (never both on the same day). This was also with the physical loading cycle taken into consideration.

▶ The **principles underpin exactly the way you want the team and players to play in all moments of the game**. This is a process that takes time.

Small Sided Games

▶ Small sided games should always be a **part of every session**.

▶ Players enjoy the games, and it is important that the games provide variety in regard to **challenge and decision making**.

▶ It is also **important the link for the whole session remains** and the players do not simply play the way they want to play.

Individual/Unit Specifics

▶ Individual **development programs** (technical, tactically and physical) are key aspects of player development.

▶ These programs were developed in line with the **position specific profiles** we wanted to create. They **enabled us to play the way we wanted to play**.

Position Specific Training

▶ Players **need to understand and be able to perform all aspects and areas of specific positions** within the team.

▶ Coaching and teaching the players all positions means they will have a **greater appreciation of each others' roles**.

Manchester City Academy Training Session Structure

PART 1 OF TRAINING SESSION (15/20 minutes)
Technical Theme / Unopposed Practices

PART 2 OF TRAINING SESSION (20/30 minutes)
Opposed Possession / Tactical Focus Practices

PART 3 OF TRAINING SESSION (30/40 minutes)
Games / Problem Solving Practices

END OF TRAINING SESSION (10 minutes)
Player Led Individual Training / Objectives

The sessions are based around the weekly theme from the rotational program.

The sessions are all delivered in the form of a session builder which includes variations dependent on the physical loading cycle and which topic is the high level of focus in the periodization **(see the next section "Building the Training Program")**.

ELITE ACADEMY COACHING

Building the Training Program

Building the Training Program

How Was Training Structured for Individuals and for the Collective?

▶ **6 Week Training Methodology Tactical Periodization Curriculum** (see next page).
▶ This ran alongside a **4 Week Physical Loading Cycle** (example shown on pages 47-50).

▶ Included in the schedule is the team training sessions, the St Bede's education program, alternate activities, and the individual physical development programs.

▶ Position specific training as **UNITS** - **Defence** / **Midfield** / **Attack**.
▶ Position specific training **INDIVIDUALLY**.

▶ **DEVELOPMENT VARIANTS** = Birth bias, relative age affect, peak height velocity, potential positions, type of runs, amount of distance to be covered, etc.

▶ Technical and Individual physical development plans tailored to individual players.
▶ Tailored to the all round holistic development (key component for all academies).

▶ We also included alternative activities in the schedule for our players development.
▶ Relates specifically to potential positions they will play and the requirements.

▶ Physical development programs should also be tailored to the specific requirements of a player's development for their future game.

Building the Training Program

6 Week Training Methodology (Tactical Periodization Curriculum)

Week	Themes		
1	Build-up Phase 1	Build-up Phase 2	Build-up Phase 3
2	Build-up Phase 2	Build-up Phase 3	Pressing from the Front
3	Build-up Phase 3	Pressing from the Front	Defending in Midfield
4	Pressing from the Front	Defending in Midfield	Defending Around the Box
5	Defending in Midfield	Defending Around the Box	Build-up Phase 1
6	Defending Around the Box	Build-up Phase 1	Build-up Phase 2

Manchester City follow this methodology religiously, and they do not react to results or performance by making changes to this structure.

Over a period of time, players have complete clarity about what is expected of them in each area of the game, each moment, and in each position.

A lot of detail goes into sessions, but the periodization is very simple, although you add set pieces too of course.

NOTE: If for instance, the team's build-up play was very good, and their pressing from the front was not, you might spend 2 weeks on pressing.

Building the Training Program

Manchester City Academy U15 Team Physical Loading Program

Week 1/4 = Low to Medium Load

THEME	MONDAY **INTENSIVE**	TUESDAY **SPECIFIC ENDURANCE**	WEDNESDAY **ADAPTATION**	THURSDAY **SPEED**	FRIDAY **REACTIVE SPEED**	SATURDAY **MATCH**
EDUCATION	9:15 to 13:15 St. Bede's College	9:15 to 13:15 St. Bede's College	9:15 to 13:15 St. Bede's College	9:15 to 13:15 St. Bede's College	9:15 to 13:15 St. Bede's College	
FOOTBALL	14:00 to 15:30 Warm up (10 min) Small Pitch & Small Numbers Possession (3 x 5 min) Game Related 3v2-2v2 (45s on/45s off) 6v6 SSG (5 x 3 min) Conditioning (20 mins)	14:00 to 15:30 Warm up (10 min) Large Pitch & Large Numbers Possession (5 x 3 min) Game Principles Phase of Play (DEF) 8v8 SSG (3 x 6 min)	14:00 to 16:00 Alternative Activities	14:00 to 15:30 Warm up (10 min) Large Pitch - Short bursts Long Distance (20m+) Possession (5 x 2.5 min) Game Related 1v1-3v2 (max 10 sec) 7v7 SSG (2 x 6 min)	14:00 to 15:30 Warm up (10 min) Small Pitch - Short bursts Short Distance (<10m) Possession (5 x 2 min) Game Principles (Reactive) 5v5 or 6v6 SSG (3 teams rotate 4 x 2 min max)	
PERF. ANALYSIS	16:00 to 16:45 Performance Analysis					
EDUCATION	16:45 to 17:45 Education Academy				16:00 to 17:00 Training for those not playing on Saturday (e.g. Technical + Conditioning)	
FOOTBALL / PHYSICAL		16:45 to 18:15 Physical Strength (30 min) Technical / Tactical Unit / Team / Individual (45 min) Physical Speed / Endurance (15 min)	16:30 to 17:30 Education Academy	16:45 to 18:15 Physical Strength (30 min) Technical / Tactical Unit / Team / Individual (45 min) Physical Speed / Endurance (15 min)		
EDUCATION		18:00 to 18:30 Homework Club Education	17:30 to 18:30 Homework Club Education			
TRAINING TIME	1 hour 30 min + 45 min	2 hours + 20 min	0 hours	2 hours + 30 min	1 hour 30 min	2 hours

Load: 1 | 2 | 3 | 4 | 5

Total = 9 hours 30 min football + 1 hour 50 min physical

Building the Training Program

Week 2/4 = Medium Load

THEME	MONDAY INTENSIVE	TUESDAY SPECIFIC ENDURANCE	WEDNESDAY ADAPTATION	THURSDAY SPEED	FRIDAY REACTIVE SPEED	SATURDAY MATCH
EDUCATION	9:15 to 13:15 St. Bede's College	9:15 to 13:15 St. Bede's College	9:15 to 13:15 St. Bede's College	9:15 to 13:15 St. Bede's College	9:15 to 13:15 St. Bede's College	
FOOTBALL	14:00 to 15:30 Warm up (10 min) Small Pitch & Small Numbers Possession (3 x 5 min) Game Related 2v2-2v1 (30s on /30s off) 5v5 SSG (5 x 3.5 min) Conditioning (20 mins)	14:00 to 15:30 Warm up (10 min) Large Pitch & Large Numbers Possession (5 x 3.5 min) Game Principles Phase of Play (DEF) 8v8 SSG (3 x 7 min)	14:00 to 16:00 Alternative Activities	14:00 to 15:30 Warm up (10 min) Large Pitch - Short bursts Long Distance (20m+) Possession (5 x 2.5 min) Game Related 1v1-3v2 (max 10 sec) 7v7 SSG (3 x 7.5 min)	14:00 to 15:30 Warm up (10 min) Small Pitch - Short bursts Short Distance (<10m) Possession (5 x 2 min) Game Principles (Reactive) 5v5 or 6v6 SSG (3 teams rotate 4 x 2 min max)	
PERF. ANALYSIS	16:00 to 16:45 Performance Analysis					
EDUCATION	16:45 to 17:45 Education Academy		16:30 to 17:30 Education Academy			
FOOTBALL / PHYSICAL		16:45 to 18:15 Physical Strength (30 min) Technical / Tactical Unit / Team / Individual (45 min) Physical Speed / Endurance (15 min)		16:45 to 18:15 Physical Strength (30 min) Technical / Tactical Unit / Team / Individual (45 min) Physical Speed / Endurance (15 min)	16:00 to 17:00 Training for those not playing on Saturday (e.g. Technical + Conditioning)	
EDUCATION		18:00 to 18:30 Homework Club Education	17:30 to 18:30 Homework Club Education			
TRAINING TIME	1 hour 30 min + 45 min	2 hours + 20 min	0 hours	2 hours + 30 min	1 hour 30 min	2 hours

Load: 1 2 3 4 5

Total = 9 hours 30 min football + 1 hour 50 min physical

Building the Training Program

Week 3/4 = High Load

	MONDAY	TUESDAY	WEDNESDAY	THURSDAY	FRIDAY	SATURDAY
THEME	INTENSIVE	SPECIFIC ENDURANCE	ADAPTATION	SPEED	REACTIVE SPEED	MATCH
EDUCATION	9:15 to 13:15 St. Bede's College	9:15 to 13:15 St. Bede's College	9:15 to 13:15 St. Bede's College	9:15 to 13:15 St. Bede's College	9:15 to 13:15 St. Bede's College	
FOOTBALL	14:00 to 15:30 Warm up (10 min) Small Pitch & Small Numbers Possession (3 x 5 min) Game Related 2v1-1v1 (20s on/20s off) 5v5 SSG (4 x 5 min) Conditioning (20 mins)	14:00 to 15:30 Warm up (10 min) Large Pitch & Large Numbers Possession (6 x 3 min) Game Principles Phase of Play (DEF) 8v8 SSG (3 x 8.5 min)	14:00 to 16:00 Alternative Activities	14:00 to 15:30 Warm up (10 min) Large Pitch - Short bursts Long Distance (20m+) Possession (5 x 2.5 min) Game Related 1v1-3v2 (max 10 sec) 7v7 SSG (3 x 7 min)	14:00 to 15:30 Warm up (10 min) Small Pitch - Short bursts Short Distance (<10m) Possession (5 x 2 min) Game Principles (Reactive) 5v5 or 6v6 SSG (3 teams rotate 4 x 2 min max)	
PERF. ANALYSIS	16:00 to 16:45 Performance Analysis					
EDUCATION	16:45 to 17:45 Education Academy		16:30 to 17:30 Education Academy		16:00 to 17:00 Training for those not playing on Saturday (e.g. Technical + Conditioning)	
FOOTBALL / PHYSICAL		16:45 to 18:15 Physical Strength (30 min) Technical / Tactical Unit / Team / Individual (45 min) Physical Speed / Endurance (15 min)		16:45 to 18:15 Physical Strength (30 min) Technical / Tactical Unit / Team / Individual (45 min) Physical Speed / Endurance (15 min)		
EDUCATION		18:00 to 18:30 Homework Club Education	17:30 to 18:30 Homework Club Education			
TRAINING TIME	1 hour 30 min + 45 min	2 hours + 20 min	0 hours	2 hours + 30 min	1 hour 30 min	2 hours

Load: 1 | 2 | 3 | 4 | 5

Total = 9 hours 30 min football + 1 hour 50 min physical

Building the Training Program

Week 4/4 = Low Load

	MONDAY	TUESDAY	WEDNESDAY	THURSDAY	FRIDAY	SATURDAY
THEME	INTENSIVE	SPECIFIC ENDURANCE	ADAPTATION	SPEED	REACTIVE SPEED	MATCH
EDUCATION	9:15 to 13:15 St. Bede's College	9:15 to 13:15 St. Bede's College	9:15 to 13:15 St. Bede's College	9:15 to 13:15 St. Bede's College	9:15 to 13:15 St. Bede's College	
FOOTBALL	14:00 to 15:30 Warm up (10 min) Small Pitch & Small Numbers Possession (3 x 5 min) Game Related 3v3 (30s on /45s off) 6v6 SSG (4 x 3.5 min) Conditioning (20 mins)	14:00 to 15:30 Warm up (10 min) Large Pitch & Large Numbers Possession (4 x 3.5 min) Game Principles Phase of Play (DEF) 8v8 SSG (4 x 5 min)	14:00 to 16:00 Alternative Activities	14:00 to 15:30 Warm up (10 min) Large Pitch & Long Distances (20m+) Possession (5 x 2.5 min) Phase of Play (ATT) or Game Related 1v1- 3v2 (max 10 sec) 7v7 SSG (2 x 7.5 min)	14:00 to 15:30 Warm up (10 min) Small Pitch - Short bursts Short Distance (<10m) Possession (5 x 2 min) Game Principles (Reactive) 5v5 or 6v6 SSG (3 teams rotate 4 x 2 min max)	
PERF. ANALYSIS	16:00 to 16:45 Performance Analysis					
EDUCATION	16:45 to 17:45 Education Academy				16:00 to 17:00 Training for those not playing on Saturday (e.g. Technical + Conditioning)	
FOOTBALL / PHYSICAL		16:45 to 18:15 Physical Strength (30 min) Technical / Tactical Unit / Team / Individual (45 min) Physical Speed / Endurance (15 min)	16:30 to 17:30 Education Academy	16:45 to 18:15 Physical Strength (30 min) Technical / Tactical Unit / Team / Individual (45 min) Physical Speed / Endurance (15 min)		
EDUCATION		18:00 to 18:30 Homework Club Education	17:30 to 18:30 Homework Club Education			
TRAINING TIME	1 hour 30 min + 45 min	2 hours + 20 min	0 hours	2 hours + 30 min	1 hour 30 min	2 hours

| Load: | 1 | 2 | 3 | 4 | 5 | Total = 9 hours 30 min football + 1 hour 50 min physical |

ELITE ACADEMY COACHING

How the 6 Week Training Methodology Works Alongside the 4 Week Physical Loading Program

There is a big challenge when incorporating a **6 Week Training Methodology** (see the Tactical Periodization Curriculum on page 46) and a **4 Week Physical Loading Program** (U15 example shown on the previous 4 pages).

What if for example, the Pressing from the Front (which is usually high intensity) fell on the down week of the Physical Loading Program?

The multi-discipline team and approach is the key to the success for this type of player development program.

Injury prevention and a comprehensive approach to the individual player's development, while also developing a clear understanding of the game model, is an extremely challenging task which takes attention to detail and forward planning.

This was mainly managed through agreement and communication involving time, space and numbers when planning the session builders for the physical and tactical periodization.

Time = How long and how many repetitions of each exercise/practice, and how much rest?

Numbers = How many players, opposed, unopposed, overloads, etc?

Playing Area = Size of the area dependent on the technical, tactical and physical objectives, and outcomes desired.

MANCHESTER CITY ACADEMY SESSION 1

Build-up Phase 1: Short Build-up from the GK (1)

Training Session 1 - Short Build-up from the GK

1. Angles of Support and Playing Through the Thirds in a 4-Line Passing Drill with Multiple Combinations

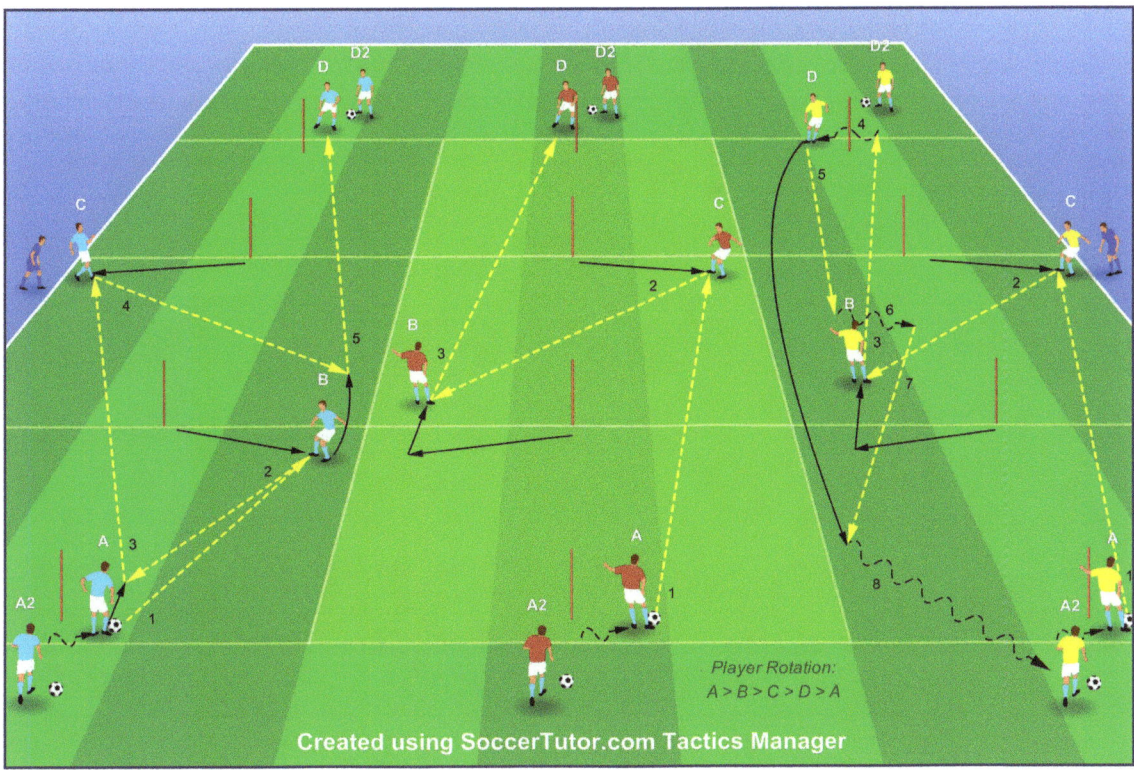

Practice Description

We start with 1 player on each pole + 1 extra player at each end. The players work in groups of 6 and practice freely using 3 different variations. The central players move wide off their poles to create angles.

1 (Left Side). A plays a one-two with **B**, then passes to **C**, who sets the ball back for **B** to play the final pass to **D**. Repeat sequence from opposite end.

2 (Middle). A passes to **C**, who sets the ball back for **B** to play the final pass to **D**. Repeat sequence from opposite end.

3 (Right Side). Player **A** passes to **C**, who sets the ball back for **B** to pass to **D**. **D** opens up past the pole and passes to **B**, who turns and passes for the deep run of **D** to receive and dribble to Position A.

→ All the players rotate to the next position (A → B → C → D → A).

Coaching Points

1. Timing of movement and pass are key to good rhythm in this practice.
2. The central players start on the poles, then time their movement away.
3. Players do not step until the ball has broken the line.
4. Pass and receive with the back foot, so you can play forward or back.

Training Session 1 - Short Build-up from the GK

2. Play Inside and Outside to Break the Line in a 3v3 (+2) Directional Possession Game

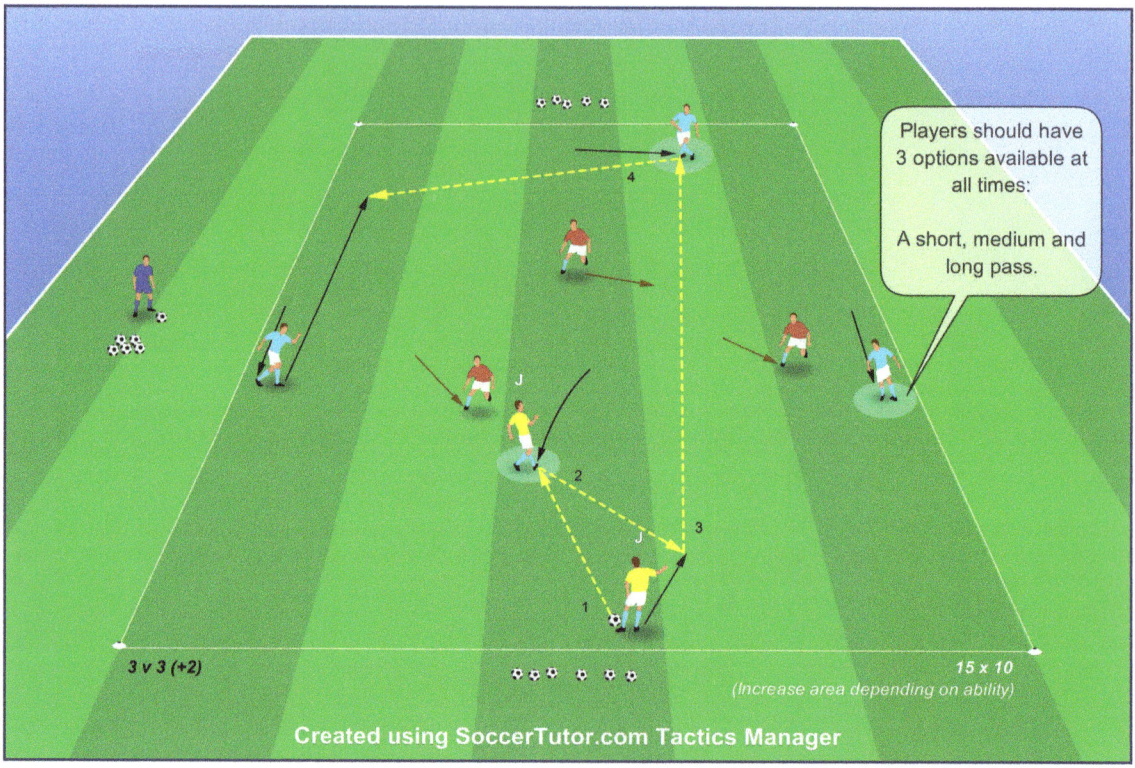

Practice Description

- The 15 x 10 yard area can be varied depending on the age and/or level of the players.
- This is a 3v3 (+2) possession game. The team in possession (blues in diagram example) effectively have a 5v3 situation with 1 player on each side + 1 in the middle against 3 defenders.
- **Concept:** Possession with a purpose, play in between and in behind, break lines. Players play their positions and try to play through the middle Joker.
- **Rule:** Ball must stay on the floor. The player in possession should always have a short, medium and long passing option.
- The team in possession aim to transfer the ball from one end to the other and continue to retain the ball.
- The 3 defenders (reds) press collectively and try to win the ball. If they do, the blues become the defenders and the possession game continues with the team roles reversed.

Coaching Points

1. Play your position.
2. Be ready to attack, ready to defend.
3. Play in between and in behind.
4. Combinations to play forward (quickly).
5. Penetration!

Training Session 1 - Short Build-up from the GK

3. End to End Game Related Attacking Overloads Wave Game (1v1 to 6v5) with Small Goals

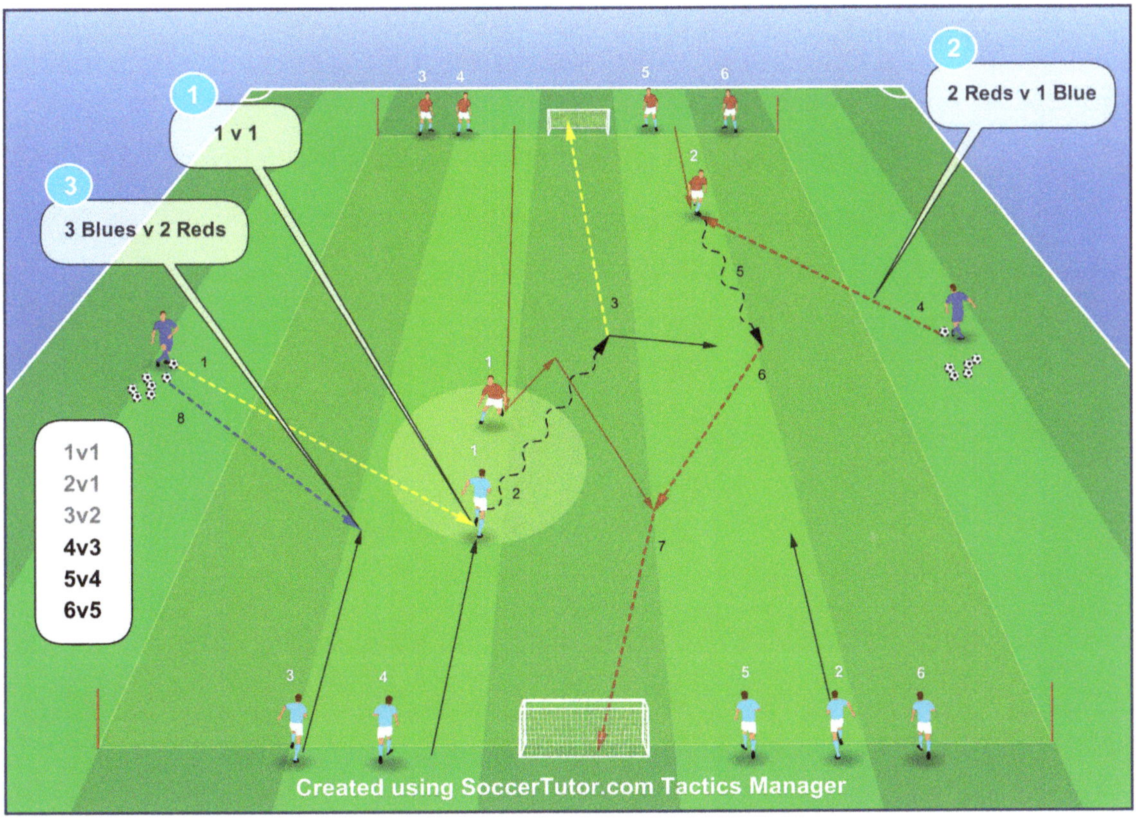

Practice Description

- In a 60 x 40 yard area, we have 2 teams of 6 and 2 small goals.

- This continuous end to end attacking overload wave game should be played with high competitiveness and intensity.

- **Ball 1:** The Coach starts by playing the ball in (yellow arrow) for a 1v1. In the diagram example, the blue player attacks and the red player defends.

- **Ball 2:** The Coach plays a new ball in (red arrow). The blue player becomes the defender and defends 2v1 against the red player + new red player who enters.

- **Ball 3:** The Coach plays a new ball in (blue arrow). 2 new blue players (2 & 3) enter for the new 3 Blues v 2 Reds attack.

- **Balls 4-6:** This continues with 4v3, then 5v4, finishing with 6v5.

- If the defender/s win the ball, they can also score and then still have the next phase of possession as the wave game continues. The winning team is the team who have scored the most goals.

- The tempo and decision making of this practice will change as more players enter the game, ranging from very fast at the start to medium tempo at the end.

Training Session 1 - Short Build-up from the GK

4. Create 3v2 Attacking Overloads in a Back to Back Goals 5v5 (+GKs) Small Sided Game

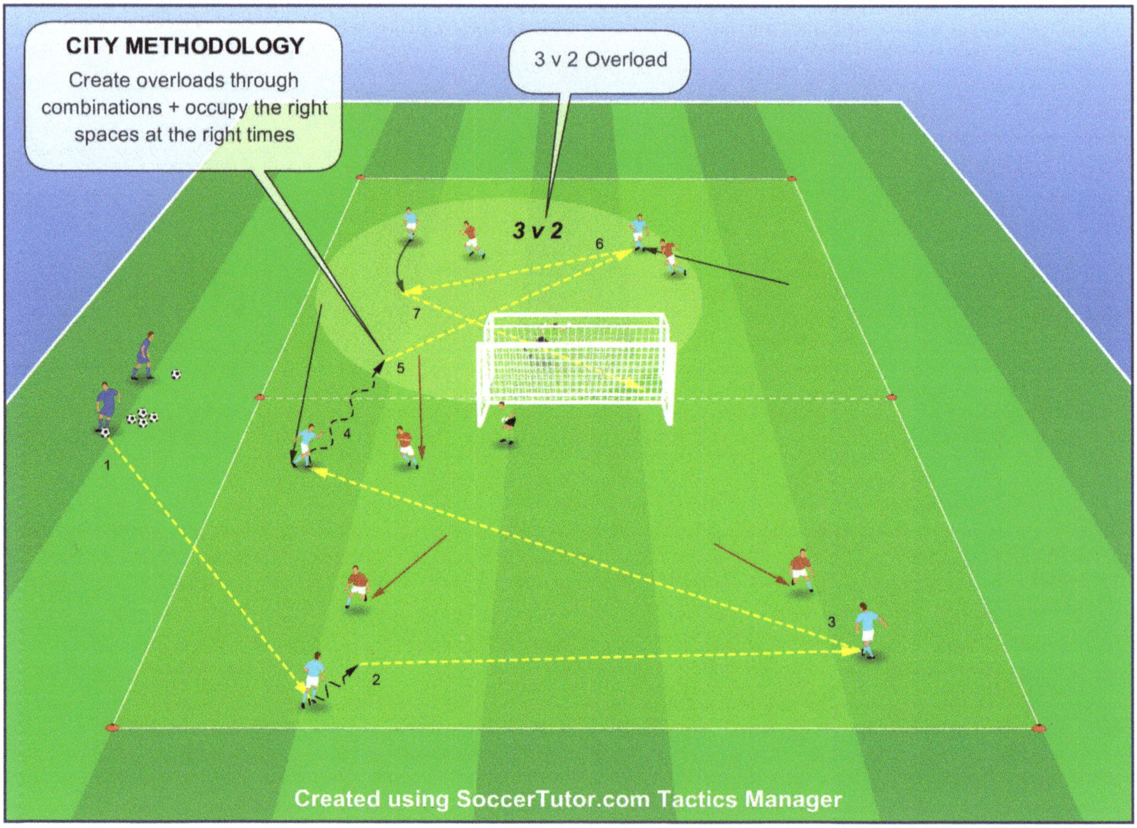

CITY METHODOLOGY
Create overloads through combinations + occupy the right spaces at the right times

3 v 2 Overload

Practice Description

- In a 60 x 40 yard area, we have 2 teams of 5 players and 2 large goals + GKs positioned back to back in the centre.

- The game starts with the Coach's pass and the team in possession (blues) aim to create a 3v2 attacking overload to score in the opposite goal.

- Implementing the City Methodology which includes creating overloads through fast combination play and occupying the right spaces at the right times helps players succeed in this game.

- High level players can be left to create 3v2, knowing the correct timings. It's about the situation and timing of when. Keep possession, then go in! The transitions should also be exploited.

Variations

1. For lower age groups/levels, start with 2v2 in both halves + 2 Jokers who float. This is easier to understand as the Jokers can easily help create a 3v2 overload.

2. Start with 3v3 in one half and 2v2 in the other.

MANCHESTER CITY ACADEMY SESSION 2

Build-up Phase 1: Short Build-up from the GK (2)

Training Session 2 - Short Build-up from the GK

1. One-Touch Technical Passing Triangle Drill with Third Man Run

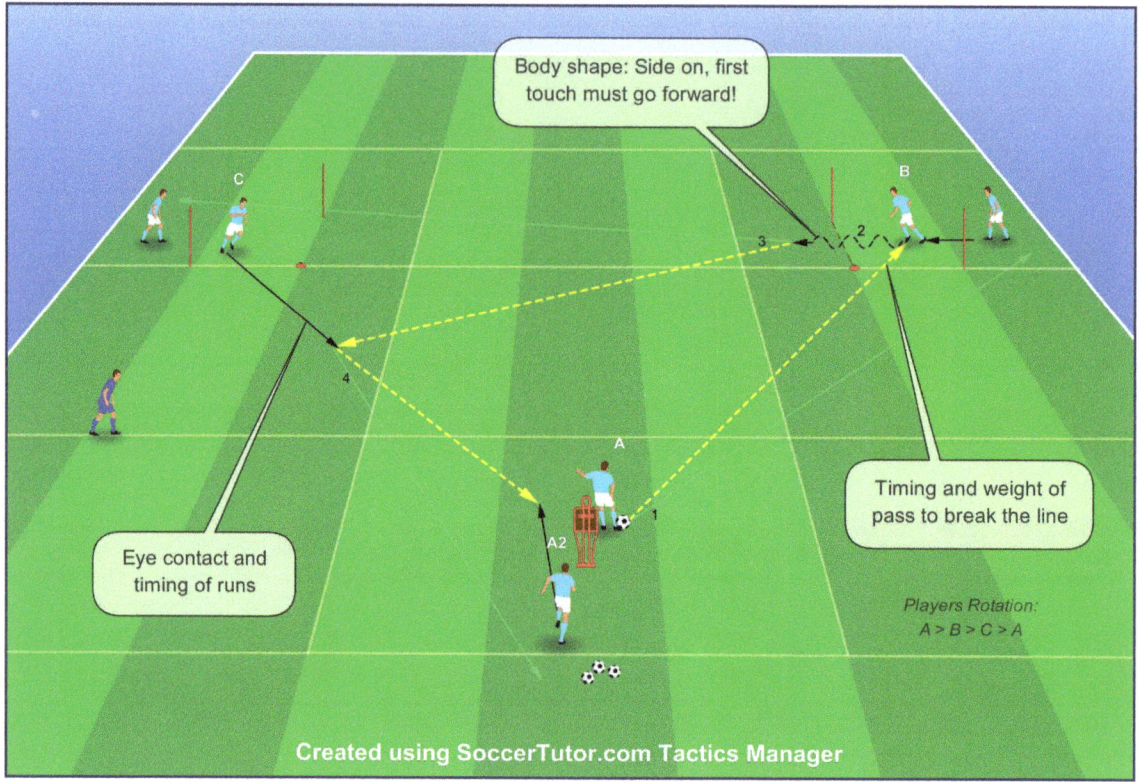

Practice Description

- Mark out the mannequins/poles 15-30 yards apart. The 2 widest poles act as defenders to check away from.
- The pole and cone creates a gate for the player to take their first touch through. The body position must be side on facing forward to break the line.
- Players use one touch with a high ball speed, so accuracy needs to be good.

Practice Sequence

1. **A** passes to **B**.
2. **B** breaks through the pole/cone gate.
3. **B** passes for the run of **C**.
4. **C** passes to **A2** and the sequence continues.

→ All the players rotate to the next position (A → B → C → A2). Change the direction often so players practice with both feet.

Coaching Points

1. Players must make eye contact to make sure the timing of their passes and movements are correct.
2. The weight of pass is key to break the line and eliminate the defender.

©SOCCERTUTOR.COM   ELITE ACADEMY COACHING

Training Session 2 - Short Build-up from the GK

2. Possession Play and Fast Transitions in Dual Directions in a Game Related 6v6 Transition Game

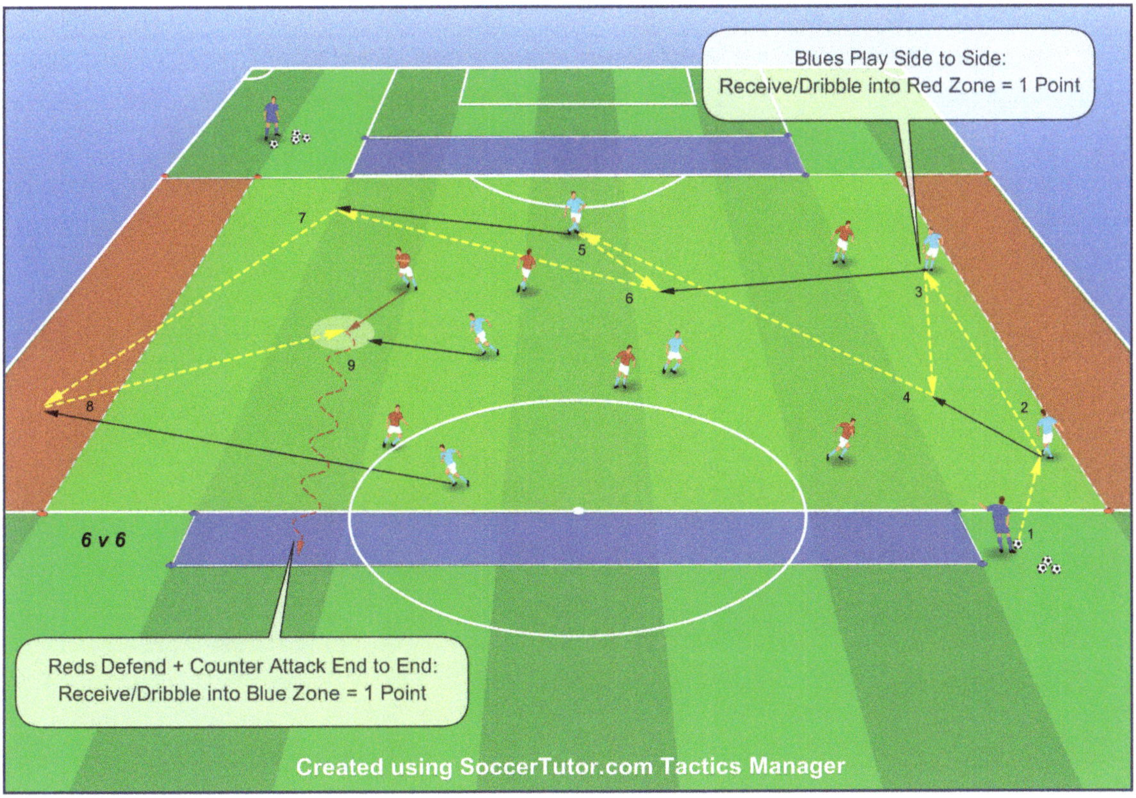

Blues Play Side to Side: Receive/Dribble into Red Zone = 1 Point

Reds Defend + Counter Attack End to End: Receive/Dribble into Blue Zone = 1 Point

6 v 6

Created using SoccerTutor.com Tactics Manager

Practice Description

- The Coach starts and the teams play 6v6. The Coach can control the game with conditions applied for time or touches to create the required game tempo.
- The blues attack side to side, aiming to receive or dribble in the red end zone (1 Point). Once they do this, they retain possession and attack the opposite red end zone.
- The reds defend and try to stop the blues. If they win the ball, they counter attack to receive or dribble into either blue end zone (1 Point). The blues make a fast transition to try and stop them.

Practice Aims (4 Phases of Game)

- Players are tasked with all 4 phases of the game (attacking, defending, and the transition phases).
- One team aims to score on the sides while also defending each end when the defensive transition happens. Another team aims to defend the sides and attack the end zones at each end after gaining possession.
- Technically gifted independent decision makers with game intelligence and understanding are the most successful in this practice.

59

©SOCCERTUTOR.COM ELITE ACADEMY COACHING

Training Session 2 - Short Build-up from the GK

3. Game Related Attacking Organisation and Overload for 3v2 Finish in a 2 Zone 3-Team SSG

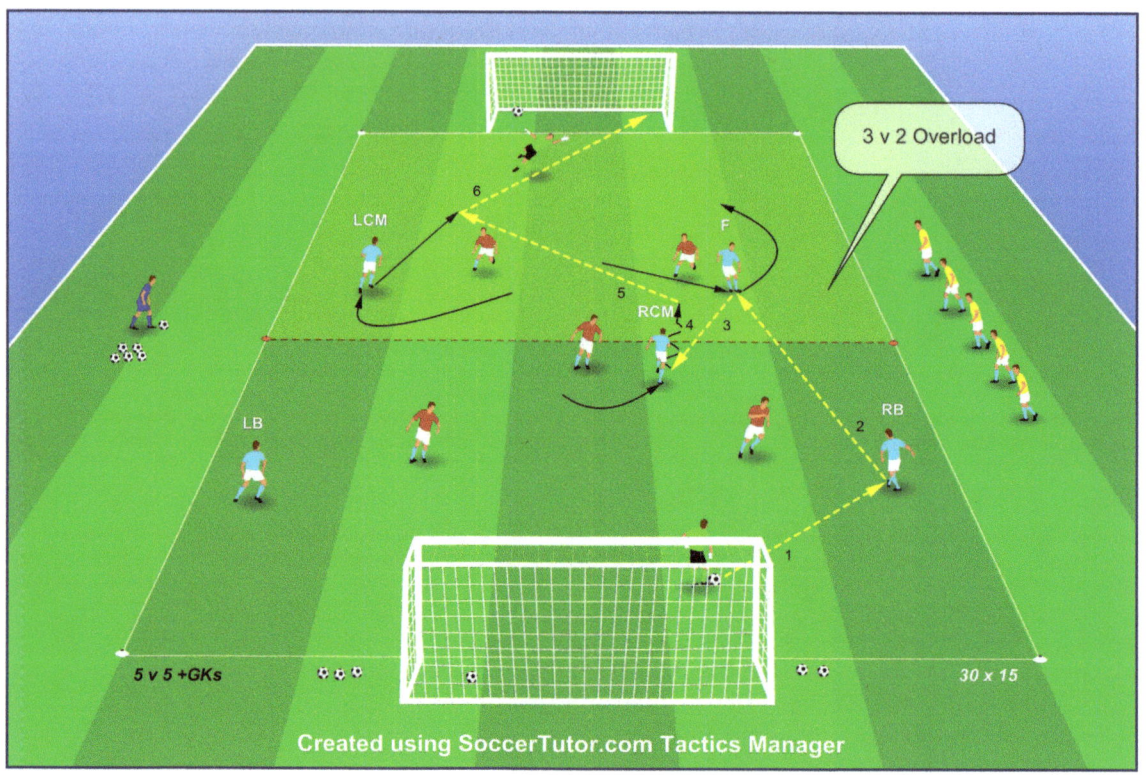

Practice Description

- In a 30 x 15 yard area, we have 3 teams of 5 players, but we only play with 2 teams at a time. Only 2 players on the defending team are allowed in their low zone (half).

- We start the game from the GK, who either passes to the **left back (LB)** or **right back (RB)**.

- *Note: The players can use multiple different patterns which you can take from other practices in the book.*

- In this example, the blue full back in possession **(RB)** plays to the **forward (F)**, who sets the ball back for either of the 2 **central midfielders (LCM or RCM)**. From that point, we have a 3v2 overload in the attacking half for the blues to try and finish the attack. Both full backs stay back and are not involved in finishing the attack.

- If the reds win the ball, they counter attack (5v5). The third team (yellows) rotates in after a goal is scored or after a set amount of time e.g. 3-5 minutes.

Coaching Points

1. Controlled possession (diamond shape) until the right moment comes to play in.
2. Dynamic counter attack before the 2 supporting players can recover.
3. Reactions, decisions, communication and positioning are all tested.

Training Session 2 - Short Build-up from the GK

4. Continuous Game Related 2v2 Duels in Pairs Wave Game with Large Goals + GKs

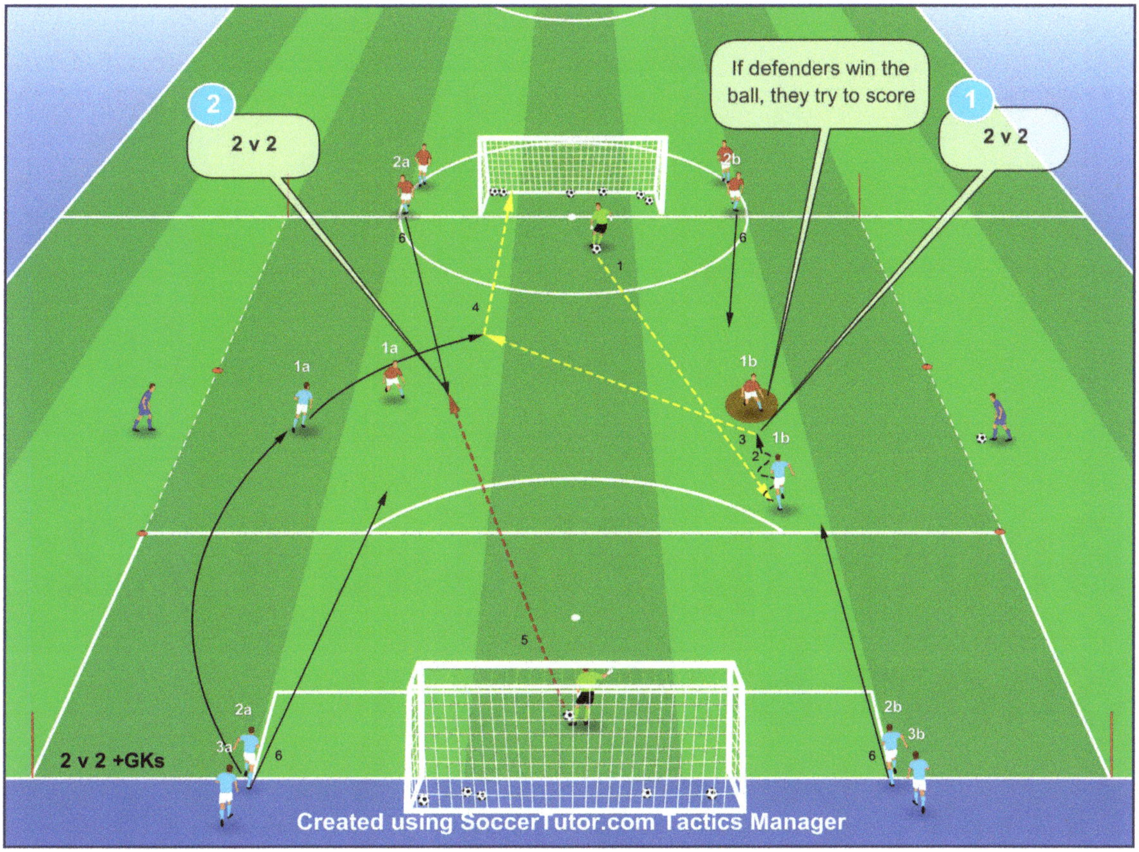

Practice Description

- In the area shown, we have 2 teams of 6 players in pairs and 2 large goals with GKs.
- **Ball 1:** The GK starts the game with a pass to a blue player (1b in diagram example).
- Blues 1a and 1b attack against Reds 1a and 1b in a 2v2 duel.
- The blues try to score quickly. If the reds win the ball, they try to score in the opposite goal.
- **Ball 2:** As soon as the first phase is over, the other GK passes to the next red pair.
- Red 2a and 2b attack the opposite goal against Blue 2a and 2b, who enter the pitch to defend.
- The game is continuous with the next pairs entering after each phase completes.

Coaching Points

1. Use overlaps, one-twos, 1v1s, one-touch lay-offs, and more when attacking.
2. Fast reactions + quick decision making for type of finish required.
3. Game should be intense and non-stop with high tempo (1v1/2v2 situations).

MANCHESTER CITY ACADEMY SESSION 3

Build-up Phase 1 + 2: Short Build-up from GK + Midfield Combination Play (1)

Training Session 3 - Short Build-up from GK + Midfield Combination Play

1. "Figure of 8" Technical Passing Diamond Drill with Free Decision Making

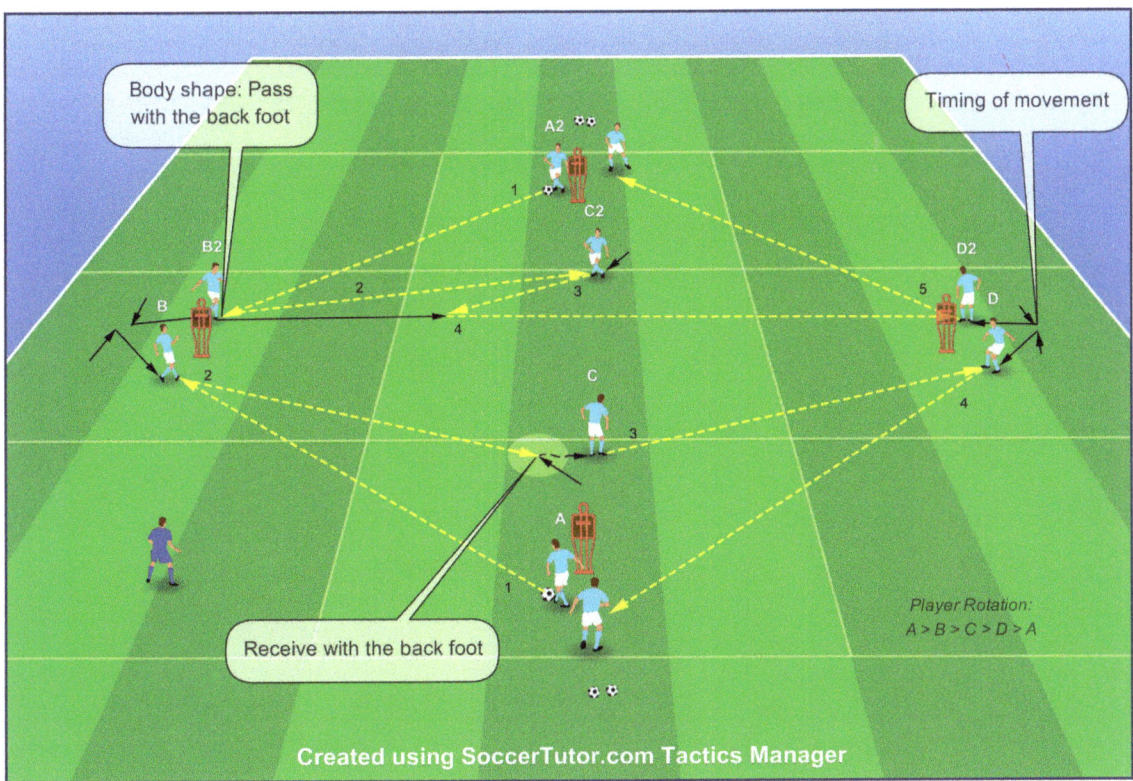

Practice Description

- In a 40 x 20 yard area, set up a diamond shape with 2 groups of players working on either side (2 triangles).
- The aim is to switch the play through the **Central Player C (DM)**.
- The focus is on challenging the players' decision making to keep possession. They can use many combinations and variations (2 are shown in the diagram).
- As they get more comfortable, they can use blind side runs, overlaps, diagonal passes into the pocket, etc.
- → All the players rotate to the next position (A → B → C → D → A).

Coaching Points

1. Open body position (half-turn) to receive the ball on the back foot.
2. Break the line with the first touch forward.
3. Switch the play → Play in between and in behind.
4. Timing and type of pass and movement is key to good rhythm in this practice.
5. Players must make eye contact and display good communication.
6. Play the pass to the player or into space.

Training Session 3 - Short Build-up from GK + Midfield Combination Play

2. Side and Central Diamond Patterns in a 7v7 (+1) Directional Possession Game with End Goal Zones

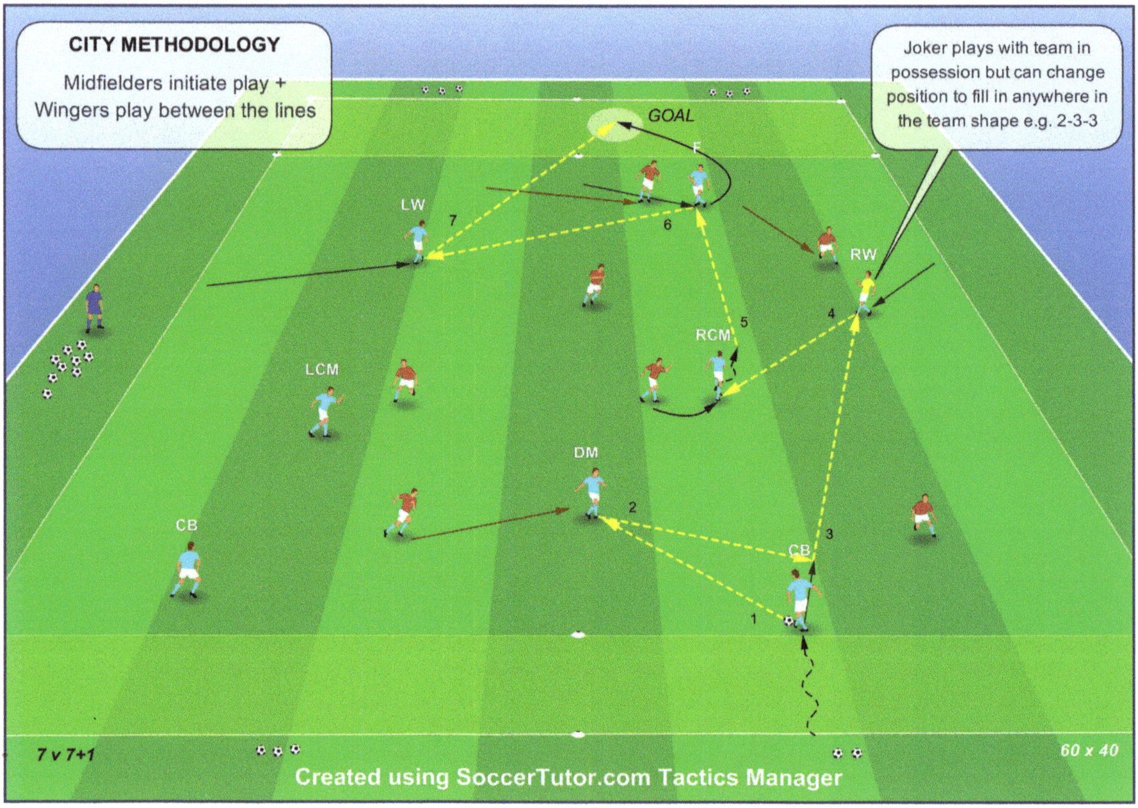

(CITY METHODOLOGY: Midfielders initiate play + Wingers play between the lines)

(Joker plays with team in possession but can change position to fill in anywhere in the team shape e.g. 2-3-3)

7 v 7+1 — 60 x 40

Practice Description

- In a 60 x 40 yard area, we play a 7v7 (+1) possession game. The yellow Joker plays with the team in possession (blues in diagram).

- The game starts with a blue player dribbling into the central zone. To score a **GOAL**, a blue player must receive within the end zone. The red defending players cannot enter this zone.

- The Coach is looking for the players to implement the side and central diamond patterns into this possession game. You can see many examples throughout the training sessions for reference.

- If a penetrative pass is played between defenders, the team score an extra point.

- When the team receives in the end zone, the red team restarts. The Joker plays with the reds as a **CB** or **DM**, trying to work the ball into the opposite end zone.

- The team shape can vary e.g. The **DM** can drop in between the 2 **CBs** to create a 3-2-3. It's all about creating +1 overloads.

Progression

- The player positions become completely fluid. The teams work the ball from end to end continuously and all the players + Joker adapt their positions constantly.

Training Session 3 - Short Build-up from GK + Midfield Combination Play

3. Game Principles and Side Diamond Patterns of Play in a 10v8 (+GKs) Functional Practice

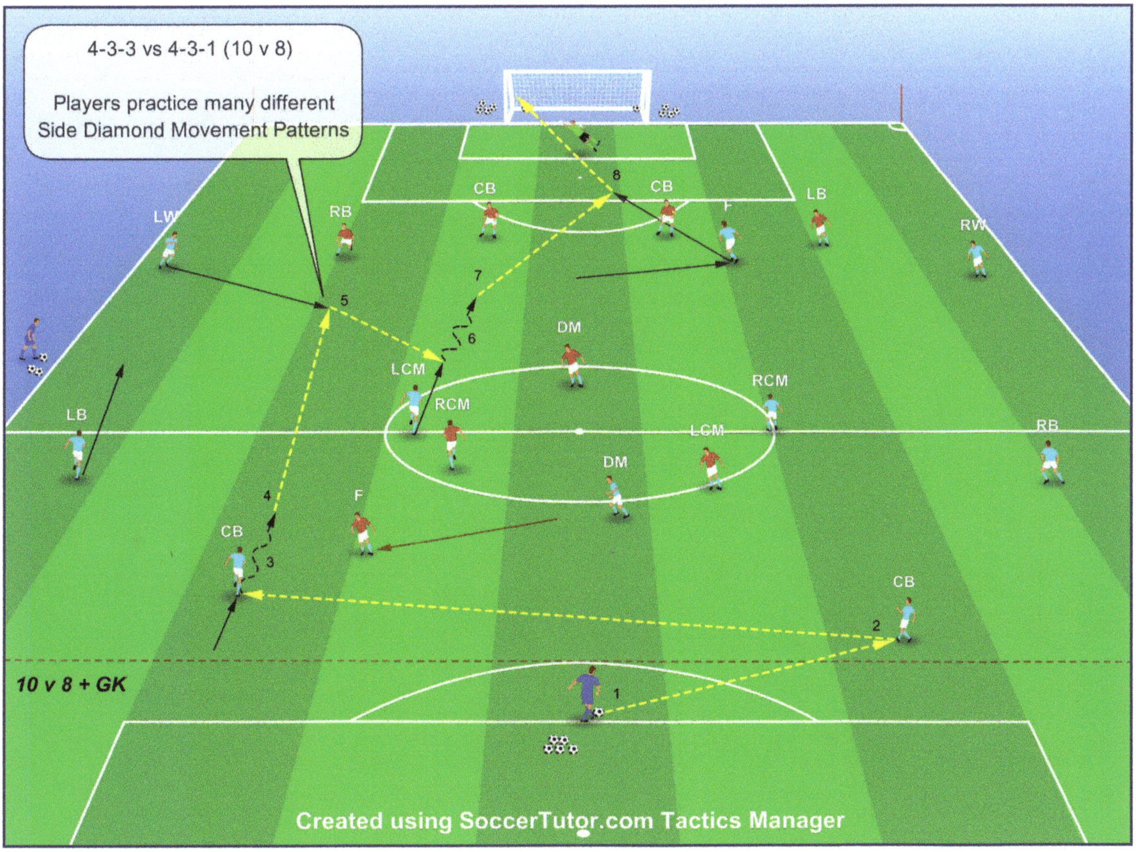

4-3-3 vs 4-3-1 (10 v 8)

Players practice many different Side Diamond Movement Patterns

10 v 8 + GK

Practice Description

- For this pattern of play practice, the Coach plays the ball in, and the blue players practice many side diamond patterns of play in the Manchester City 4-3-3 formation (you can see many examples throughout the training sessions for reference).

- The red team defend in a 4-3-1 formation.

- The blues use a side diamond pattern to create an overload in the wide area and exploit their numerical advantage (10 v 8). They must recognise what pattern to use at the right time.

- In the diagram example, the side diamond pattern enables them to receive in between the lines **(LW)**, set the ball for the **central midfielder (LCM)**, and then play a through pass for the movement of the **forward (F)** in behind to finish.

- The Coach must observe all the technical and tactical detail in line with the methodology.

- **NOTE:** This kind of opposed pattern of play practice was used in the later stages of the season when we wanted it to be opposed, making the players create overloads for success.

Training Session 3 - Short Build-up from GK + Midfield Combination Play

4. Break the Lines and Create Attacking Overloads in a Position Specific 7v7 (+1) +GKs 3-Zone SSG

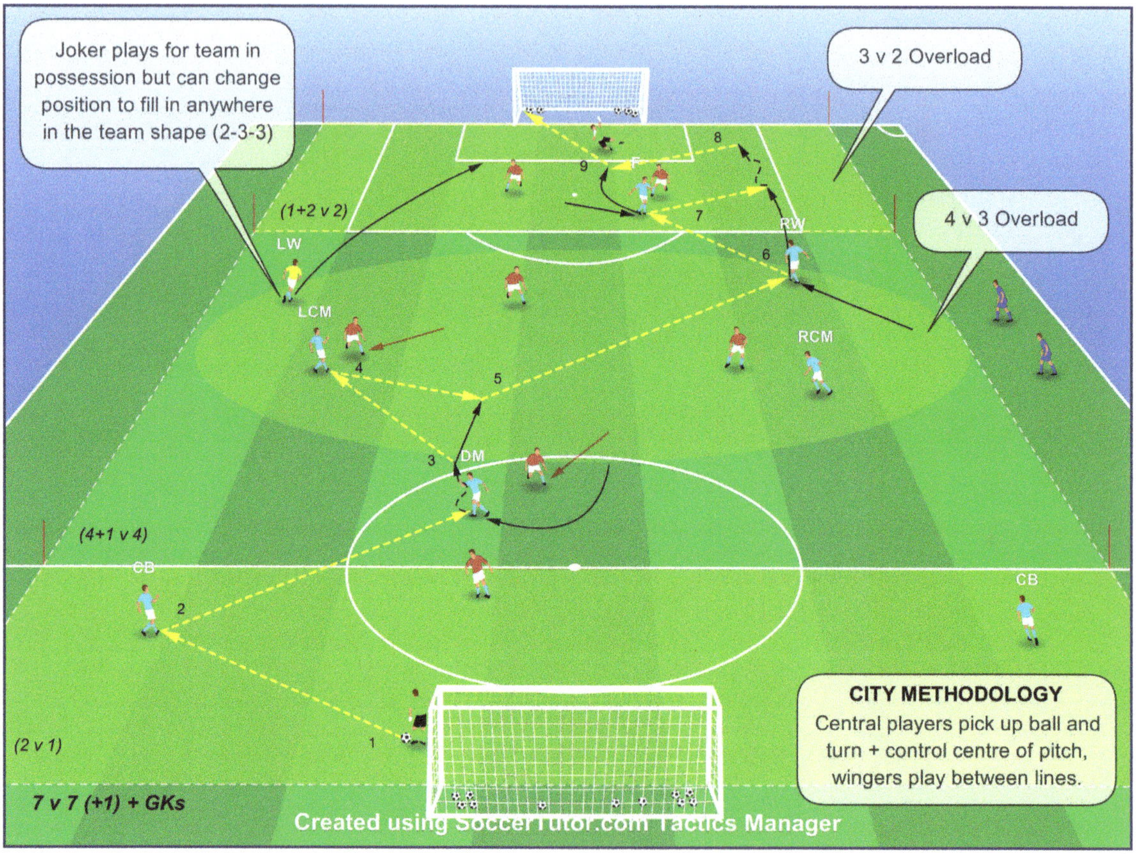

(Diagram: Joker plays for team in possession but can change position to fill in anywhere in the team shape (2-3-3). 3 v 2 Overload. 4 v 3 Overload. (1+2 v 2), (4+1 v 4), (2 v 1). 7 v 7 (+1) + GKs.)

CITY METHODOLOGY
Central players pick up ball and turn + control centre of pitch, wingers play between lines.

Practice Description

- This functional game is all about creating +1 overloads around the ball area using the extra Joker. The Coach controls the practice (rules) and can change where the players are allowed to move.

- This example has 3 marked out zones and starts with the blues playing out from the back with a 2v1 +GK advantage. The blues are in a 2-3-3 shape and the reds are using a 2-3-2.

- If the **DM** drops, it creates a 4v3 overload in the middle area (highlighted), as the closest red forward must mark him.

- **NOTE:** 1 x CB is allowed to step into the middle zone to create +1 if he wants to).

- The wingers **(LW & RW)** can drop into the pockets in the middle zone to create overloads in midfield. They can also enter the end zone to create a 3v2 attacking overload to finish the attack.

- When the attack finishes, the red team restarts from their GK. The yellow Joker plays with the reds as a **DM** or **CM** (the other players adjust their positions), trying to work the ball the opposite way with the same aims.

MANCHESTER CITY ACADEMY SESSION 4

Build-up Phase 1 + 2: Short Build-up from GK + Midfield Combination Play (2)

Training Session 4 - Short Build-up from GK + Midfield Combination Play

1a. Side Diamond Pattern to Play Through the Thirds in a Technical Pass and Move Circuit

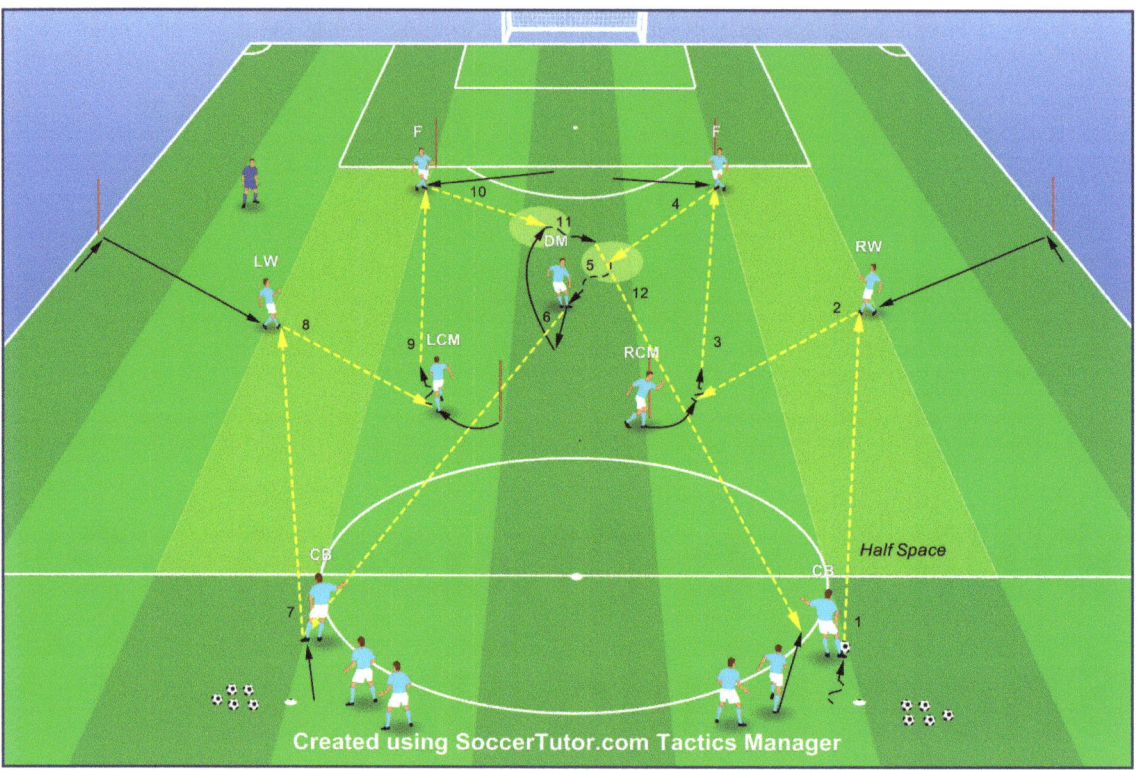

Practice Description

- The first **centre back (CB)** steps in with the ball taking their first touch forward into the space.

- The **winger (RW)** times the movement of when to come in off the line and receive in the half space.

- The **central midfielders (RCM)** starts behind the pole to keep the passing channels open.

- When the **CB** plays the pass into **RW** (breaking midfield line), the **RCM** steps forward to receive the set pass back from **RW**. **RCM** must take the first touch forward to open up all options.

- The **forward (F)** must stay high and central to receive the pass from **RCM**, then pass back to the **defensive midfielder (DM)**, who acts as the pivot to transfer the ball to the other side.

- The **DM** must receive on the half-turn and pass the ball to the other centre back on the opposite side. The same sequence is repeated on the other side (mirrored image) ending at the start position.

Coaching Point:

- **RW** uses a right foot pass and **RCM** receives with his left foot. **LW** uses a left foot pass and **LCM** receives with his right foot. This makes sure the players play at maximum speed through the lines.

Training Session 4 - Short Build-up from GK + Midfield Combination Play

1b. Technical Side Diamond Pattern Box to Box Pass and Move Circuit

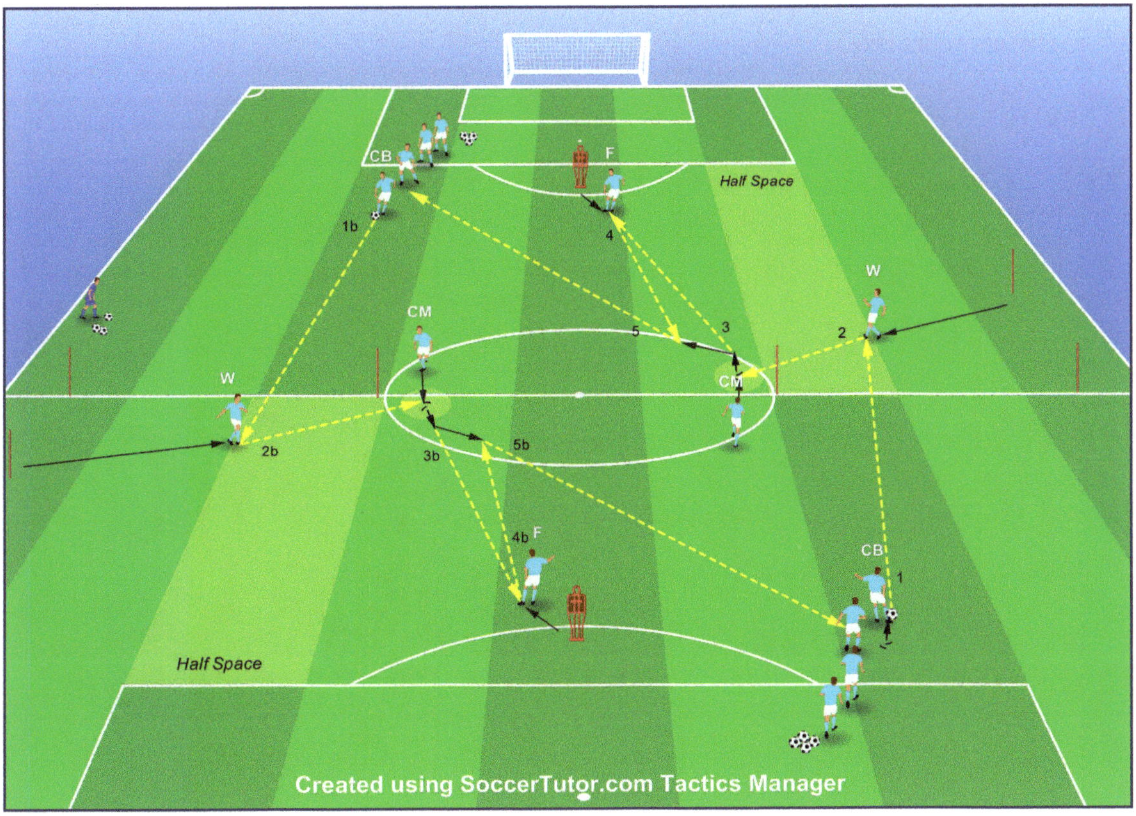

Practice Description

1. The practice starts with 2 balls in opposite corners. Both **centre backs (CB)** take a touch forward and pass into the half space for the **winger (W)**, who moves inside to receive.
2. **W** sets the ball for the **central midfielder (CM)** to receive beyond the pole.
3-4. **CM** passes to the **forward (F)**, who sets the ball back to the **CM** (one-two).
5. **CM** completes the sequence by passing to the opposite start position.

→ The practice continues with all the players rotating to the next position.

Coaching Points

1. The **centre backs (CB)** must step into play with their first touch when receiving the pass.
2. Focus on the timing of movement for the **wingers (W)** arriving in the half space to play a 1 touch set.
3. The **central midfielders (CM)** must take their first touch forward when receiving the set from **W**.
4. Play with a high ball speed to replicate match conditions.

Training Session 4 - Short Build-up from GK + Midfield Combination Play

2. Side and Central Diamond Patterns in a 7v7 (+1) Directional Possession Game with End Goal Zones

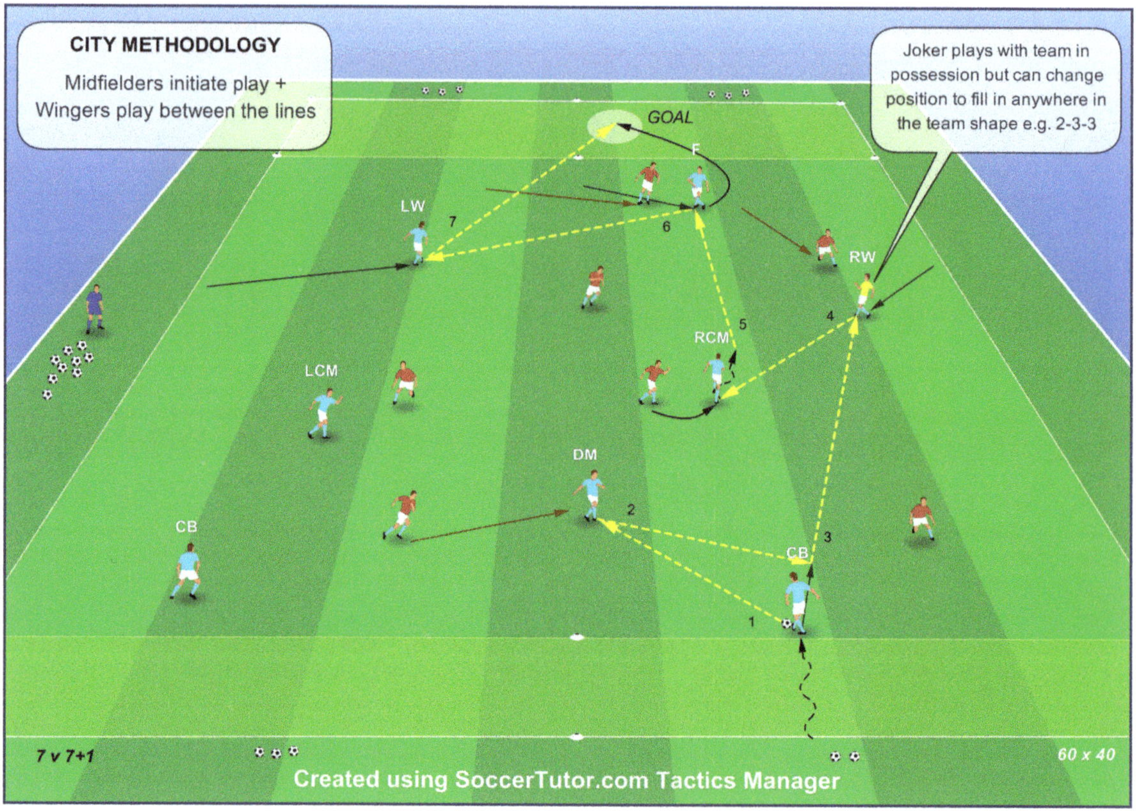

(CITY METHODOLOGY: Midfielders initiate play + Wingers play between the lines)

(Joker plays with team in possession but can change position to fill in anywhere in the team shape e.g. 2-3-3)

Practice Description

- In a 60 x 40 yard area, we play a 7v7 (+1) possession game. The yellow Joker plays with the team in possession (blues in diagram).

- The game starts with a blue player dribbling into the central zone. To score a **GOAL**, a blue player must receive within the end zone. The red defending players cannot enter this zone.

- The Coach is looking for the players to implement the side and central diamond patterns into this possession game.

- If a penetrative pass is played between defenders, the team score an extra point.

- When the team receives in the end zone, the red team restarts. The Joker plays with the reds as a **CB** or **DM**, trying to work the ball into the opposite end zone.

- The team shape can vary e.g. The **DM** can drop in between the 2 **CBs** to create a 3-2-3. It's all about creating +1 overloads.

Progression:

- The teams work the ball from end to end continuously and all the players + Joker adapt their positions constantly.

This is a repetition of the practice on Page 64 - it is placed here again as that is how sessions were built at the Manchester City Academy

Training Session 4 - Short Build-up from GK + Midfield Combination Play

3. Break Lines and Create Attacking Overloads in a Position Specific 7v7 (+GKs) 2-Zone SSG

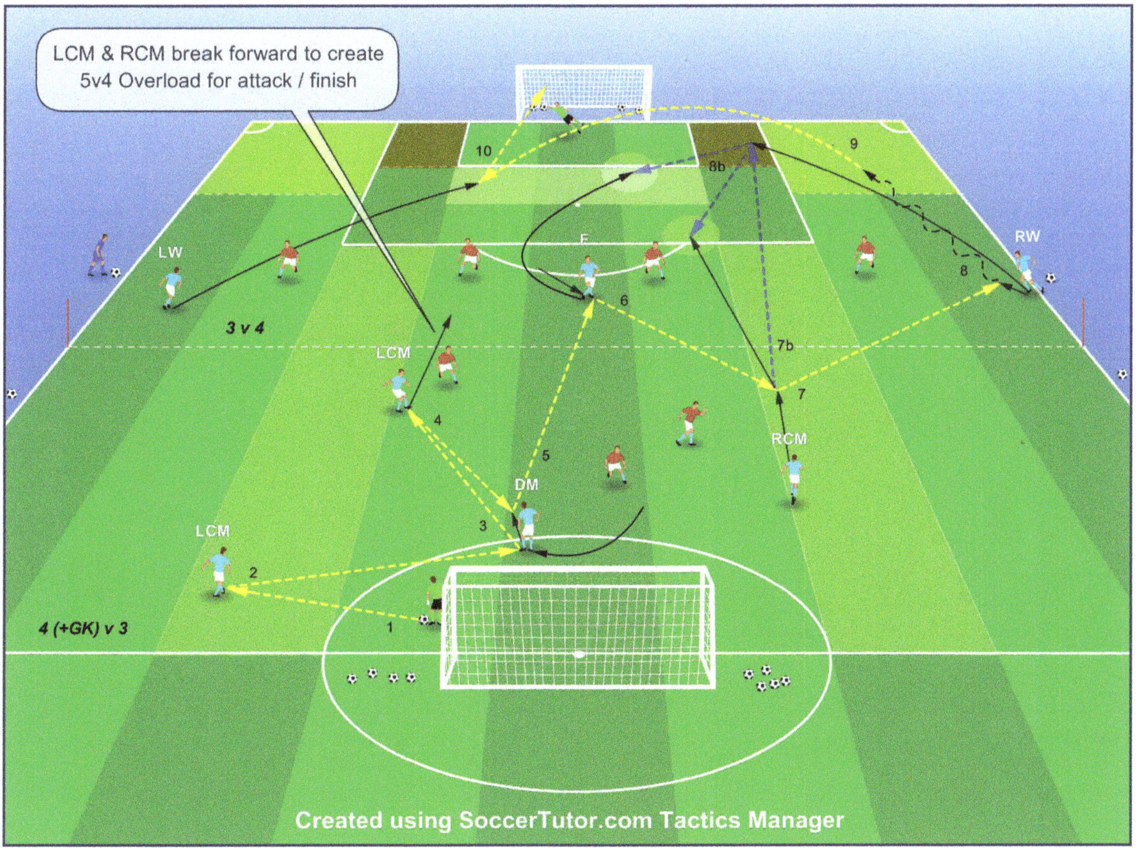

Practice Description

- Using half a pitch, we split the area into 2 equal halves as shown. We play a 7v7 (+GKs) small sided game.

- Start with the GK and an attacking overload in the low half (4 +GK v 3) and a 3v4 defensive overload in the high half.

- The blues keep controlled possession until the right moment to play into the attacking half **(DM → F in diagram)**. When this happens, both central midfielders **LCM** and **RCM** break forward to create a 5v4 overload to join and help finish the attack.

- If the reds win the ball in the low half, 2 red defenders can move forward to create a 5v5 attack to try and score.

- If the reds win the ball in the high half, it becomes a normal 7v7 (+GKs) game.

Coaching Points

1. Players reactions, decisions, positioning, and communication are all tested. You will quickly see the players who make the right decisions in the quickest time.

2. The tempo of this session is high so the players/teams have to identify when they can take a rest with the ball.

Training Session 4 - Short Build-up from GK + Midfield Combination Play

4. Break the Lines and Create Attacking Overloads in a Position Specific 7v7 (+1) +GKs 3-Zone SSG

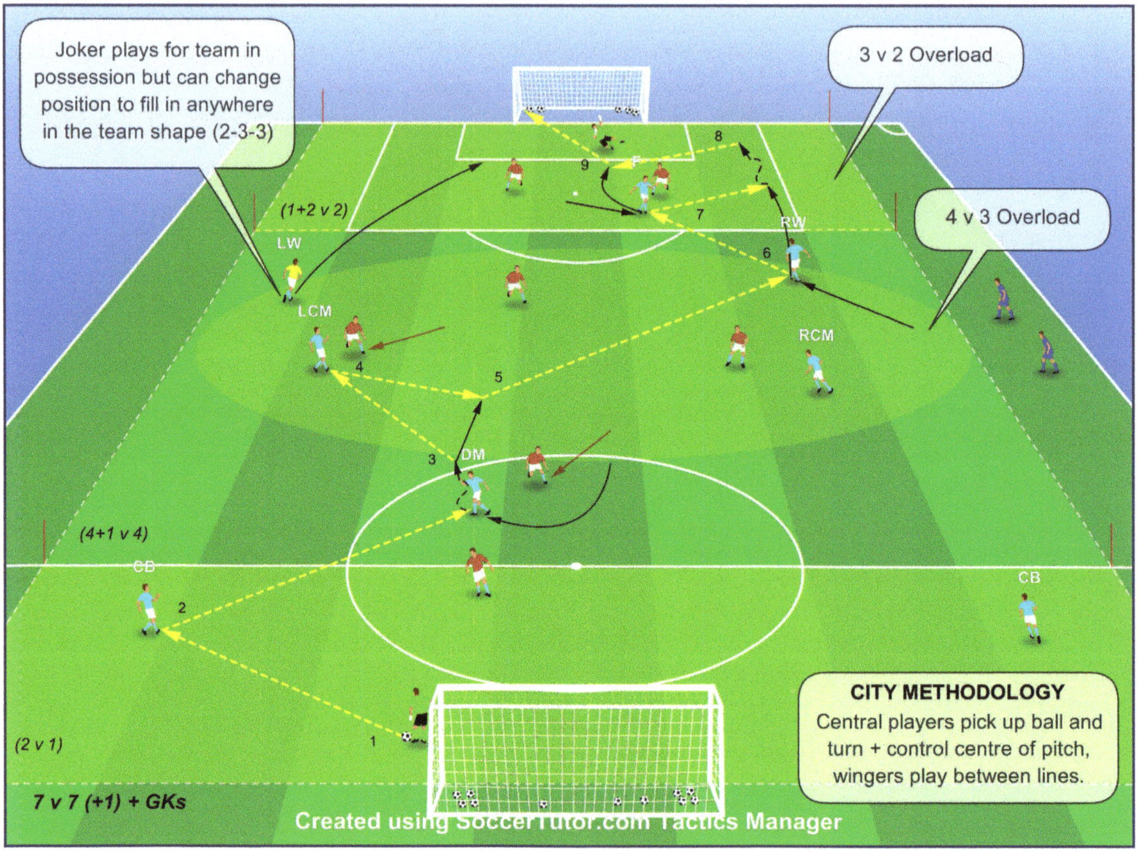

Practice Description

- This functional game is all about creating +1 overloads around the ball area using the extra Joker. The Coach can change where the players are allowed to move.

- This example has 3 marked out zones and starts with the blues playing out from the back with a 2v1 +GK advantage. The blues are in a 2-3-3 shape and the reds are using a 2-3-2.

- If the **DM** drops, it creates a 4v3 overload in the middle area (highlighted), as the closest red forward must mark him.

- **NOTE:** 1 x CB is allowed to step into the middle zone to create +1 if he wants to).

- The wingers **(LW & RW)** can drop into the pockets in the middle zone to create overloads in midfield. They can also enter the end zone to create a 3v2 attacking overload to finish the attack.

- When the attack finishes, the red team restarts from their GK. The yellow Joker plays with the reds as a **DM** or **CM** (the other players adjust their positions), trying to work the ball the opposite way with the same aims.

This is a repetition of the practice on Page 66 - it is placed here again as that is how sessions were built at the Manchester City Academy

MANCHESTER CITY ACADEMY SESSION 5

Build-up Phase 3: Finishing the Attack (Final Third)

Training Session 5 - Finishing the Attack (Final Third)

1a. Break Past Opponent and Play Final Pass in a Technical Triangle Drill with Finish

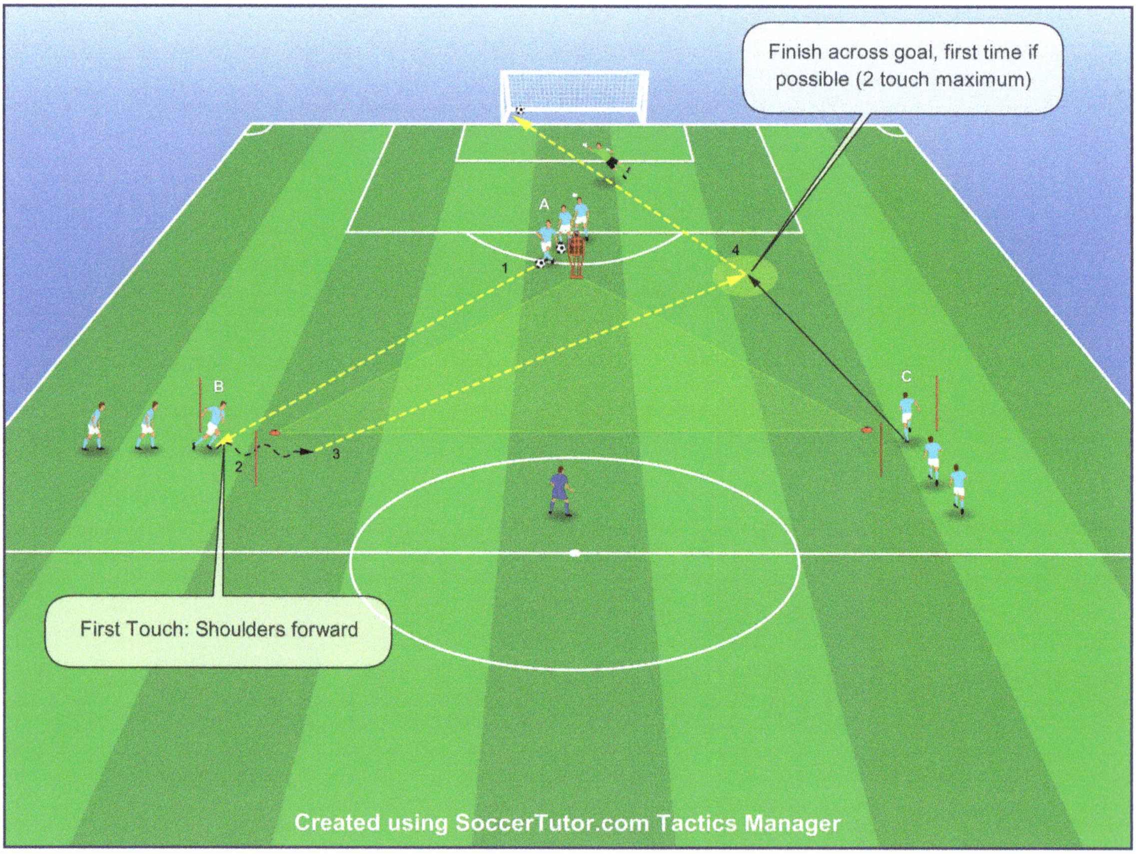

Finish across goal, first time if possible (2 touch maximum)

First Touch: Shoulders forward

Practice Description

- Mark out a triangle shape as shown and play at match speed with firm ground passes.
- The pole and cone creates a gate for the player to take their first touch through. The body position must be side on facing forward to break the line.

Practice Sequence

1-2. **A** passes to **B**, who breaks through the pole/cone gate.

3. **B** plays a diagonal pass for the run of **C**.

4-5. Depending on how close to goal he receives, **C** uses 1 or 2 touches to try and score past the GK.

→ All the players rotate to the next position (A → B → C → A). Change the direction often so players practice with both feet.

Coaching Points

1. First touch through the pole/cone gate with shoulders forward → past opponent, always forward to break the line.

2. The finish needs to be across goal and first time if possible (2 touch maximum).

Training Session 5 - Finishing the Attack (Final Third)

1b. Open Up and Switch Play with Diagonal Pass in a Technical Triangle Drill with Finish

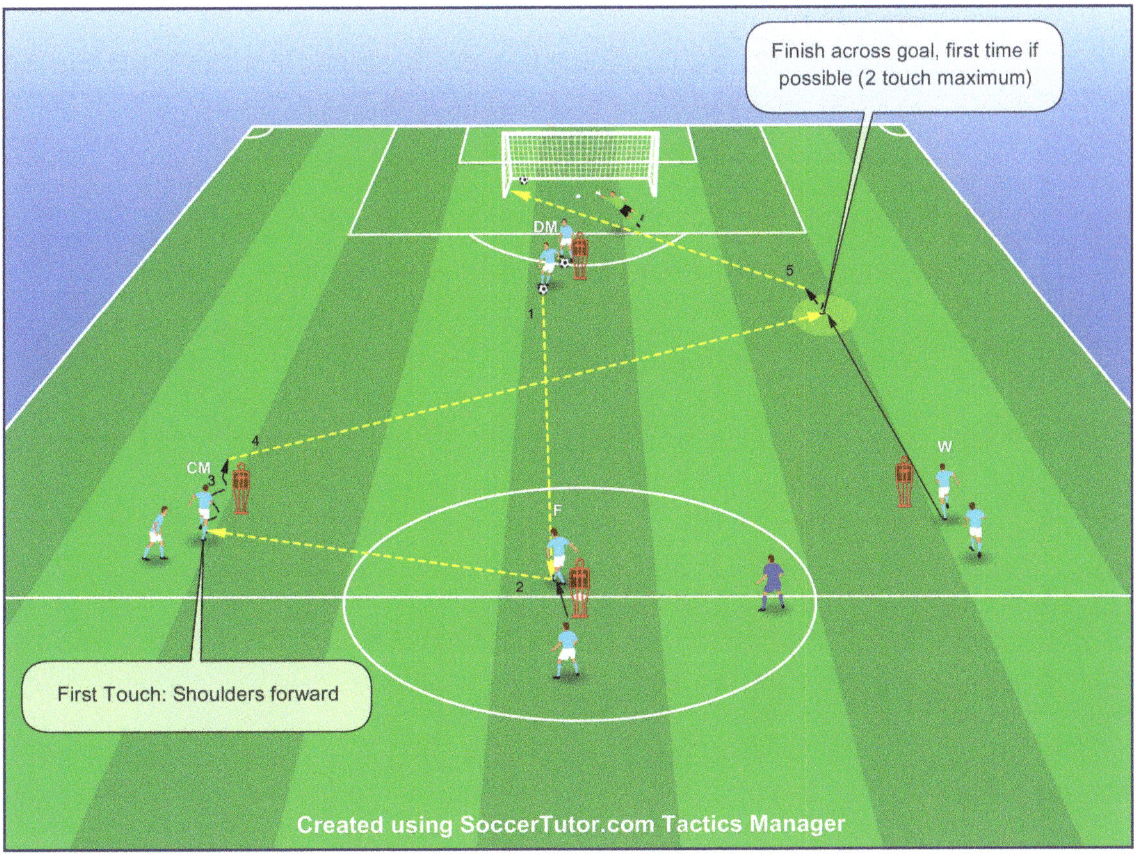

Finish across goal, first time if possible (2 touch maximum)

First Touch: Shoulders forward

NOTE: This practice can be position specific or not. If it is, the player positions may look unorthodox because this pattern includes a reverse for a finish at the end. However, the players are still making the type of passes relevant for their specific positions.

Practice Sequence

1-3. The **defensive midfielder (DM)** passes to the **forward (F)**, who passes across to the **central midfielder (CM)**.

CM opens up and receives, moving past the mannequin.

4-5. **CM** plays a diagonal pass for the third man run of the **winger (W)**, who takes a forward touch and shoots across the goal.

→ All the players rotate to the next position and the practice continues. Practice on both sides.

Training Session 5 - *Finishing the Attack (Final Third)*

1c. One-Two, Set, and Final Pass in a Technical Triangle Drill with Finish

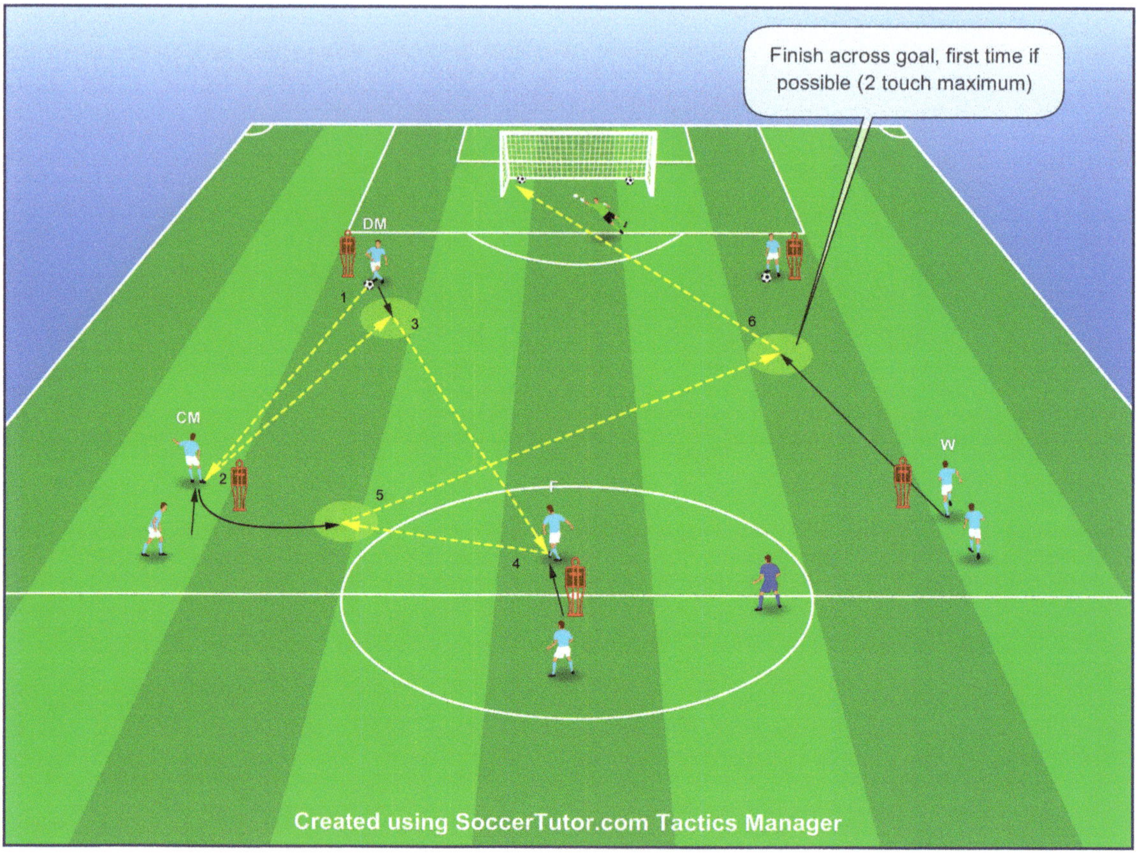

Finish across goal, first time if possible (2 touch maximum)

NOTE: *This practice can be position specific or not. If it is, the player positions may look unorthodox because this pattern includes a reverse for a finish at the end. However, the players are still making the type of passes relevant for their specific positions.*

Practice Sequence

1-3. The **defensive midfielder (DM)** plays a one-two with the **central midfielder (CM)**, then passes to the **forward (F)**.

4. **F** sets the ball for **CM** to run around the mannequin and receive.

5-6. **CM** plays a diagonal pass for the third man run of the **winger (W)**, who shoots at goal.

→ All the players rotate to the next position and the practice continues. Practice on both sides.

Training Session 5 - Finishing the Attack (Final Third)

1d. One-Two, Set, and Give & Go in a Technical Triangle Drill with Finish

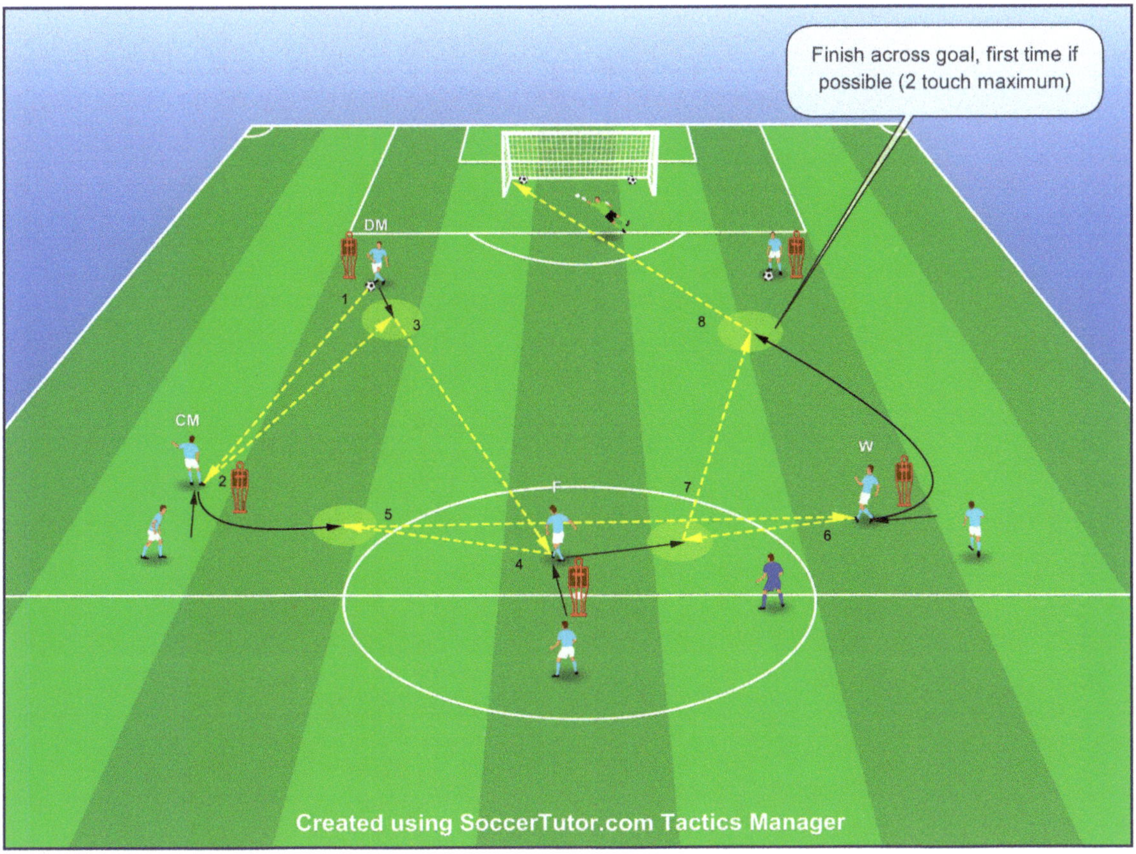

Finish across goal, first time if possible (2 touch maximum)

NOTE: This practice can be position specific or not. If it is, the player positions may look unorthodox because this pattern includes a reverse for a finish at the end. However, the players are still making the type of passes relevant for their specific positions.

Practice Sequence

1-3. The **defensive midfielder (DM)** plays a one-two with the **central midfielder (CM)**, then passes to the **forward (F)**.

4. **F** sets the ball for **CM** to run around the mannequin and receive.

5. **CM** passes across to the **winger (W)**.

6-7. **W** sets the ball for **F** to play a final pass for the run of **W** around the mannequin (give & go).

8. **W** shoots at goal.

→ All the players rotate to the next position and the practice continues. Practice on both sides.

Training Session 5 - Finishing the Attack (Final Third)

2. Side Diamond Pattern of Play to Receive in Between Lines, Set + Through Pass and Finish

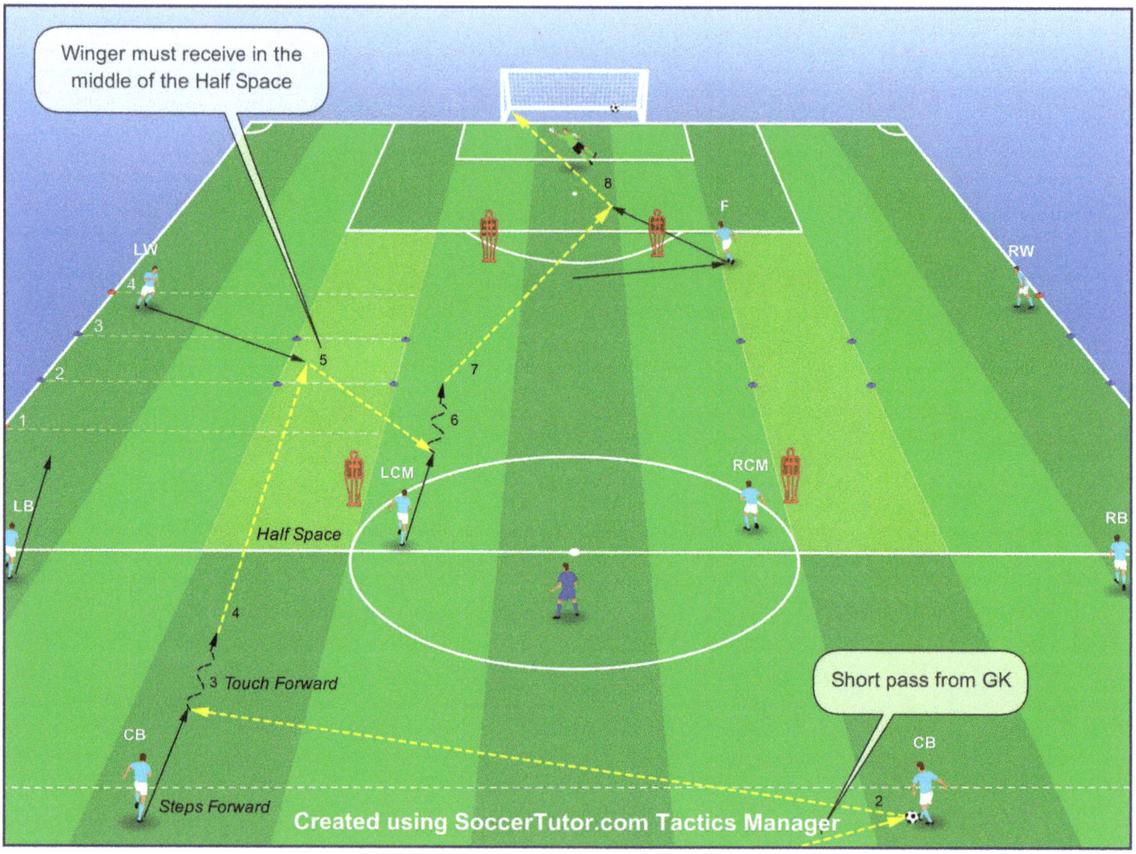

Practice Description

The players practice different patterns of play set out by the coach. There are many examples included in the book. This one shows the **Side Diamond Combination** (centre back, full back, central midfielder, & winger on one side).

1-3. The **GK** passes short to a **CB**. The **CB** passes across to the other **CB**, who has stepped forward and takes a touch.

4. The **CB** passes forward into the half space for the **LW**, who drops off the line and inside to receive.

5-6. The **LW** sets the ball back for the oncoming **LCM**, who takes a touch to open up all the options on both sides of the pitch rather than playing first time.

7-8. In this example, the **LW** plays in between the mannequins for the **forward (F)**, who has made a double movement to receive in behind and score.

Winger Receiving in the Half Space:
Use markers as a reference for arriving in the half space. Too high and the ball takes longer to travel, so it can get cut out. Too low, you cannot set the ball back to the CM because of the opposing midfielder.

Training Session 5 - Finishing the Attack (Final Third)

3. Game Principles for Switching Play in a Corners End Zones Possession Game

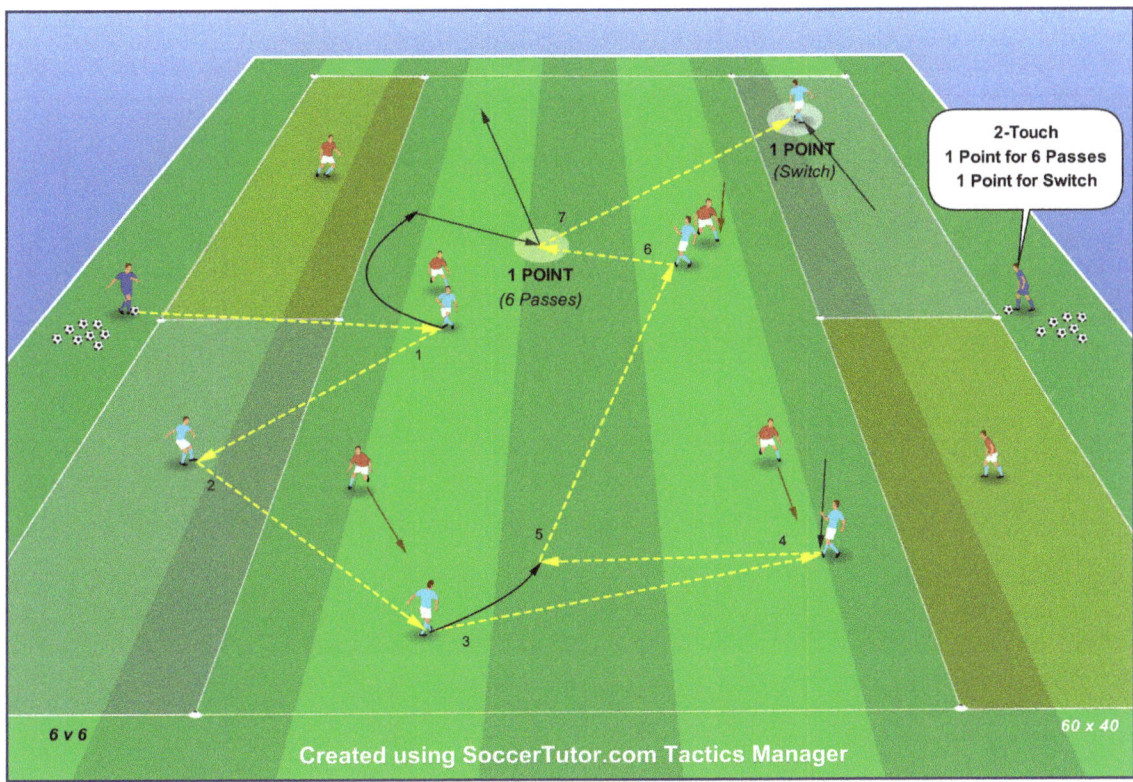

Practice Description

- In a 60 x 40 yard area, mark out 4 zones which are 10 yards wide. The zones are split in half with 2 players from each team in the 4 zones, as shown. The possession game is 4 (+2) v 4 (+2).

- The Coaches stand on each side centrally with balls to start and feed in a new ball if play breaks down.

- The team in possession (blues) score **1 Point** each time they play from one corner zone to the other + when they complete 6 passes.

- The corner zone players can only use 1 touch to bounce the ball back into play.

- The defending team (reds) aim to win the ball before 6 passes are played = **1 Point**. The blue players make a fast transition to try and win the ball back as quickly as possible.

Progression:

- The players in the end zones rotate with the players on the inside after receiving.

Coaching Points

1. Players need to keep shape in and out of possession and execute combinations and patterns of play to move the ball from zone to zone.

2. Be ready to attack, ready to defend.

Training Session 5 - Finishing the Attack (Final Third)

4. Possession Play and Transitions in a 4-Goal Conditioned Small Sided Game with Variations

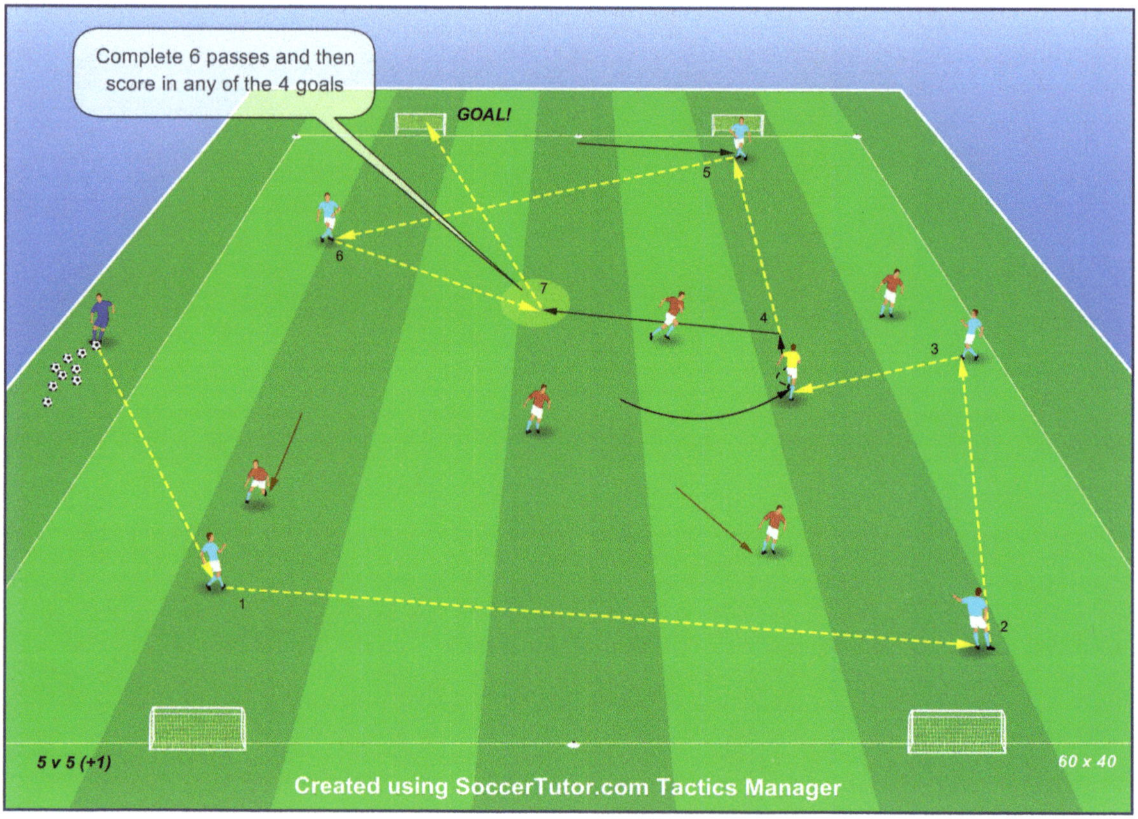

Complete 6 passes and then score in any of the 4 goals

GOAL!

5 v 5 (+1) *60 x 40*

Practice Description

- In a 60 x 40 yard area, we play a 5v5 (+1) small sided game with 4 small goals.
- The Coach starts and the team in possession (blues) must first complete 6 passes and can then try to score in any of the 4 goals.
- If the reds win the ball, they must also complete 6 passes and then try to score in any of the 4 goals.
- **Variation 1:** Score in any goal without any conditions (except completing 6 passes).
- **Variation 2:** All goals must be scored with a 1 touch finish.
- **Variation 3:** One team simply tries to keep possession to complete 10 passes (1 Point). The other team tries to win the ball and then score in any of the 4 goals (2 touch max + 1 touch finish). The same team always starts until the team roles are reversed.
- **Variation 4:** Use large goals + GKs.

Coaching Points

1. Social development with encouragement and good communication.
2. Quick decision making and transitions from attack to defence.
3. Control the tempo of the game.

MANCHESTER CITY ACADEMY SESSION 6

Build-up Phase 2 + 3: Midfield Combination Play and Finishing the Attack (1)

Training Session 6 - Midfield Combination Play + Finishing the Attack

1. Technical Attacking Combination Play and Finishing Circuit

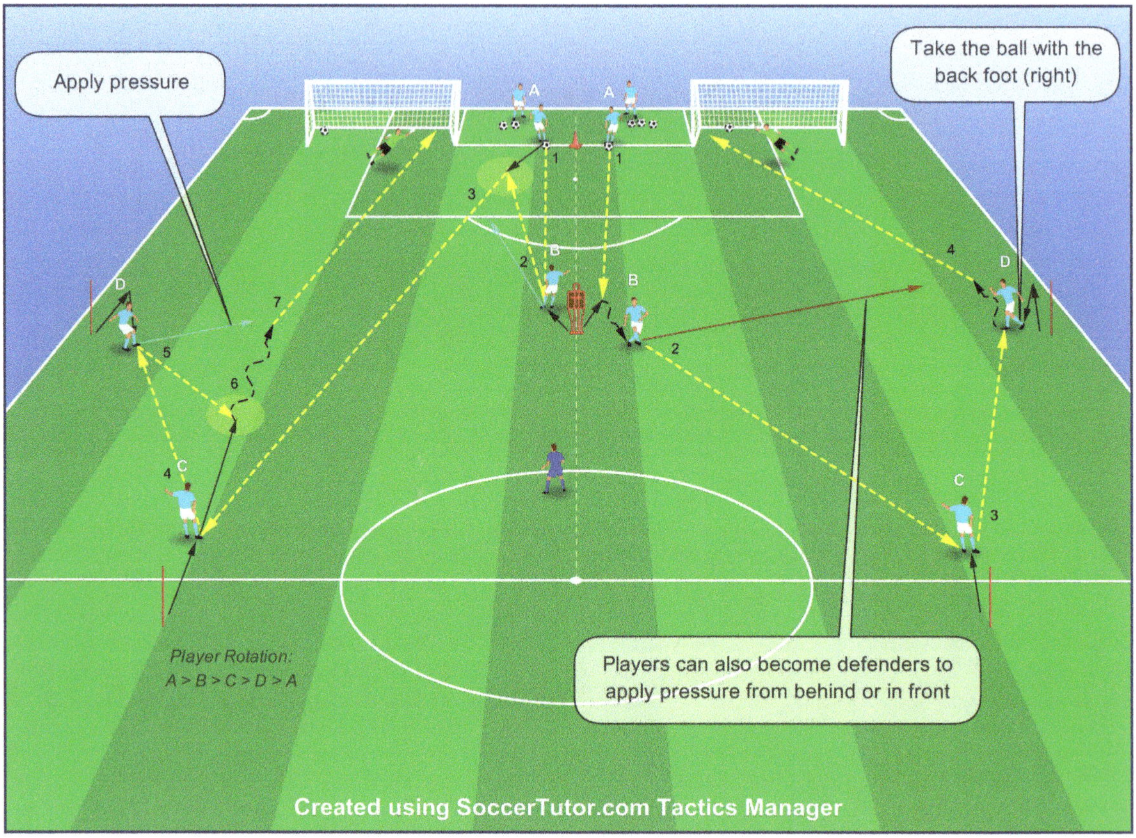

Practice Description

We position 2 large goals with GKs and cones or poles in the positions shown. The players use this circuit to practice different combinations + finishing.

Players can also become defenders to apply pressure (from behind or in front).

Practice Sequence Example (Left)

1-2. **A** plays a one-two with **B**.

3. **B** plays a long ground pass to **C**.

4-5. **C** plays a one-two with **D** and moves forward at pace to receive the return.

6-7. **D** takes a forward touch towards goal and shoots with the second touch.

Coaching Points

1. Use the correct weight of pass.
2. Body position to receive = Half-turn.
3. Correct angles/positioning when receiving + take ball on the back foot.
4. Break the line with the first touch.
5. Use the correct finish for the situation.
6. The Coach may add forfeits for players missing the target or add time limits for intensity and competition.

Training Session 6 - Midfield Combination Play + Finishing the Attack

2. Midfield Combinations + Crossing in Functional 6v5 (+GK) Attacking Overloads

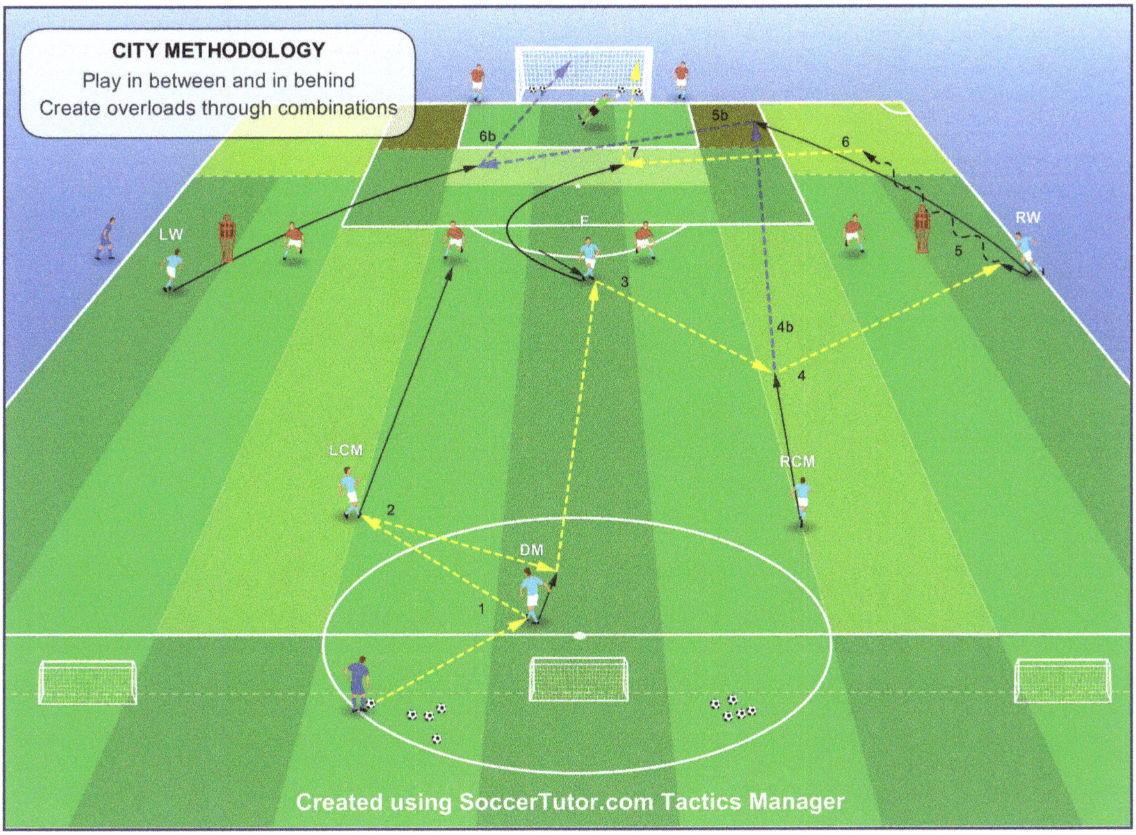

Practice Description

- The practice starts with the Coach's pass to the defensive midfielder **(DM)**.
- The blue team use the typical Manchester City combinations (shown throughout the training sessions) in midfield, and the **forward (F)** sets the ball back for one of the central midfielders to play the ball wide.
- The aim is for a winger to dribble or receive in behind and then cross into the box for oncoming runners.
- If the reds win the ball, they then try to score in any of the 3 small goals.

- **NOTE:** It is important that the Coach manages the defensive unit to get the realism required for the practice. The Coach must demand that the defensive unit's positioning, angles, and distance in relation to the ball are correct in real time. They must also defend with the correct levels of aggression (especially in the final third of the pitch) to challenge the attackers to make the right decisions under pressure.

Training Session 6 - Midfield Combination Play + Finishing the Attack

3a. Game Related 3v2 (+GK) Attacking Overload Duels

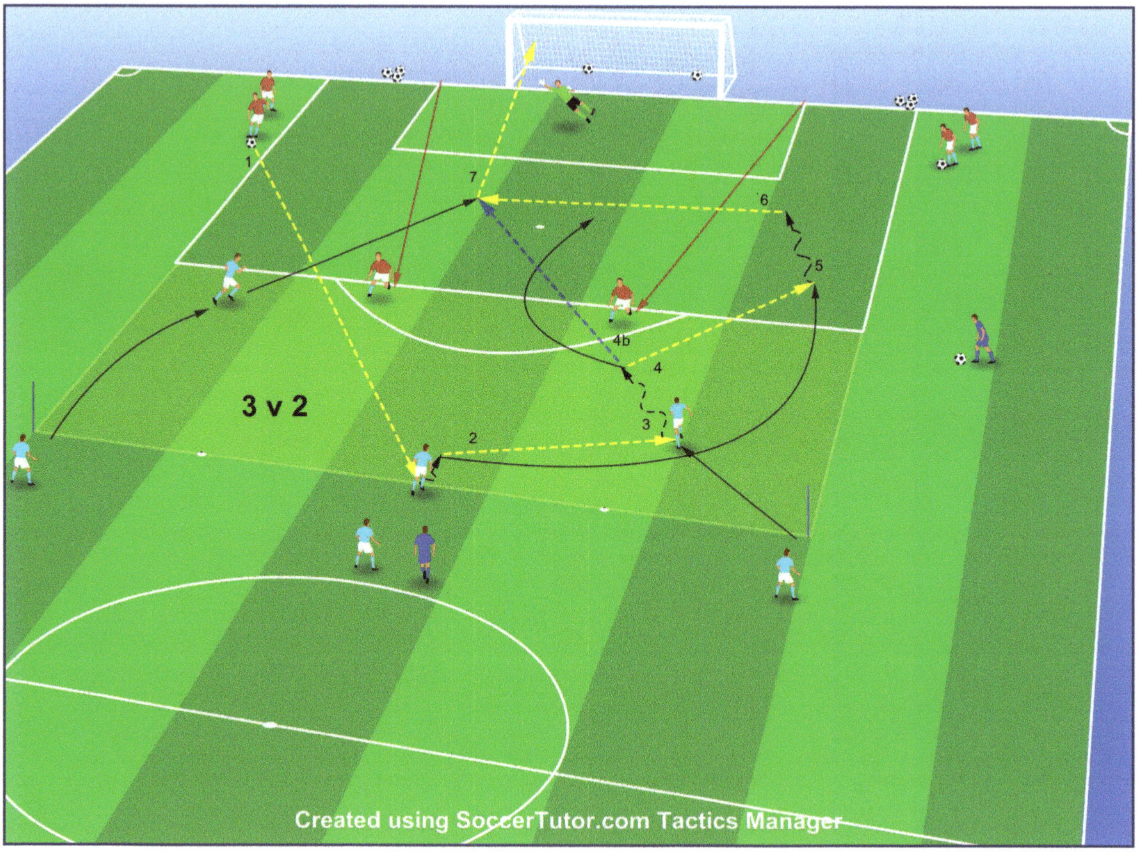

Practice Description

- The red defenders work in pairs and the blue attackers work in groups of 3.
- A red defender or GK serves the ball to a blue attacker and 2 defenders move forward.
- The 3 blues try to score with their 3v2 advantage, and the 2 reds try to defend their goal.

Coaching Points

1. Use diagonal runs and overlaps.
2. Time the run to get in behind.
3. Monitor the correct type of pass and timing of pass.
4. The attacker should use their first touch to change the angle of attack and disrupt the defenders.
5. Decision making of when to penetrate and when to keep possession is key.

Possible Practice Conditions

- Time limit to score.
- Use rewards for defenders.
- Use other conditions which help make the practice competitive at high intensity.

Training Session 6 - Midfield Combination Play + Finishing the Attack

3b. Game Related 4v3 (+GK) Attacking Overload Duels

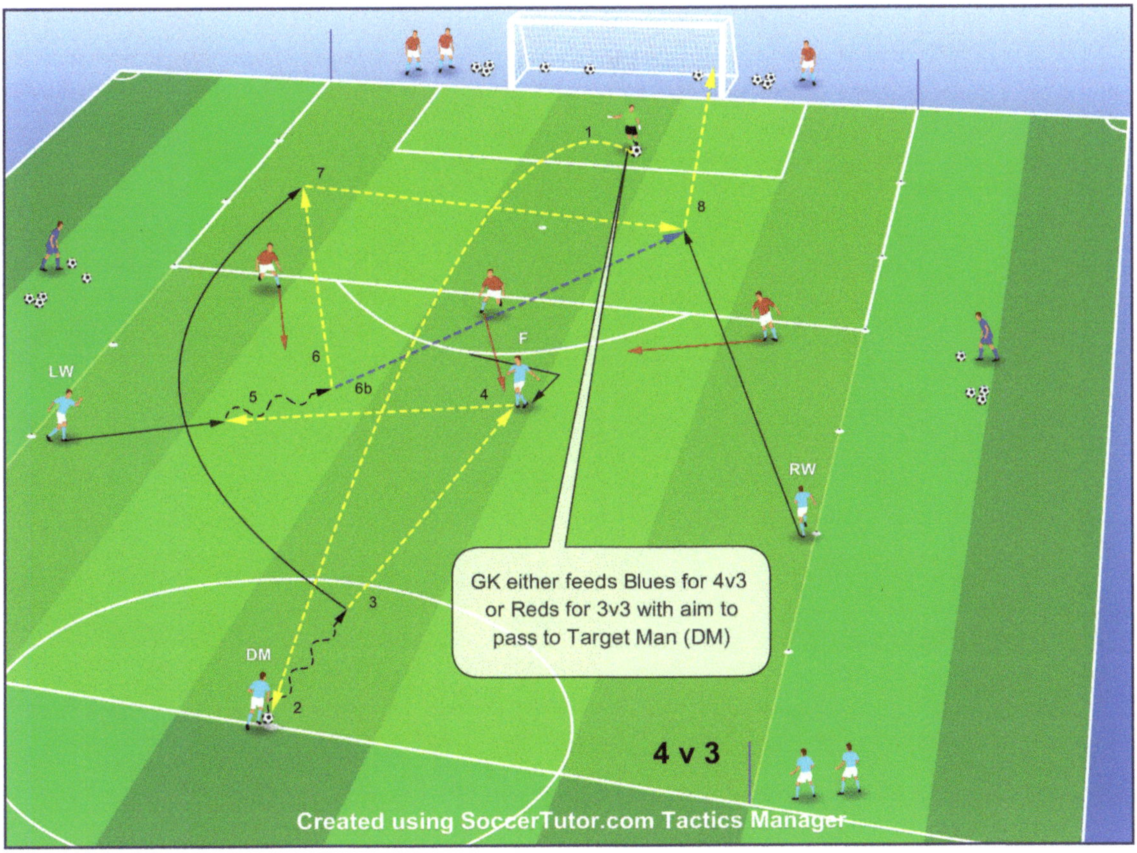

GK either feeds Blues for 4v3 or Reds for 3v3 with aim to pass to Target Man (DM)

4 v 3

Practice Description

- The red defenders work in groups of 3 and the blue attackers work in groups of 4 (1 defensive midfielder, 2 wingers, and 1 forward).
- **Option 1:** The GK feeds the ball to the halfway line for the blues to attack in a 4v3 situation. Once the phase is complete, we restart from the GK.
- **Option 2:** The GK feeds the ball to a red defender to attack in a 3v3 situation. Their aim is to pass to the Target Man (the blue DM who stays on halfway line).

Coaching Points

1. Focus on creating and exploiting 1v1 situations.
2. Fast combination play with good communication.
3. Make the extra player count (4v3) with different types of movement and overloads.
4. Decision making of when to penetrate and how/when to keep possession is key.
5. Choose the right type of finish for the situation.

Training Session 6 - Midfield Combination Play + Finishing the Attack

4. Attacking Overloads in a Dynamic 2-Zone 5v5 (+GKs) Small Sided Game

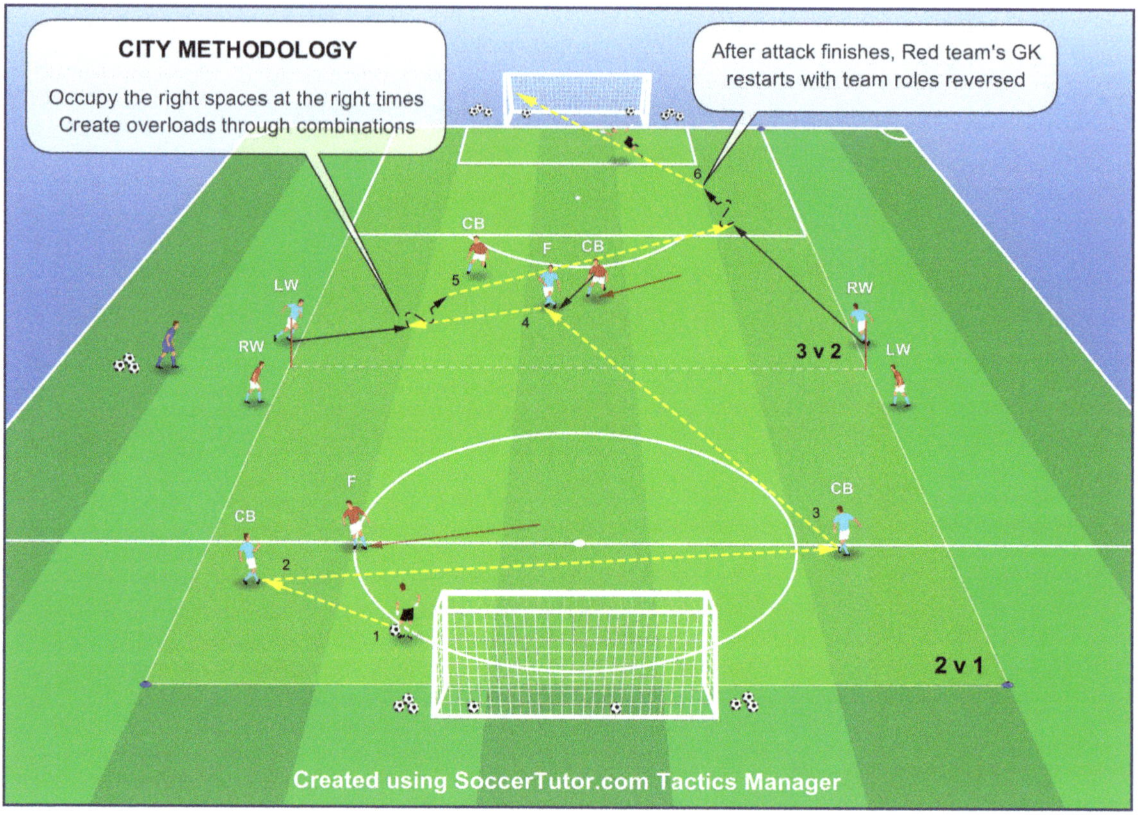

CITY METHODOLOGY
Occupy the right spaces at the right times
Create overloads through combinations

After attack finishes, Red team's GK restarts with team roles reversed

Practice Description

- In the area shown, we play 5v5 (+GKs). Adjust the size of the area depending on the age and/or level.

- The halfway line splits 2 zones. The GK starts and there is a 2v1 situation in the low zone. The blues keep controlled possession and wait for the right time to play into the **forward (F)**.

- **F** sets the ball back for either of the 2 wide players who join from their outside positions shown to create a 3v2 attack.

- In this example, the **left winger (LW)** receives and takes a forward touch.

- The opposite winger **(RW)** keeps the width on the opposite side and makes a run in behind to try and score.

- Restart from the red team's GK and repeat the practice in the opposite direction with the team roles reversed.

MANCHESTER CITY ACADEMY SESSION 7

Build-up Phase 2 + 3: Midfield Combination Play and Finishing the Attack (2)

Training Session 7 - Midfield Combination Play + Finishing the Attack

1. One-Touch Technical Passing Triangle Drill with Set Through Combination

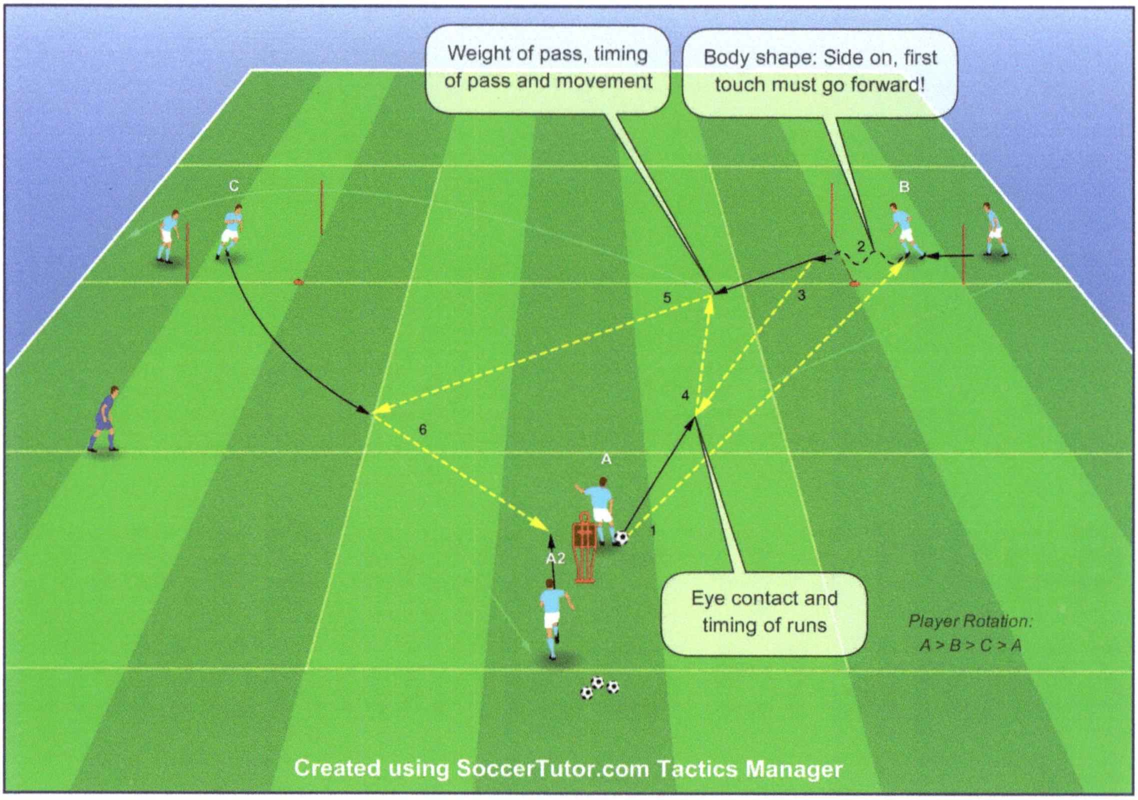

Practice Description

- Mark out the mannequins/poles 15-30 yards apart. The 2 widest poles act as defenders to check away from.
- The pole and cone creates a gate for the player to take their first touch through. The body position must be side on facing forward to break the line.
- Players use one touch with a high ball speed, so accuracy needs to be good.

Practice Sequence

1-2. **A** passes to **B**, who breaks through the pole/cone gate.

3-4. **B** plays a one-two with **A**.

5. **B** passes to **C**, who makes a third man run to receive (set by A → through pass).

6. **C** passes to the start position and the practice continues with **A2**.

→ All the players rotate to the next position (A → B → C → A). Change the direction often so players practice with both feet.

Coaching Points

1. Players must make eye contact to make sure the timing of their passes and movements are correct.

2. The weight of pass is key to break the line and eliminate the defender.

Training Session 7 - Midfield Combination Play + Finishing the Attack

2. Central Diamond Pattern of Play, Crossing, and Finishing vs 2 Box Defenders

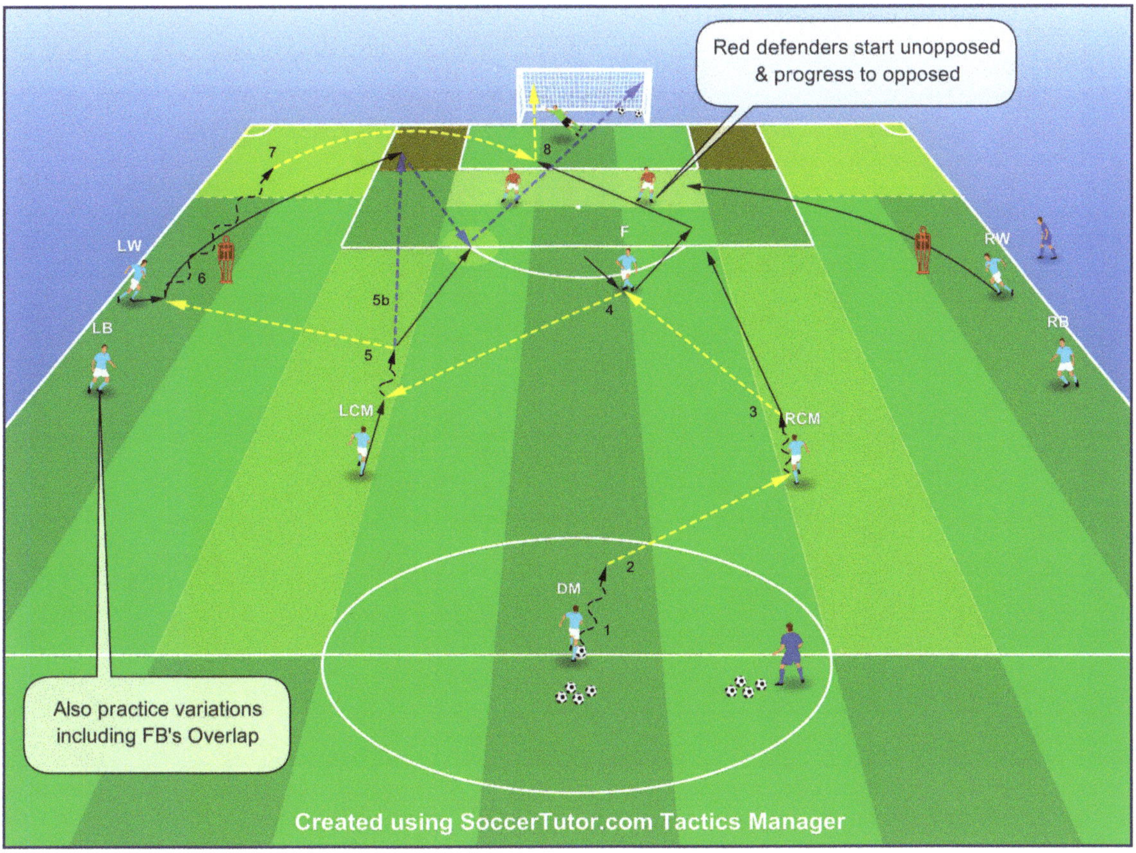

Practice Description

The 2 defenders operate inside the box - they start as passive, then progress to fully active to defend the crosses.

1-2. The **defensive midfielder (DM)** starts by taking a touch forward and passing to either **central midfielder (LCM or RCM)**.

3. In this example, **RCM** receives and passes to the **forward (F)**, who operates within the width of the semi-circle.

4. **F** sets the ball back for **LCM**, who takes a touch forward to open up all the passing options.

5. **LCM** either passes directly into the **left winger's (LW)** feet or in behind and into the box, depending on the movement. In a different variation, **LW** can move inside to be involved in the combination and create space for the **left back (LB)** on the overlap.

6-8. **RULE:** *The area the wide player receives determines the type of cross.* From the wide yellow zone, cross to the front post to **F** or the back post to **RW**. From the small red zone, cut the ball back to the closest central midfielder **(LCM)** on the edge of the box (blue arrows).

Training Session 7 - Midfield Combination Play + Finishing the Attack

3. Game Related Attacking Organisation and Overload for 3v2 Finish in a 5v2 (+GKs) SSG

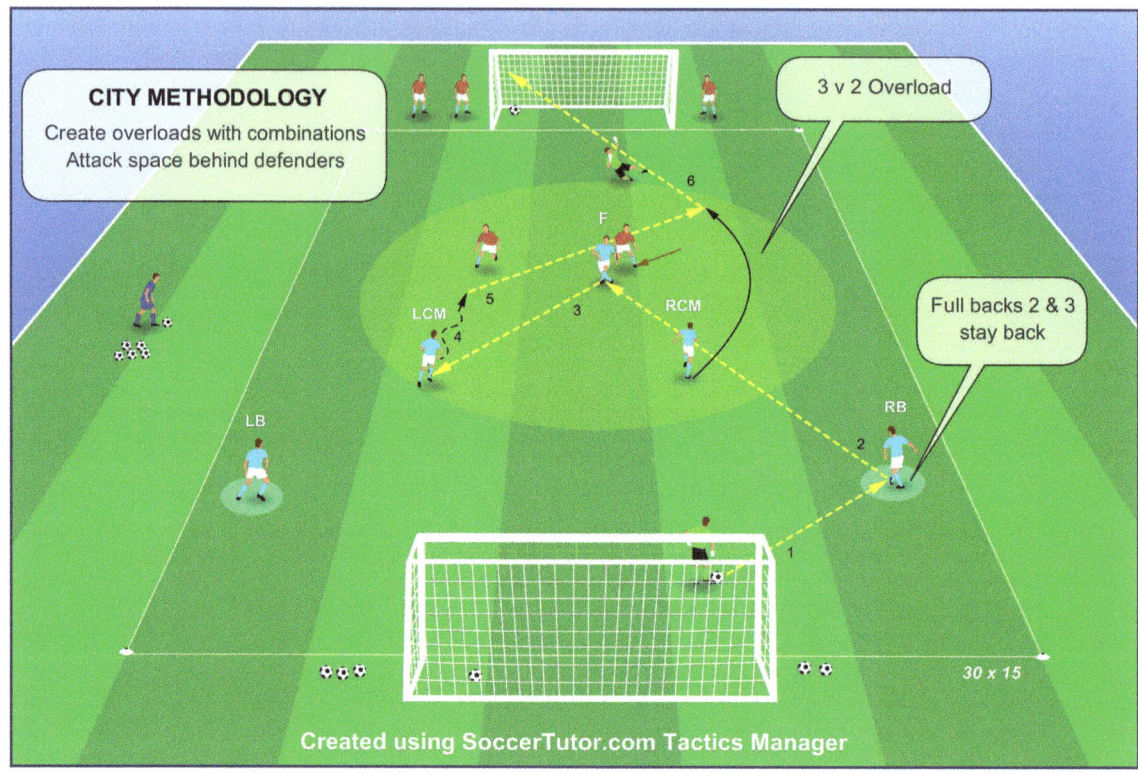

Practice Description

- In a 30 x 15 yard area, we have 2 teams of 5 players, but we play with 5v2 (+GKs).
- We start from the GK, who passes to the **left back (LB)** or **right back (RB)**.
- Note: The players can use multiple different patterns which you can take from other practices in the book.
- In this example, the full back in possession **(RB)** plays to the **forward (F)**, who sets the ball back for either of the 2 **central midfielders (LCM or RCM)**.
- From that point, we have a 3v2 overload for the blues to try and finish the attack.
- Both blue full backs stay back and are not involved in finishing the attack.
- Rotate the defenders for rest.
- Change the team roles after a set amount of time.

Progression:

Add 1 red defender and the blue team create 4v3 overloads with 1 x **full back (LB or RB)** joining the attack

Training Session 7 - Midfield Combination Play + Finishing the Attack

4. Attacking Organisation and Overloads in a Position Specific 7 v 7 (+GKs) 2-Zone SSG

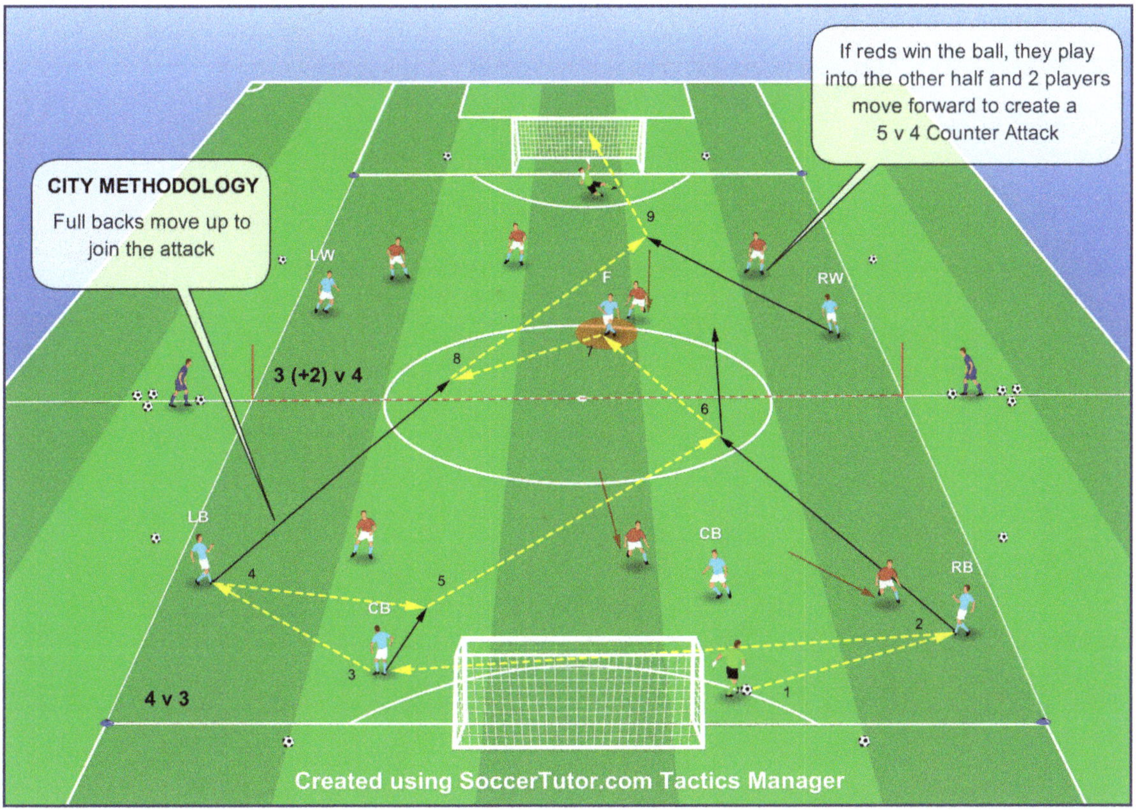

(Diagram: If reds win the ball, they play into the other half and 2 players move forward to create a 5 v 4 Counter Attack. CITY METHODOLOGY — Full backs move up to join the attack. 3 (+2) v 4 in high zone; 4 v 3 in low zone.)

Practice Description

- In the box to box area, the halfway line splits 2 zones. The GK starts and there is a 4v3 situation in the low zone. The blues keep controlled possession and wait for the right time to play into their front 3.

- Once this happens, the 2 blue full backs **(LB & RB)** move forward to create a 5v4 advantage to attack in the high zone and try to score.

- This leaves 2v3 in the low zone, so if the reds win the ball, they play quickly forward so they can finish a quick and dynamic 3v2 counter attack before the 2 blue full backs recover back.

- If the reds win ball in the first phase, the 2 red full backs move forward to create a 5v4 advantage to attack the blue back 4.

- The tempo of this session will be high so the players have to identify when they can take a rest with the ball.

- Reactions, decisions, communication, and positioning will all be tested during this practice. You will quickly see the players who make the right decisions in the quickest time.

- **Progression:** The practice flows into a SSG without the halfway line (no zones). The principles of the practice should continue.

ELITE ACADEMY COACHING

MANCHESTER CITY ACADEMY SESSION 8

Build-up Phase 2 + 3: Midfield Combination Play and Finishing the Attack (3)

Training Session 8 - Midfield Combination Play + Finishing the Attack

1a. One-Touch Technical Passing Triangle Drill with Overlapping Runs to Receive

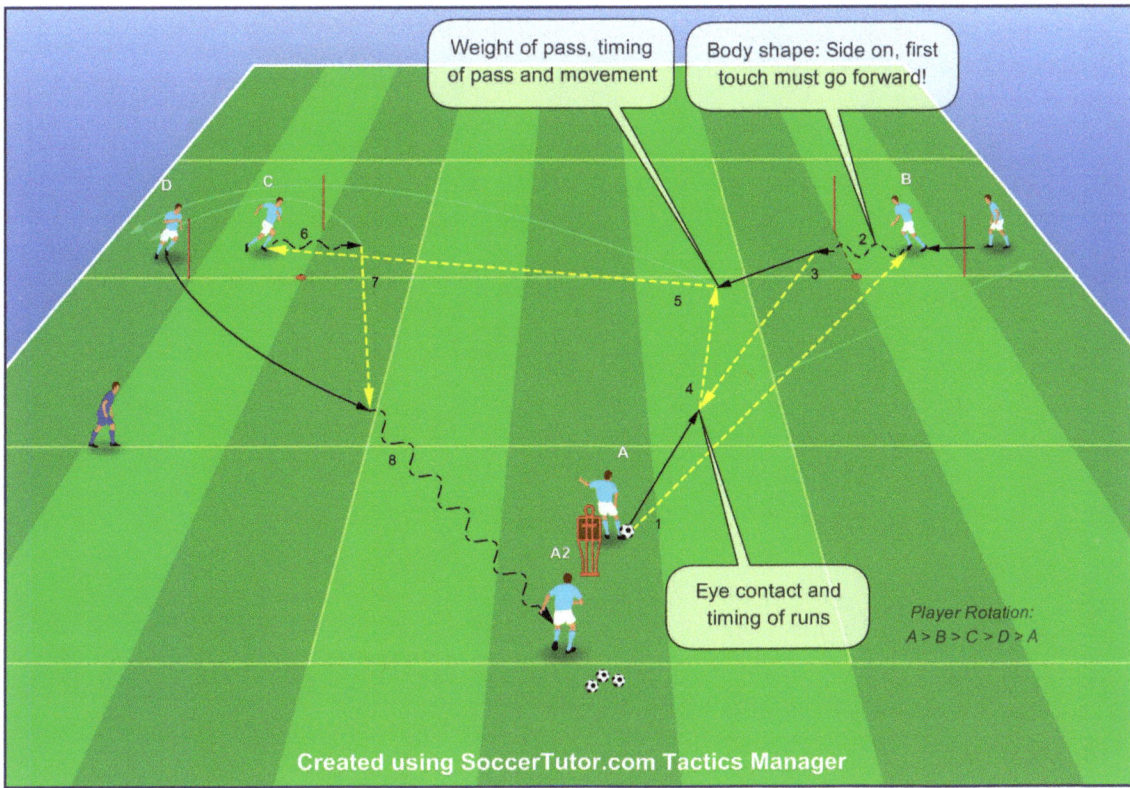

Practice Description

- Mark out the mannequins/poles 15-30 yards apart. The 2 widest poles act as defenders to check away from.

- The pole and cone creates a gate for the player to take their first touch through. The body position must be side on facing forward to break the line.

- Players use one touch with a high ball speed, so accuracy needs to be good.

Practice Sequence

1-2. **A** passes to **B**, who breaks through the pole/cone gate.

3-4. **B** plays a one-two with **A**.

5-6. **B** passes to **C**, who breaks forward through the pole/cone gate.

7-8. **C** passes for the overlapping run of **D**, who dribbles to the start position.

→ All the players rotate to the next position (A → B → C → D → A). Change direction often so players practice with both feet.

Coaching Points

1. Players must make eye contact to make sure the timing of their passes and movements are correct.

2. The weight of pass is key to break the line and eliminate the defender.

Training Session 8 - Midfield Combination Play + Finishing the Attack

1b. One-Touch Technical Passing Triangle Drill with Quick One-Two Combinations

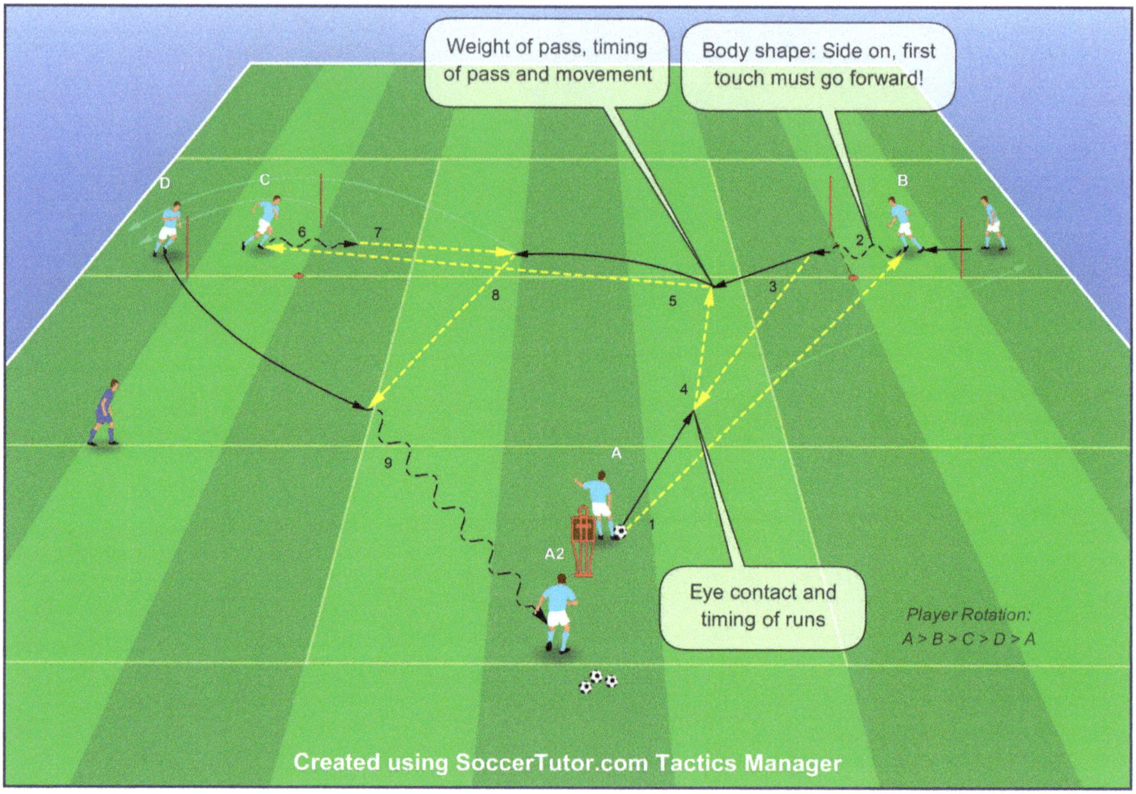

Practice Description

- Mark out the mannequins/poles 15-30 yards apart. The 2 widest poles act as defenders to check away from.
- The pole and cone creates a gate for the player to take their first touch through. The body position must be side on facing forward to break the line.
- Players use one touch with a high ball speed, so accuracy needs to be good.

Practice Sequence

1-2. A passes to **B**, who breaks through the pole/cone gate.

3-4. B plays a one-two with **A**.

5-7. B passes to **C**, who breaks forward through the pole/cone gate, and then passes back to **B**.

8-9. B passes for the run of **D**, who dribbles to the start position.

→ All the players rotate to the next position (A → B → C → D → A). Change direction often so players practice with both feet.

Coaching Points

1. Players must make eye contact to make sure the timing of their passes and movements are correct.
2. The weight of pass is key to break the line and eliminate the defender.

Training Session 8 - Midfield Combination Play + Finishing the Attack

2. Central Diagram Pattern of Play with Wing Play, Crossing, and Finishing

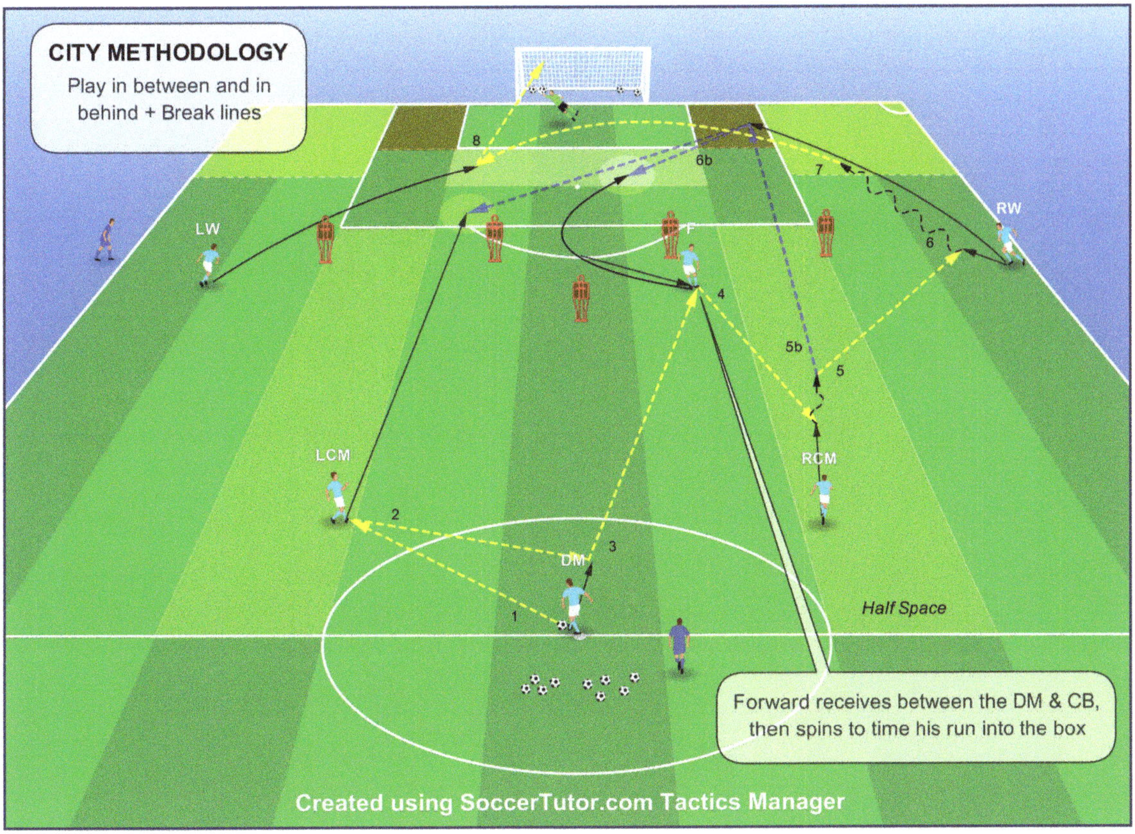

CITY METHODOLOGY
Play in between and in behind + Break lines

Forward receives between the DM & CB, then spins to time his run into the box

Half Space

Practice Description

- For this pattern, both of the **attacking midfielders (LCM & RCM)** play in the half spaces. The **DM** passes to either of them to set the ball back (one-two).

- The pass to the left **(LCM)** should be set back with the left foot, and vice versa with **RCM** on the right side.

- The **forward (F)** starts central and high. The **DM** passes forward for **F**, who moves across and back between the centre back (5) and DM (6) mannequins to receive.

- **F** would move to the opposite side if **RCM** had set the ball back to **DM**.

- **F** sets the ball back to the central midfielder on that side **(RCM)**, who takes a touch forward and either passes directly into the **winger's (RW)** feet or in behind and into the box, depending on the movement.

- **RULE:** *The area the winger receives determines the type of cross*. If he dribbles into the wide yellow zone, he crosses to the front or back post. If he receives in the small red zone, he cuts the ball back. **F** attacks the front post and the opposite winger **LW** attacks the back post. **LCM** or **RCM** (or both) move for the cut back to the edge of the box.

Training Session 8 - Midfield Combination Play + Finishing the Attack

3. Game Related 3v2 to 4v3 Attacking Overload Duels

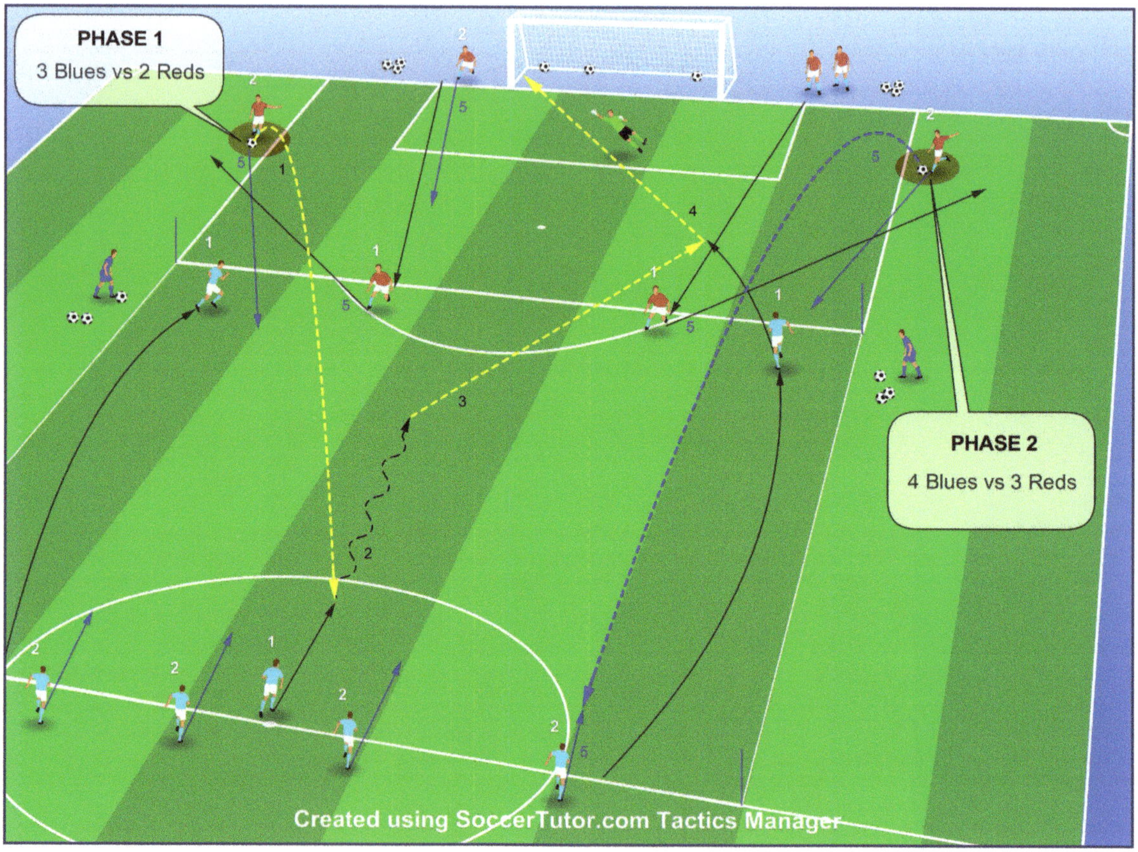

PHASE 1
3 Blues vs 2 Reds

PHASE 2
4 Blues vs 3 Reds

Practice Description

- **Phase 1:** A red defender or GK feeds the ball to a blue attacker and 2 defenders move forward (No1s). The 3 blues (No1s) try to score with their 3v2 advantage, and the 2 reds try to defend their goal.

- **Phase 2:** A red defender or GK feeds the ball to a new blue attacker and 3 red defenders move forward (No2s). The 4 new blues (No2s) try to score with a 4v3 advantage, and the 2 reds again try to defend their goal.

- Consider time restraints to score and rewards for defenders.

Coaching Points

1. The practice should be competitive and played with a high intensity.
2. Timing and choosing the right types of passes and movements is key.
3. The attacking players should look to take a first touch which alters the angle of attack and disrupts the defenders.
4. Monitor the correct decision making for when to penetrate and how and when to retain possession.

Training Session 8 - Midfield Combination Play + Finishing the Attack

4. Game Principles and Patterns of Play in an 8v8 (+GKs) Small Sided Game

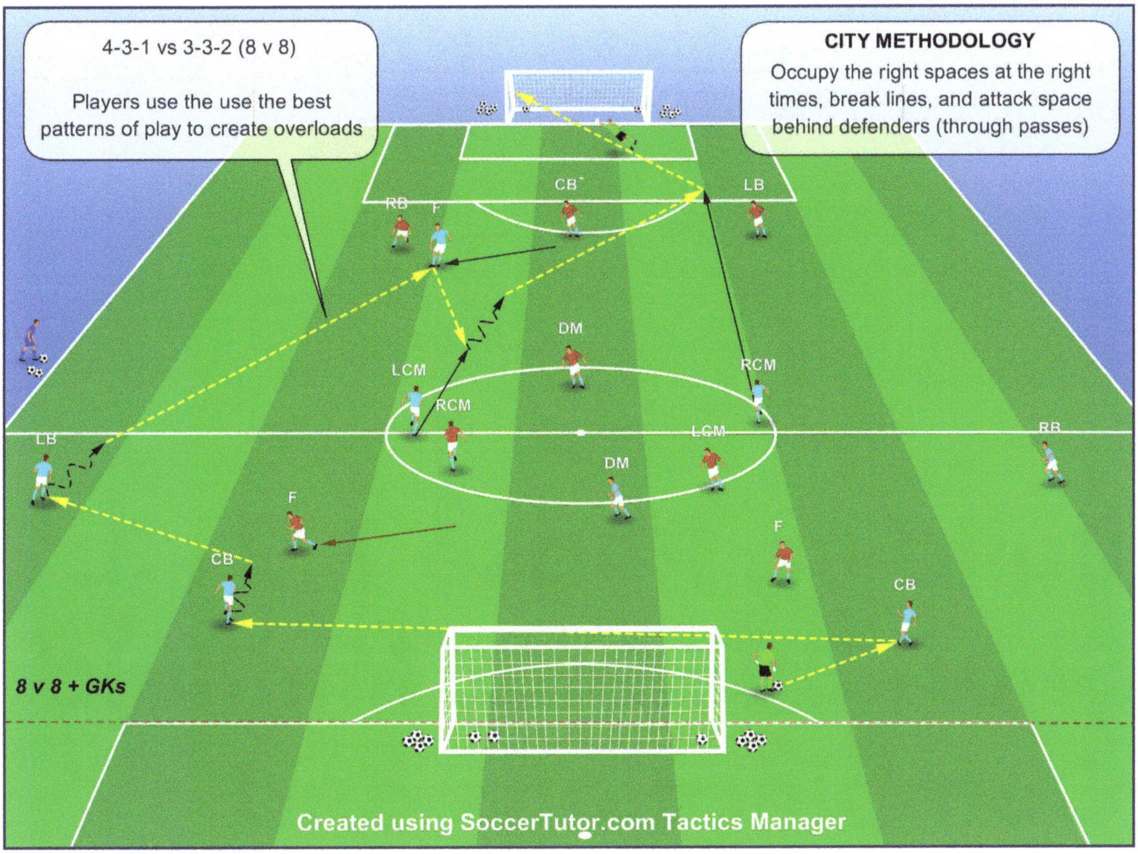

4-3-1 vs 3-3-2 (8 v 8)
Players use the use the best patterns of play to create overloads

CITY METHODOLOGY
Occupy the right spaces at the right times, break lines, and attack space behind defenders (through passes)

8 v 8 + GKs

Practice Description

- This small sided game has even numbers (8v8) but the team in possession should always be looking to use the best patterns of play to create overloads and gain an advantage over their opponents.

- The blues play with a 4-3-1 formation and the reds play with a 3-3-2.

- In the diagram example, the blue team use a side diamond variation. The red forward (F) blocks the forward pass, so the blue **centre back (CB)** passes to the left back who passes to the **forward (F)**.

- The **forward (F)** sets the ball back for one central midfielder **(LCM)**, who then plays a through pass for the deep run of the other central midfielder **(RCM)**.

- You can utilise all the different patterns which are displayed in the training sessions in this book, all of which we used at the Manchester City academy regularly.

- **NOTE:** This kind of game practicing patterns of play was used in the later stages of the season when we wanted it to be opposed, making the players create overloads for success.

MANCHESTER CITY ACADEMY SESSION 9

Build-up Phase 1, 2 + 3: Short Build-up, Midfield Combinations and Finishing the Attack (1)

Training Session 9 - Build-up, Midfield Combinations + Finish the Attack

1a. Switching Play and Attacking Combination in the Final Third Pattern with Crossing & Finishing

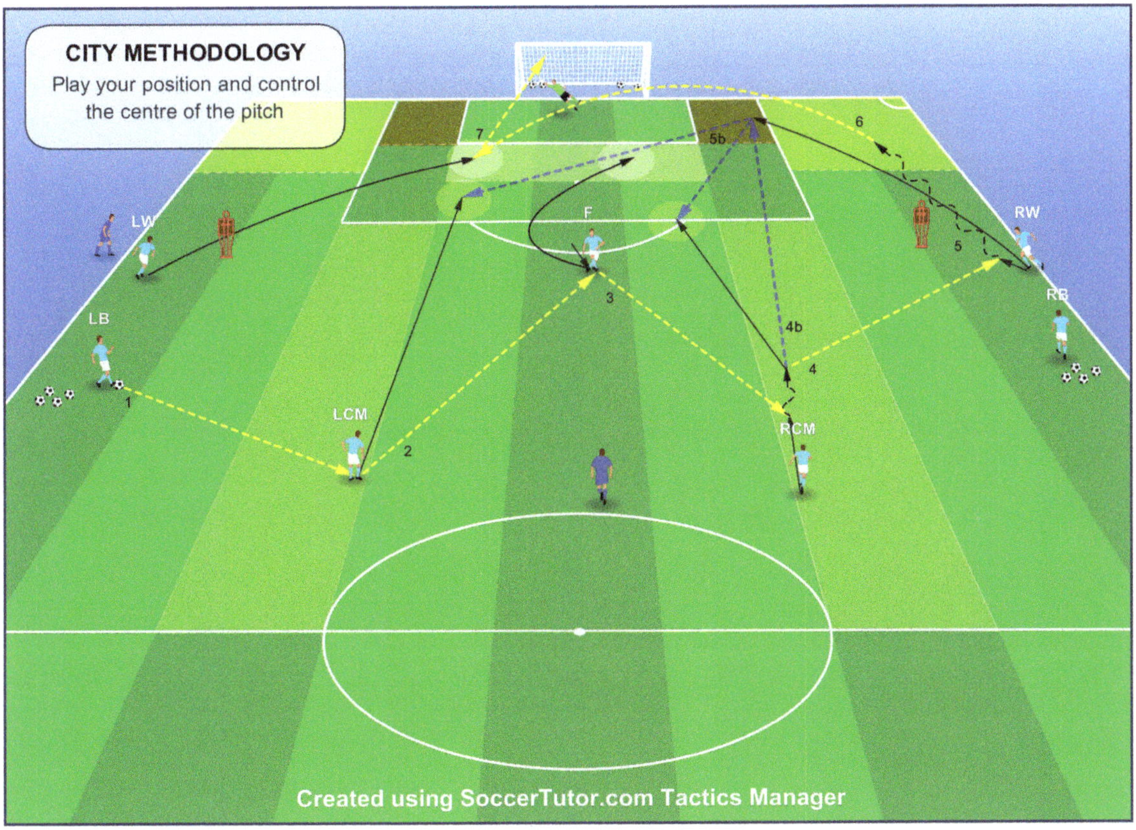

Practice Description

1. The **left back (LB)** starts by passing back to the **central midfielder (LCM)**.

2-3. **LCM** passes to the **forward (F)**, who sets the ball back for the oncoming **RCM**.

4-5. **RCM** takes a forward touch and passes to the **winger (RW)** near the sideline. **RW** receives and dribbles into the wide yellow zone.

4b-5b. If **RCM** plays a through pass into the small red zone instead (4b), then **RW** cuts the ball back to either of the central midfielders **(LCM or RCM)** near the edge of the box.

6-7. **RW** crosses to the front or back post. **F** attacks the front post and the opposite winger **LW** attacks the back post.

→ The practice is repeated starting from the other side **(RB)**.

→ A variation which includes the full back using an overlapping run is on the next page.

Coaching Point:

Whether or not the central midfielder plays to the winger's feet or in behind depends on the winger's decision and movement.

Training Session 9 - Build-up, Midfield Combinations + Finish the Attack

1b. Combination Play in the Final Third Pattern with Winger Receiving Inside + Overlapping Full Back

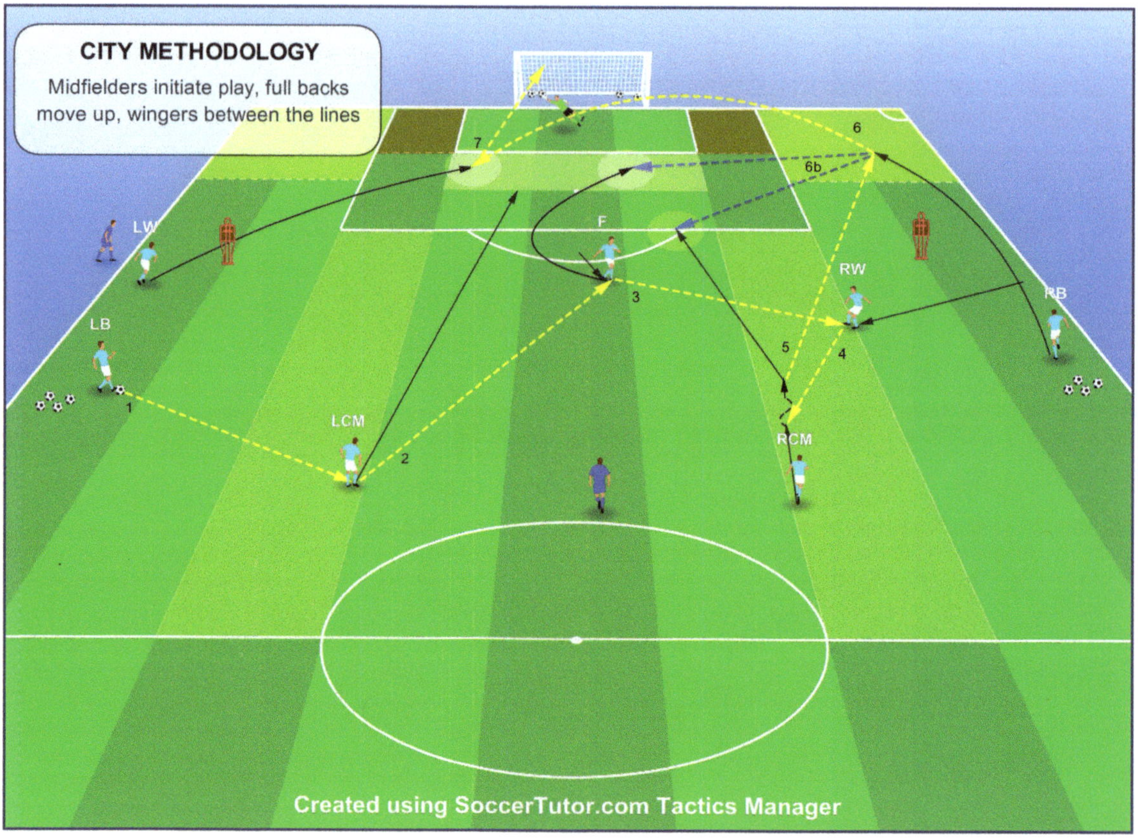

CITY METHODOLOGY
Midfielders initiate play, full backs move up, wingers between the lines

Practice Description

1. The **left back (LB)** starts by passing back to the **central midfielder (LCM)**.

2-3. **LCM** passes to the **forward (F)**, who sets the ball back for the **winger (RW)**.

4. **RW** has moved inside to receive within the half space and set the ball back to **RCM**, and also create space for the full back **(RB)** to exploit on the flank.

5. **RCM** takes a forward touch and passes in behind for the overlapping run of **RB** to receive in the wide yellow zone.

6. **RB** crosses to the back post to **LW**.

6b. Alternatively, **RB** can cut the ball back to either of the central midfielders **(LCM or RCM)** or pass across for the forward **(F)** to score, as shown.

→ The practice is repeated starting from the other side **(RB)**.

Training Session 9 - Build-up, Midfield Combinations + Finish the Attack

2. Break the Line in a Game Related Directional 4v4 End Zone Possession Game

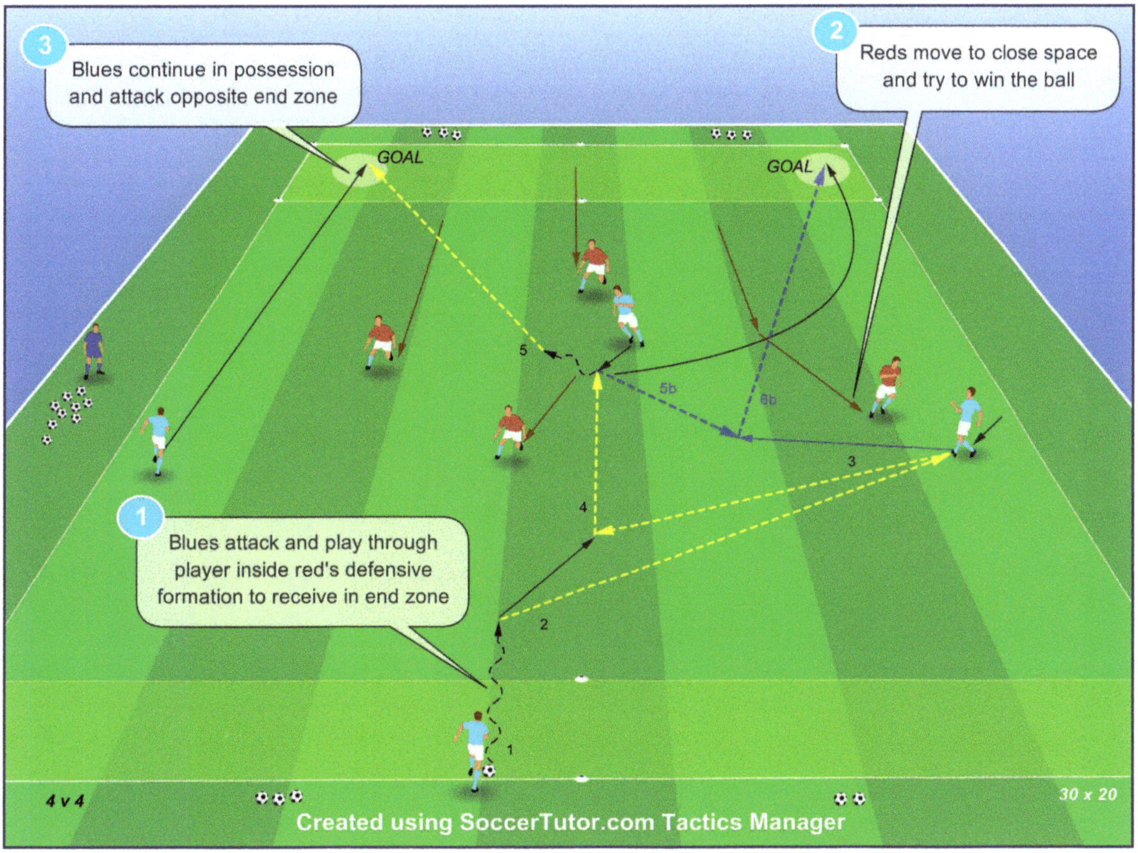

Practice Description

We play 4v4 here, but you can also have an attacking or defending overload e.g. 5v4. The area can be 30 x 20 to 60 x 40 yards depending on numbers, age, ability, etc.

Start with a player dribbling into the middle zone. The blues aim to score by receiving in the end zone, then attack the opposite end zone. The aim is to play in between opponents and in behind. A penetrative pass between defenders = Extra Point.

The reds try to win the ball and reverse the team roles.

Coaching Points

1. Open up in possession (diamond shape).
2. Quick combination play to penetrate.
3. Support from behind and ahead of ball.
4. Play in between and in behind.
5. Be ready to attack ready to defend.
6. Ball comes to you, don't go to the ball.
7. Use the first touch to break the line and create overloads.

Progression: Play in full area (defenders can enter end zones to apply pressure).

Training Session 9 - Build-up, Midfield Combinations + Finish the Attack

3. Game Related Position Specific Attacking Overloads in a Functional Practice with Channels

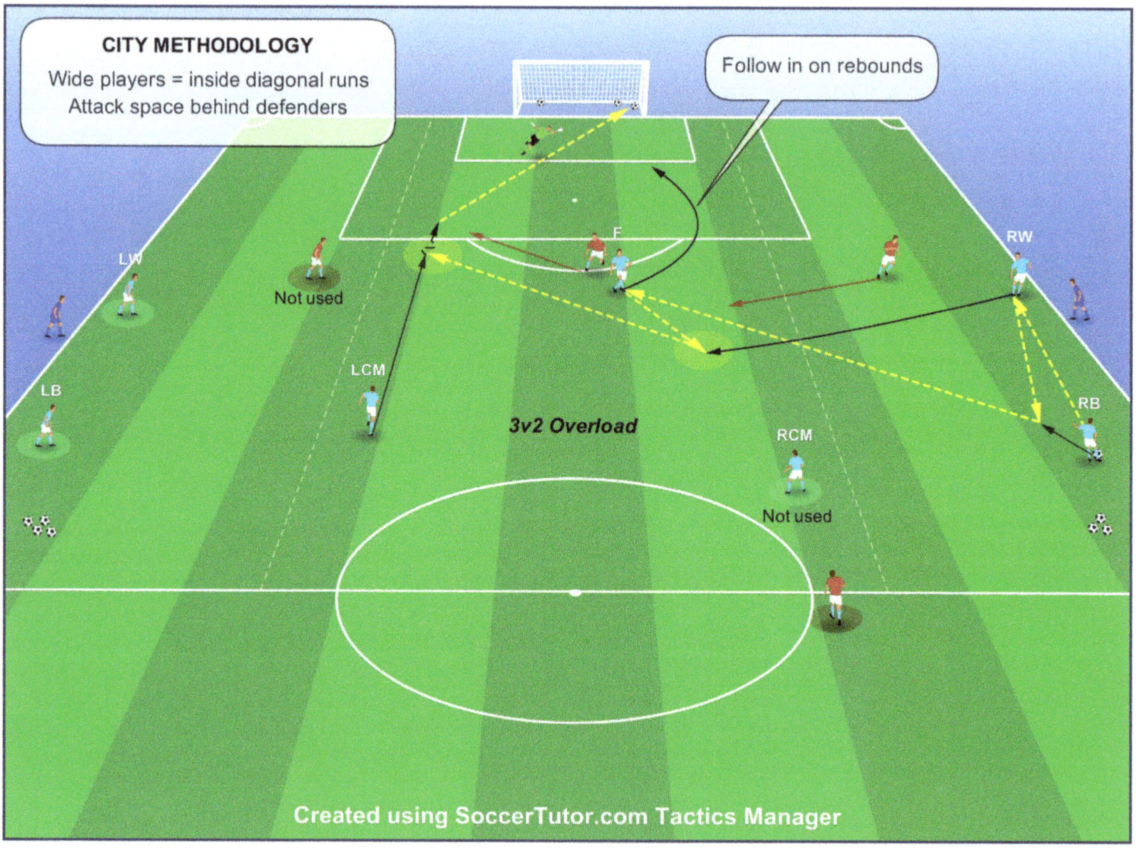

Practice Description

- Using half a pitch, we mark out 3 channels as shown. The practice starts from either full back alternately.

- In this example, the active players are the **right back (RB), right winger (RW), left central midfielder (LCM)** and **forward (F)** versus 2 red defenders (4v2).

- The attacking team must play within 2 channels and try to create an attacking overload to score with the **central midfielder (LCM in diagram)** making a penetrating run in behind.

- This example sequence starts with **RB's** one-two with **RW**, followed by the pass into the **forward (F)**. From there, **RW** moves inside at pace to receive **F's** lay-off and then play a through pass for the forward run of **LCM** to score.

- The finish should be across goal so the **forward (F)** can have the opportunity to score on the rebound if the GK saves.

- As soon as the first phase is finished, the left back starts a new one with play only within the left and central channels with **LB, LW, RCM**, and **F** involved.

Training Session 9 - Build-up, Midfield Combinations + Finish the Attack

4. Attacking Overloads in a Dynamic 2-Zone 5v5 (+GKs) Small Sided Game

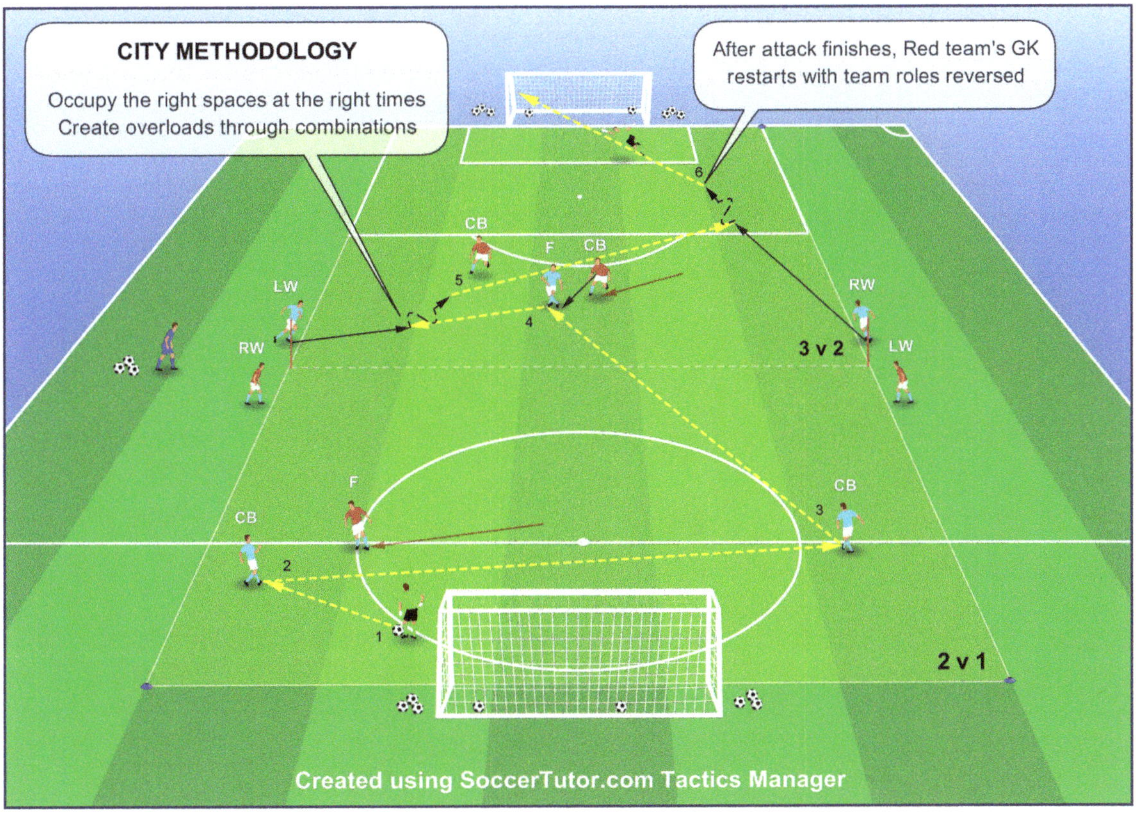

Practice Description

- In the area shown, we play 5v5 (+GKs). Adjust the size of the area depending on the age and/or level.

- The halfway line splits 2 zones. The GK starts and there is a 2v1 situation in the low zone. The blues keep controlled possession and wait for the right time to play into the **forward (F)**.

- **F** sets the ball back for either of the 2 wide players who join from their outside positions shown to create a 3v2 attack.

- In this example, the **left winger (LW)** receives and takes a forward touch.

- The opposite winger **(RW)** keeps the width on the opposite side and makes a run in behind to try and score.

- Restart from the red team's GK and repeat the practice in the opposite direction with the team roles reversed.

This is a repetition of the practice on Page 86 - it is placed here again as that is how sessions were built at the Manchester City Academy

MANCHESTER CITY ACADEMY SESSION 10

Build-up Phase 1, 2 + 3: Short Build-up, Midfield Combinations and Finishing the Attack (2)

Training Session 10 - Build-up, Midfield Combinations + Finish the Attack

1. Support Play and Attacking Combination in the Final Third Pattern with Crossing & Finishing

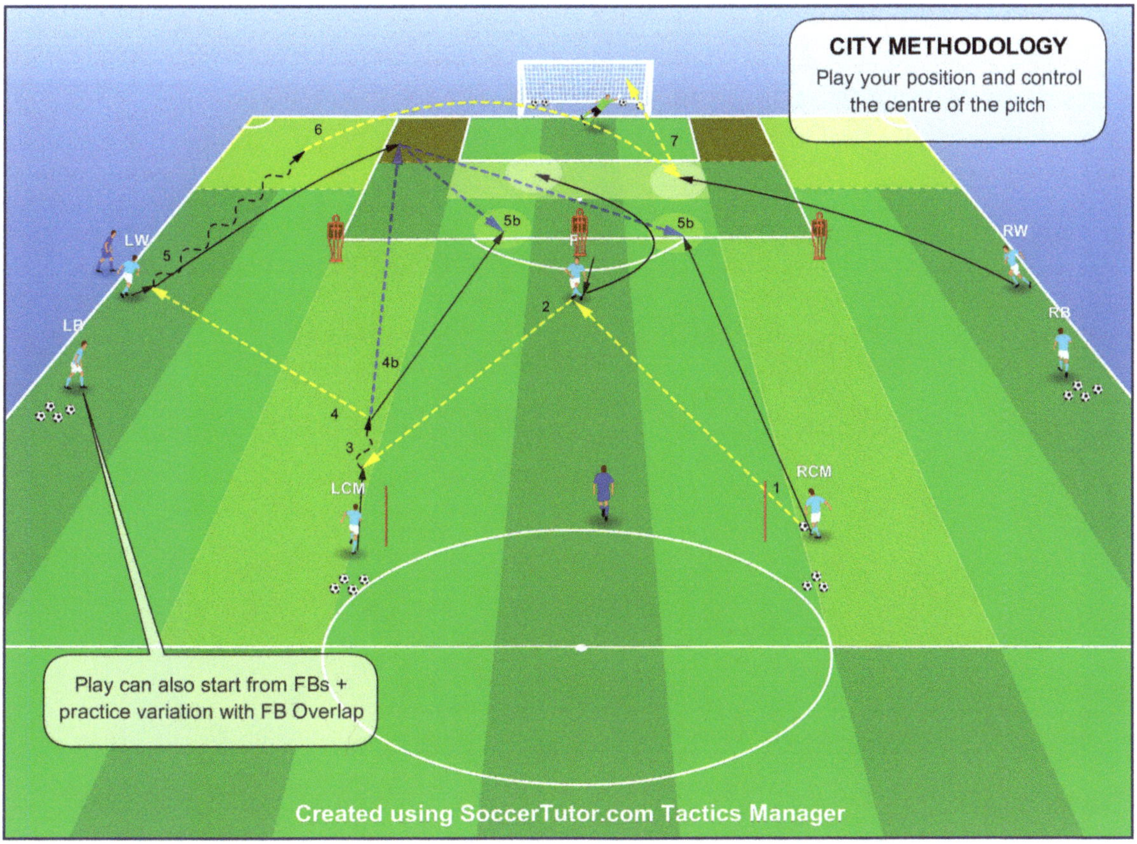

CITY METHODOLOGY
Play your position and control the centre of the pitch

Play can also start from FBs + practice variation with FB Overlap

Practice Description

1-2. The **central midfielder (RCM)** passes to the forward **(F)**, who sets the ball back for the oncoming **LCM**.

3-5. **LCM** takes a forward touch and passes to the **winger (LW)** near the sideline. **LW** receives and dribbles into the wide yellow zone.

4b-5b. If **LCM** plays a through pass into the small red zone instead *(4b)*, then **LW** cuts the ball back to either of the central midfielders **(LCM or RCM)** near the edge of the box.

6-7. **LW** crosses to the front or back post. **F** attacks the front post and the opposite winger **RW** attacks the back post.

→ The practice is repeated starting from the other side **(RB)**.

→ Variations which includes winger moving inside and the full back using an overlapping run should also be practiced.

Coaching Point:

Whether or not the central midfielder plays to the winger's feet or in behind depends on the winger's decision and movement.

Training Session 10 - Build-up, Midfield Combinations + Finish the Attack

2. Runs from Deep in Behind the Defensive Line + Crossing and Finishing Functional Practice

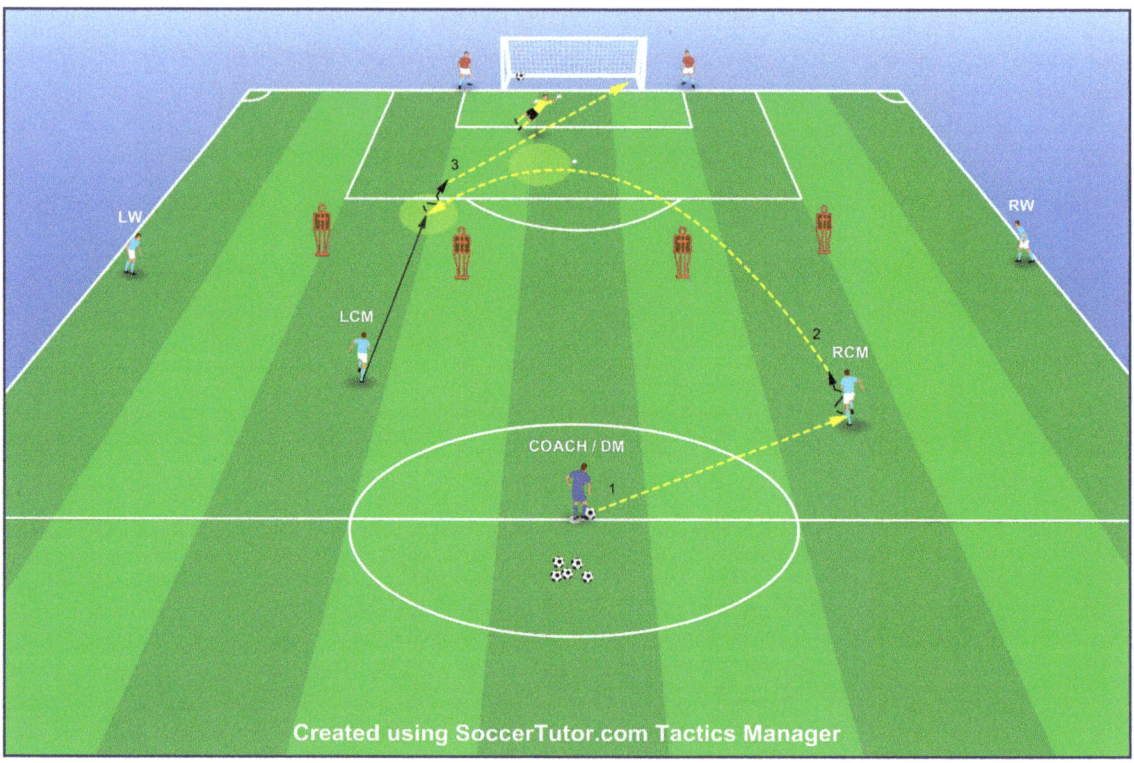

Description

- We have 2 blue central midfielders, 2 wingers and either a defensive midfielder or a Coach with balls.

- There is also a GK and 2 red defenders either side of the goal. The Coach decides if and when to introduce the 2 defenders into the practice.

- To start, the DM or Coach passes to either **central midfielder (RCM in diagram example)**.

- **Option 1:** The central midfielder **(RCM)** must receive the pass on the back foot (half-turn) and open up to play a pass in behind. They must use a maximum of 2 touches (control + pass).

- The other central midfielder **(LCM)** times a straight line run in between the full back and centre back mannequins to receive the diagonal aerial pass on the full.

- The **LCM** uses a maximum of 2 touches to receive and move towards goal + finish.

- **Option 2:** The central midfielder passes wide to either **winger (LW or RW)** and the wide player delivers a cross into the box. The other 3 players all make runs to try and score.

- When using this practice, make sure to practice on both sides.

Training Session 10 - Build-up, Midfield Combinations + Finish the Attack

3. Game Principles and Side Diamond Patterns of Play in a 10v8 (+GKs) Functional Practice

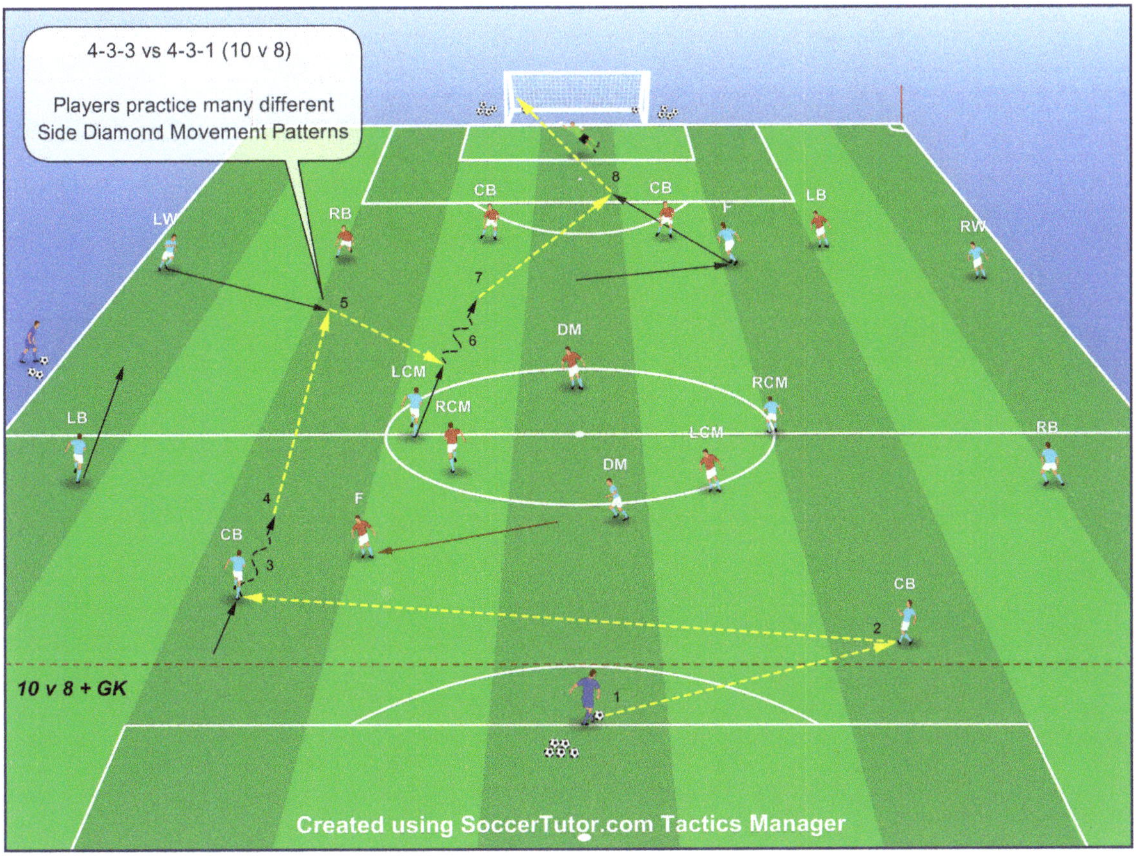

4-3-3 vs 4-3-1 (10 v 8)

Players practice many different Side Diamond Movement Patterns

Practice Description

- For this pattern of play practice, the Coach plays the ball in, and the blue players practice many side diamond patterns of play in the 4-3-3 formation (you can see many examples throughout the training sessions for reference). The red team defend in a 4-3-1 formation.

- The blues use a side diamond pattern to create an overload in the wide area and exploit their numerical advantage (10v8). They must recognise what pattern to use at the right time.

- In the diagram example, the side diamond pattern enables them to receive in between the lines **(LW)**, set the ball for the **central midfielder (LCM)**, and then play a through pass for the movement of the **forward (F)** in behind to finish.

- The Coach must observe all the technical and tactical detail in line with the methodology.

- **NOTE:** This kind of opposed pattern of play practice was used in the later stages of the season (opposed), making the players create overloads for success.

This is a repetition of the practice on Page 65 - it is placed here again as that is how sessions were built at the Manchester City Academy

ELITE ACADEMY COACHING

Training Session 10 - Build-up, Midfield Combinations + Finish the Attack

4. Create 3v2 Attacking Overloads in a Back to Back Goals 5v5 (+GKs) Small Sided Game

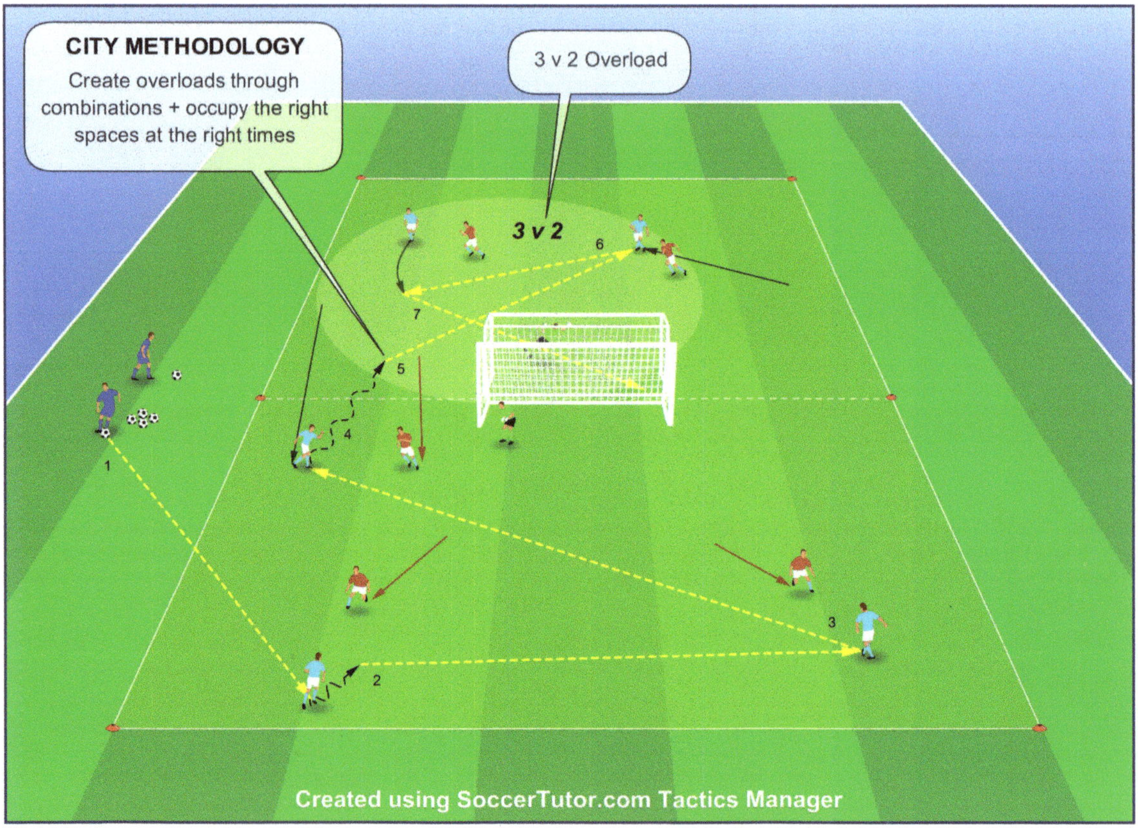

CITY METHODOLOGY
Create overloads through combinations + occupy the right spaces at the right times

3 v 2 Overload

Practice Description

- In a 60 x 40 yard area, we have 2 teams of 5 players and 2 large goals + GKs positioned back to back in the centre.

- The game starts with the Coach's pass and the team in possession (blues) aim to create a 3v2 attacking overload to score in the opposite goal.

- Implementing the City Methodology which includes creating overloads through fast combination play and occupying the right spaces at the right times helps players succeed in this game.

- High level players can be left to create 3v2, knowing the correct timings. It's about the situation and timing of when. Keep possession, then go in! The transitions should also be exploited.

Variations

1. For lower age groups/levels, start with 2v2 in both halves + 2 Jokers who float. This is easier to understand as the Jokers can easily help create a 3v2 overload.

2. Start with 3v3 in one half and 2v2 in the other.

This is a repetition of the practice on Page 56 - it is placed here again as that is how sessions were built at the Manchester City Academy

MANCHESTER CITY ACADEMY SESSION 11

Pressing from the Front (1)

Training Session 11 - Pressing from the Front

1a. Side Diamond Pattern when Forward Pass is Blocked & Full Back Plays into Forward (Left)

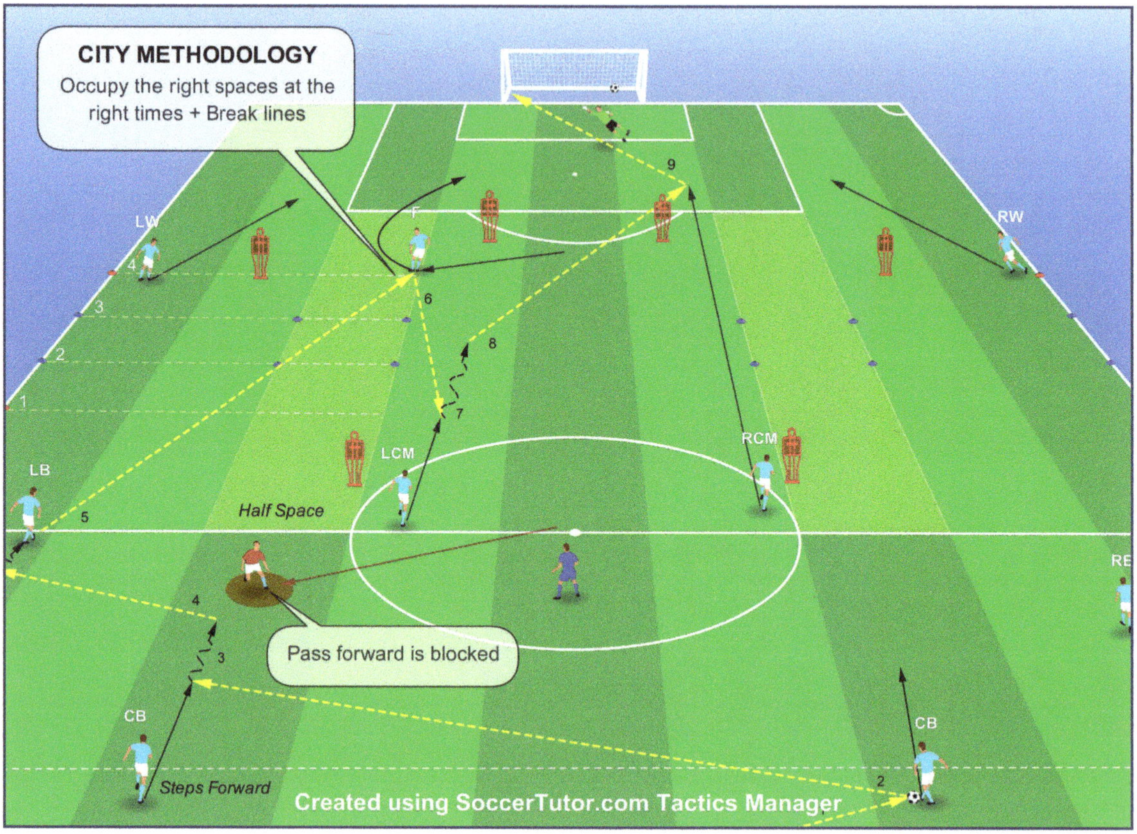

Practice Description

The players practice different patterns of play set out by the coach. There are many examples included in the book. This one shows the **Side Diamond Combination** (centre back, full back, central midfielder, & winger on one side) when the centre back is blocked from playing forward.

1-3. If the space in front of the **CB** is closed (as shown by red player in diagram moving across to press him), the diagram above shows a good combination.

4. The **LB** should be level with the ball carrier (**CB**) to receive the next pass.

5-6. The **winger (LW)** stays high and wide, opening up the channel for the **full back (LB)** to play the pass into the **forward (F)**, who sets the ball back for the oncoming **central midfielder (LCM)**.

7. The **LCM** takes a touch to open up all the options on both sides of the pitch rather than playing first time.

8-9. In this example, the other central midfielder **(RCM)** makes a penetrating run in behind the defensive line in between the 2 red CB mannequins. The **LCM** plays a well timed diagonal pass into the box for **RCM** to receive and score.

Training Session 11 - Pressing from the Front

1b. Side Diamond Pattern when Forward Pass is Blocked & Full Back Plays into Forward (Right)

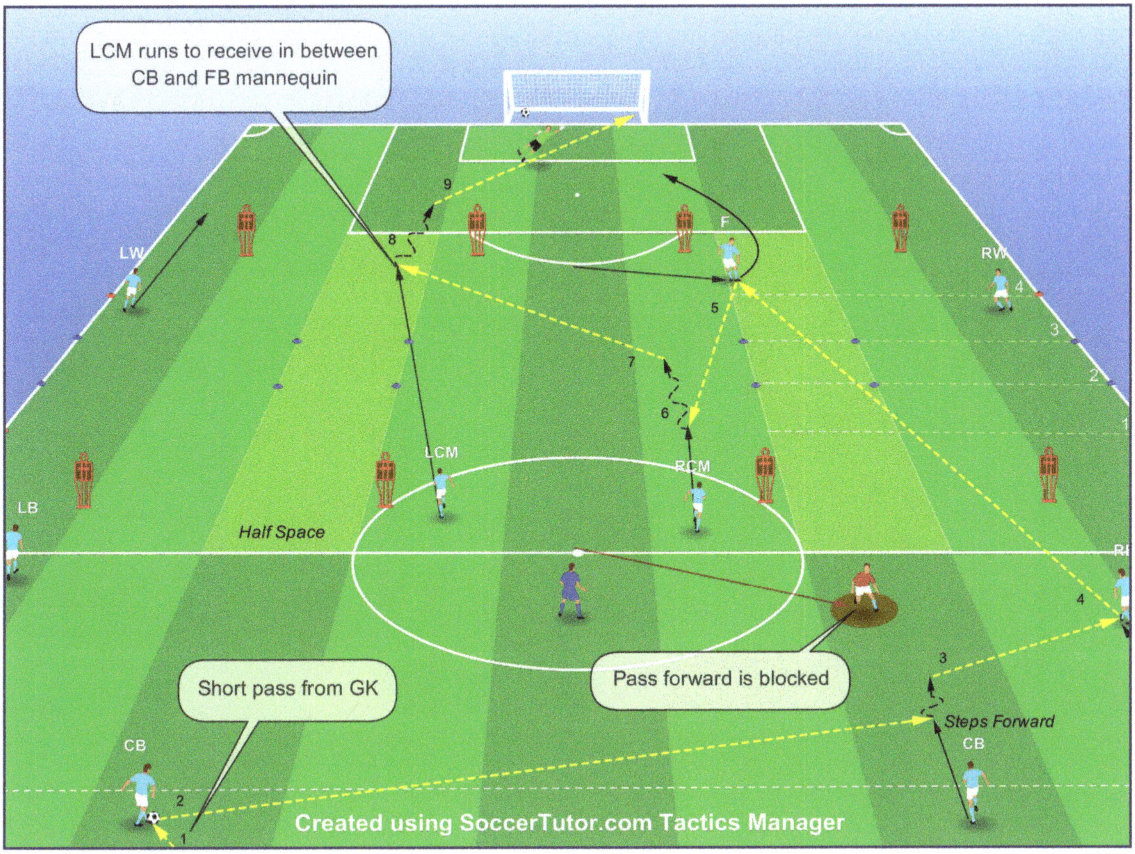

Practice Description

This is a variation of the example on the previous page with the side diamond combination now being played on the right side of the pitch.

1-6. These passes and movements are the same as example on the previous page but just mirrored on the right side.

7. In this example, the central midfielder **(RCM)** makes a penetrating run to receive in between the CB and FB mannequins. **RCM** plays a well timed diagonal pass into the half space for **LCM's** forward run.

8-9. **LCM** takes the ball into the box and shoots across the GK to try and score.

Training Session 11 - Pressing from the Front

2. Defensive Organisation and Pressing in a 4v4 (+3) Directional Possession Game

(Diagram: 4 v 4 (+3) directional possession game. Note 1: "3 Yellows play with team in possession." Note 2: "Blues lose the ball = Switch roles with Reds.")

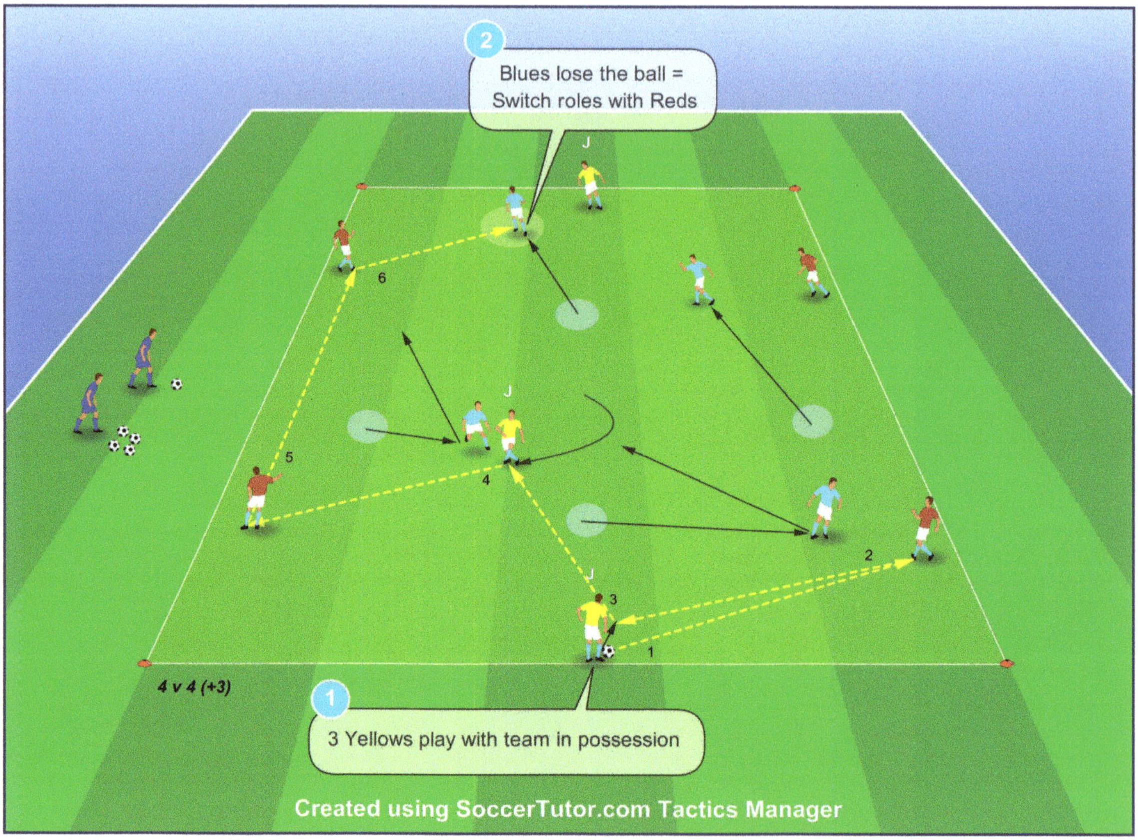

Practice Description

- In a 10 x 15 yard area, we have 2 teams of 4 players (blue and red) + 3 yellow jokers who play with the team in possession.
- The practice starts with the Coach and the red team try to maintain possession with help from the 3 yellow jokers.
- The blue team work together (pressing) to close off the angles and try to win the ball. If they are able to win the ball, the teams switch roles.
- If you make it position specific, the blue players would be the forward, 2 central midfielders, and 1 defensive midfielder.

Coaching Points

1. The focus is on defensive organisation: How can the 4 defenders stop the 7 playing through and penetrating? Stop the ball being played through the centre.
2. Force the ball down the sides of the defensive diamond to create 1v1 and 2v2 situations
3. Keep the ball in front and protect space in behind. Press quickly as a unit with correct angles and distances.
4. Recognise when to press and when to drop and regroup.

Training Session 11 - Pressing from the Front

3. Pressing from the Front to "Set the Trap" in a Dynamic 6v8 (+GK) Phase of Play

Practice Description

- Start from the red team's GK, who plays out to either centre back. The blue **central midfielder (RCM)** moves forward to mark the red defensive midfielder (DM), which releases the **forward (F)** to be able to press from the front.

- The **forward (F)** positions himself between the 2 centre backs and tries to force the play one way (wide), then applies pressure. By making the play predictable to "set the trap," the blue team can implement their coordinated pressing plan.

- The blue winger on that side **(LW)** presses the ball once it travels wider (to red RB). The central midfielder on that side **(LCM)** marks his opponent tightly and the defensive midfielder **(DM)** moves into a balanced position to mark red F and cover LCM.

- The other blue winger **(RW)** discourages a switch of play by taking up a balanced position.

- **Coaching Points:** Get compact, stop the switch of play, apply pressure on ball ("squeeze"), keep the ball in front, protect the depth and drop if no pressure on ball.

Training Session 11 - Pressing from the Front

4. Defensive Organisation and Pressing in Midfield in a 5v5 (+1) 4-Goal Small Sided Game

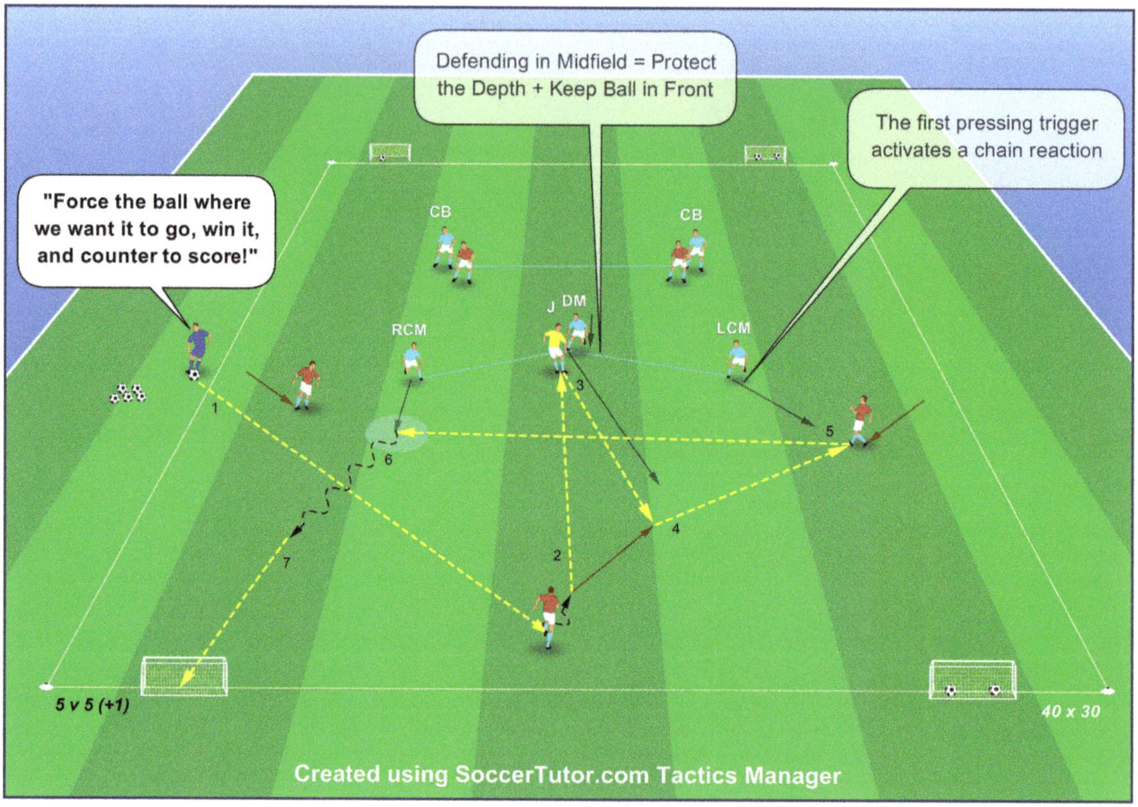

Defending in Midfield = Protect the Depth + Keep Ball in Front

The first pressing trigger activates a chain reaction

"Force the ball where we want it to go, win it, and counter to score!"

5 v 5 (+1) 40 x 30

Practice Description

- In a 40 x 30 yard area, we play a 5v5 (+1) small sided game with 4 small goals.

- The Coach starts and the red team try to score in 2 small goals without any conditions. The focus is on the blue team defending the numerical disadvantage they have (5v6).

- The blue team use a good defensive shape (2-1-2) and organisation to defend their goals. Once the first pressing trigger is initiated, it activates a chain reaction to try and win the ball.

- If the blues win the ball, they try to score in the other 2 goals as quickly as possible.

Coaching Points

1. Individual roles and responsibilities are key, so the players are ready to attack, and ready to defend.

2. Players need to execute the information given to them by the Coach during the practice e.g. "Force the ball where we want it to go, win it, and counter to score!"

MANCHESTER CITY ACADEMY SESSION 12

Pressing from the Front (2)

Training Session 12 - Pressing from the Front

1. Side Diamond Pattern of Play to Receive in Between Lines, Set + Overlapping Full Back Cross

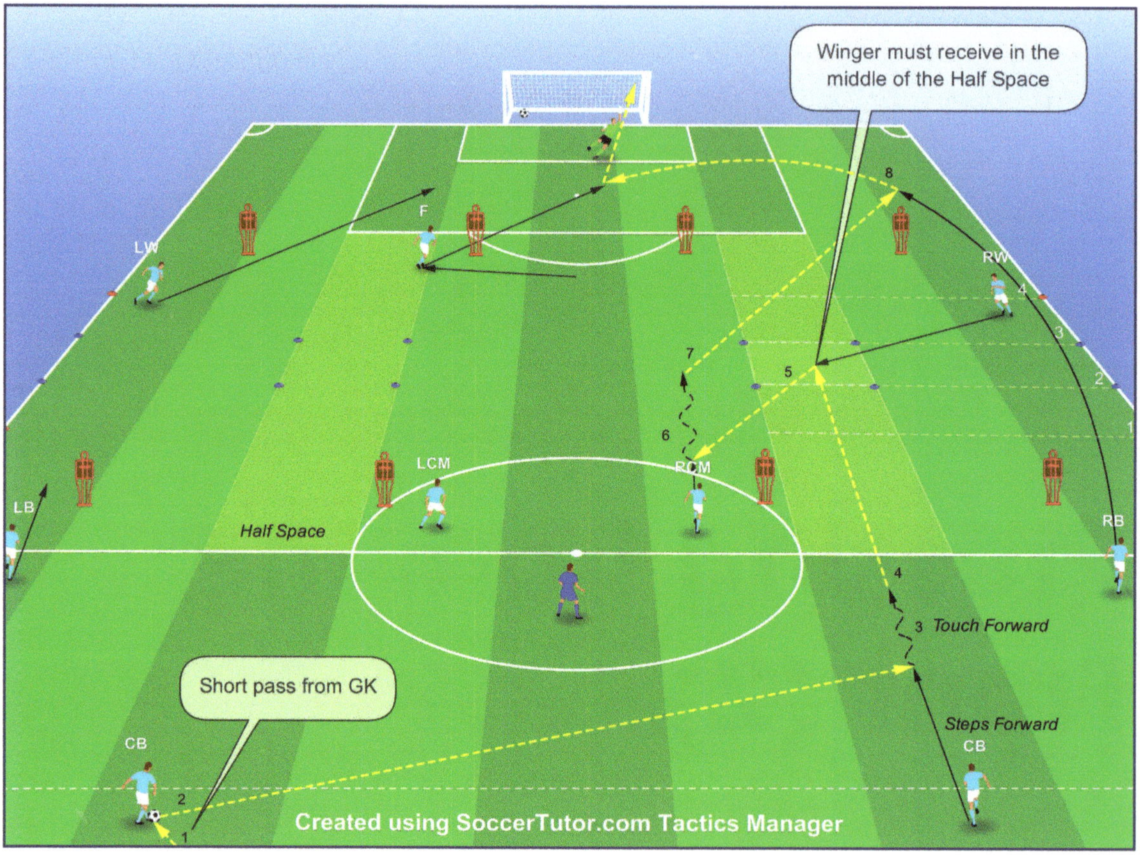

Practice Description

The players practice different patterns of play set out by the coach. There are many more examples in the book. This one shows the **Side Diamond Combination** (centre back, full back, central midfielder, & winger on one side).

1-3. The **GK** passes short to a **centre back (CB)**. He passes across to the other **CB**, who has stepped forward (takes a touch).

4. The **CB** passes forward into the half space for the **winger (RW)**, who drops off the line and inside to receive.

5. The **RW** sets the ball back for the oncoming **central midfielder (RCM)**.

6-7. **RCM** takes a touch to open up all the options on both sides of the pitch rather than playing first time, then plays in between the full back and centre back mannequins for the overlapping run of the **right back (RB)**.

8-9. **RB** delivers a cross into the box and the **forward (F)** and opposite winger **(LW)** make runs into the box to try and score. In this example, **F** scores from a central position.

Training Session 12 - Pressing from the Front

2. Pressing with a Numerical Disadvantage in a Game Related 2-Zone 5v5 Transition Game

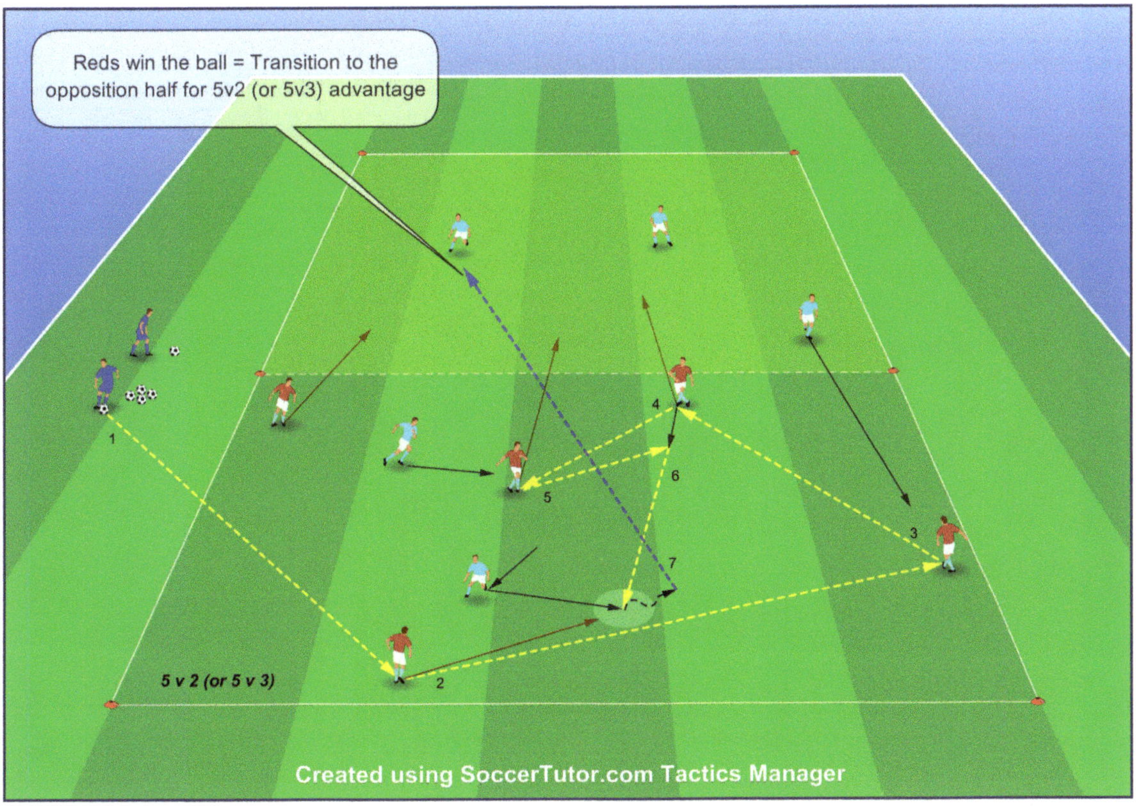

Reds win the ball = Transition to the opposition half for 5v2 (or 5v3) advantage

5 v 2 (or 5 v 3)

Practice Description

- In a 30 x 20 yard area, we split it into 2 equal zones. Both teams have 5 players. The transition game starts with the Coach's pass as shown.
- The team in possession (reds) try to retain possession and **2 or 3 blue players press them**, trying to win the ball. Set the reds a target e.g. **10 Passes = 1 Point**.
- If the blues win the ball, they pass to a teammate in the other zone.
- 2 or 3 red players must make a very fast transition and sprint across to the other zone to press. The team roles are reversed with the same aims.

Coaching Points

1. In possession, keep the ball moving with good decision making.
2. Out of possession = keep shape.
3. Press collectively and win the ball!
4. Create even numbers around the ball (1v1 / 2v2).
5. Win possession and move the ball quickly to a free teammate in the other zone.
6. Quick reactions on the defensive transition to try and regain possession.

Training Session 12 - Pressing from the Front

3. Pressing from the Front to "Set the Trap" in a Full Man for Man Pressing Game (10v10 +GK)

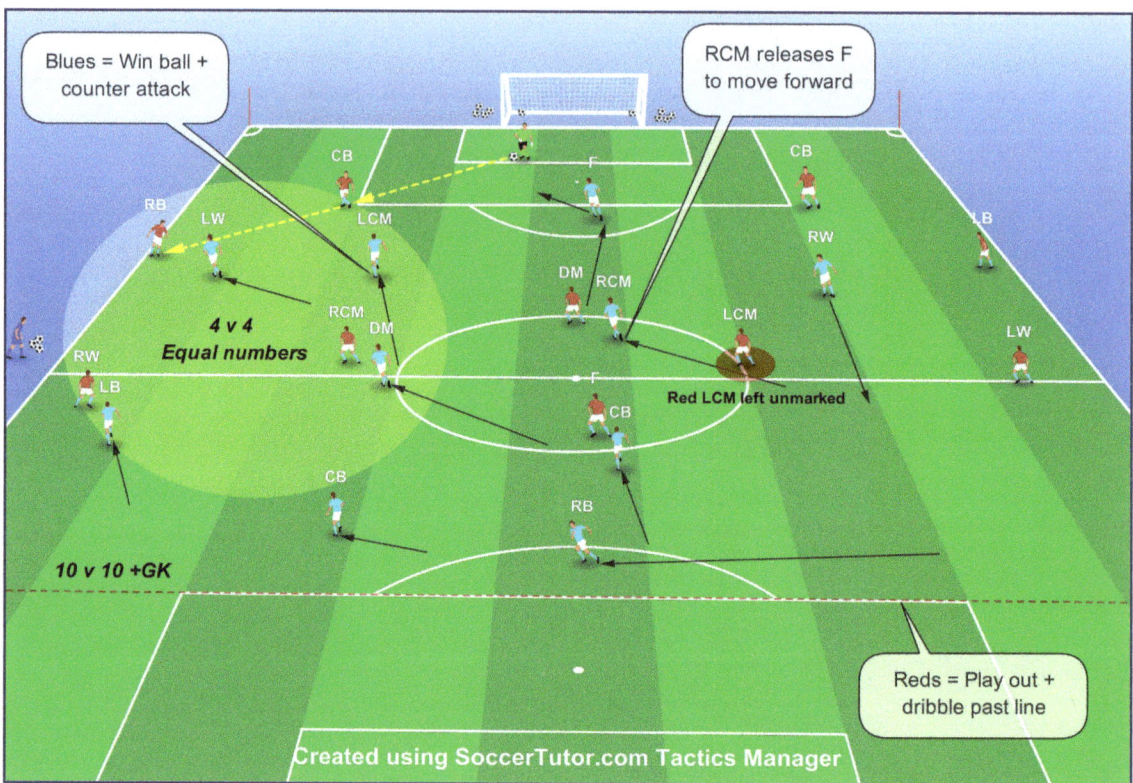

Practice Description

- The red team's GK plays out to a defender and the reds build up play trying to play through the red line. The blues try to win the ball and then score on the counter attack.

- The blues implement a full man to man press. The blue **central midfielder (RCM)** moves forward to mark the red defensive midfielder (DM), which releases the **forward (F)** to be able to press from the front.

- The GK passes to the red CB and the **left central midfielder (LCM)** sprints forward to press the ball. The **defensive midfielder (DM)** moves to mark red RCM.

- This chain reaction is completed with the **centre back (CB)** moving forward to mark the red forward (F).

- The blue **left winger (LW)** moves to press the red RB once the ball is played to him.

- The blue **left back (LB)** moves forward to mark the red RW. This creates equal numbers (4v4) around the ball area on one side and a good chance for the blues to win the ball.

- The other **centre back (CB)** and the **right back (RB)** shift across to provide balance at the back. The **right winger (RW)** drops back to prevent a switch of play towards the red LW.

Training Session 12 - Pressing from the Front

4. Defensive Organisation and Pressing from the Front in a Rotational 3-Team 6v6 (+GKs) SSG

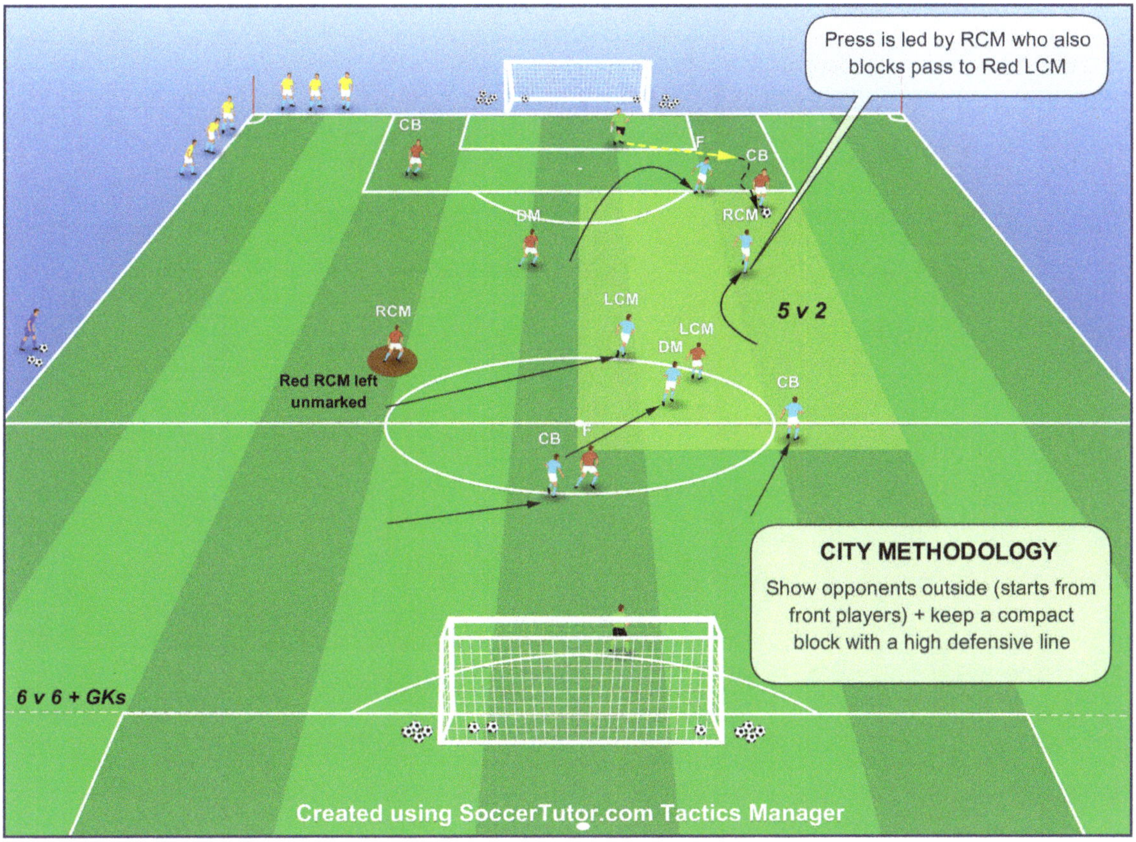

Press is led by RCM who also blocks pass to Red LCM

Red RCM left unmarked

5 v 2

CITY METHODOLOGY
Show opponents outside (starts from front players) + keep a compact block with a high defensive line

6 v 6 + GKs

Practice Description

- Using the area shown, two teams have 6 players (2 centre backs, 1 defensive midfielder, 2 central midfielders, and 1 forward) +GKs. There is also an extra third team waiting outside (yellows).

- The focus is **pressing from the front and defending in a compact shape** to stop penetrating passes.

- The players must identify pressing triggers dependent on the angles and distances of the units to be able to press aggressively. Once the first player presses, a chain reaction follows.

- The game starts with the GK and the team in possession (reds) try to build-up/play through their opponents to score.

- The defending team (blues) defend, try to win the ball + counter attack to score.

- The diagram shows exactly how the Manchester City players were coached to press in this situation. They press from the front and try to create a numerical advantage around the ball. The opposite side red central midfielder (RCM) is left unmarked as it is difficult to pass to him.

- Rotate the teams after conceding a goal or after a set amount of time e.g. 5 mins.

MANCHESTER CITY ACADEMY SESSION 13

Defending in Midfield

Training Session 13 - Defending in Midfield

1. Winger Comes Inside to Set Att. Midfielder's Pass for Forward to Open Up and Finish Pattern of Play

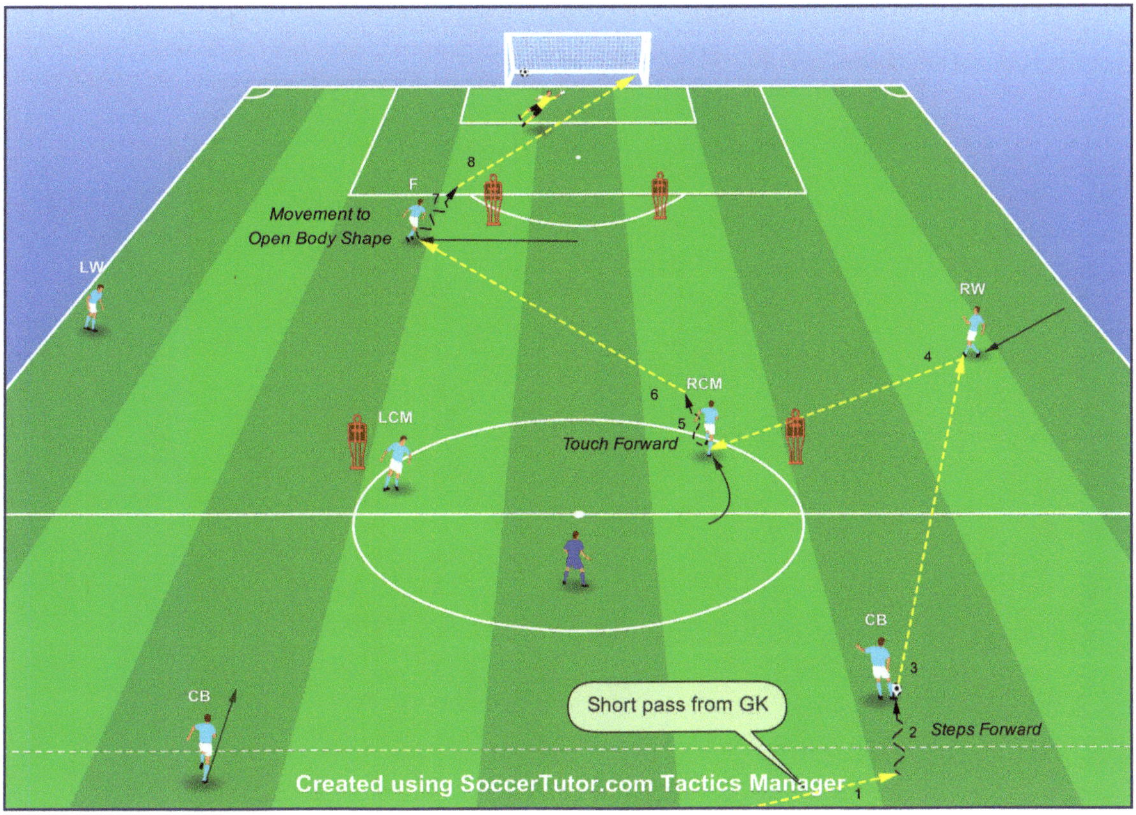

Practice Description

1-2. The **GK** passes short to a **centre back (CB)**, who steps forward with the ball.

3. The **CB** passes to the **winger (RW)**, who comes off the line at the correct angle to receive.

4. **RW** sets the ball back for the oncoming **central midfielder (RCM)**, who must first be positioned on the inside of the mannequin (defender), so the passing channel is open. **RCM** starts the forward movement as soon as the **CB** plays the pass into the **RW** and has broken the line.

5. **RCM** must take his first touch forward to open up all options on both sides of the pitch, rather than playing the pass first time.

6-8. **RCM** passes for the movement of the **forward (F)**, who must first stay high and central to receive the pass and look to exploit the space wide of the mannequin. He opens up, takes a touch into the box and shoots across the goal into the far corner.

→ The sequence is then repeated on the left side of the pitch using the **LCM** and **LW**, with **F** opening up towards the right side to receive.

Training Session 13 - Defending in Midfield

2. Pressing with Numerical Disadvantage in a Game Related 2-Zone 6v6 Transition Game

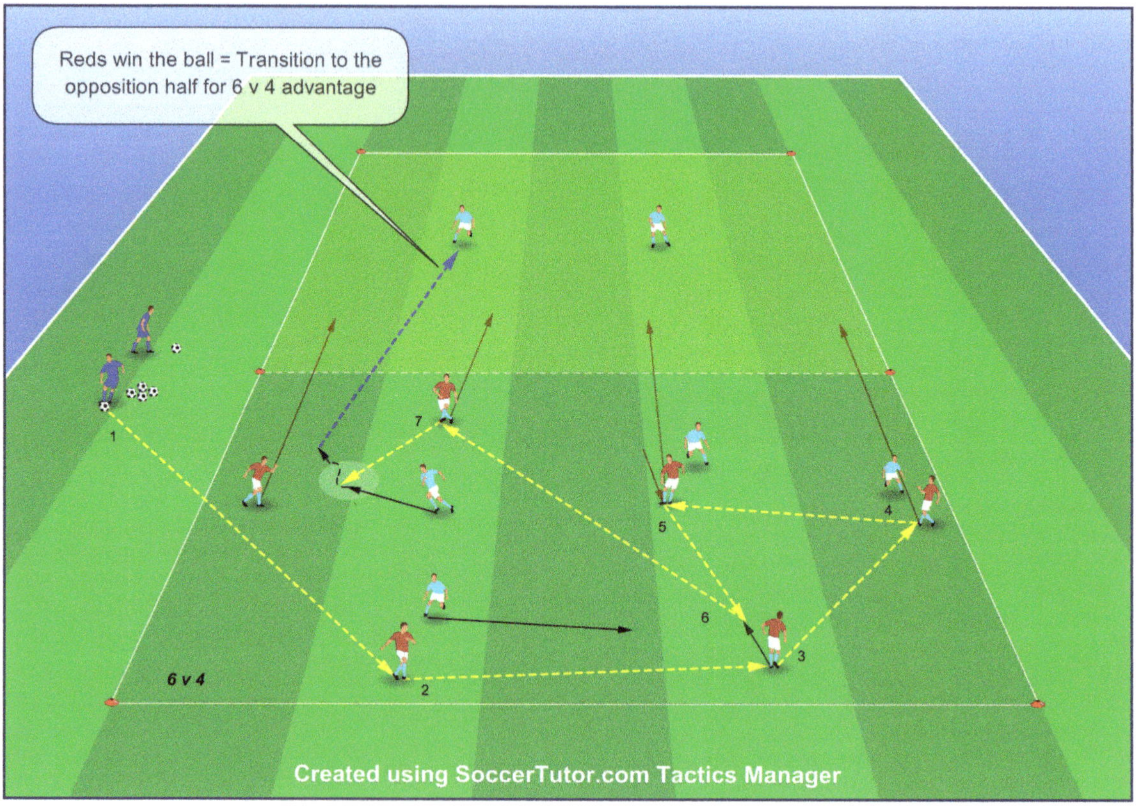

Reds win the ball = Transition to the opposition half for 6 v 4 advantage

Practice Description

- In a 35 x 25 yard area, we split it into 2 equal zones. Both teams have 6 players. The possession game starts with the Coach's pass as shown.
- The team in possession (reds) try to retain possession and **4 blue players press** them, trying to win the ball. Set the reds a target e.g. **10 Passes = 1 Point**.
- If the blues win the ball, they pass to a teammate in the other zone.
- 4 red players must make a very fast transition and sprint across to the other zone to press. The team roles are reversed with the same aims.

Coaching Points

1. In possession, keep the ball moving with good decision making.
2. Out of possession = keep shape.
3. Press collectively and win the ball!
4. Create even numbers around the ball (1v1 → 4v4).
5. Win possession and move the ball quickly to a free teammate in the other zone.
6. Quick reactions on the defensive transition to try and regain possession.

Training Session 13 - Defending in Midfield

3. Continuous Overloads in Game Related Situations (2v1, 3v2, 4v3, 5v4, 6v5)

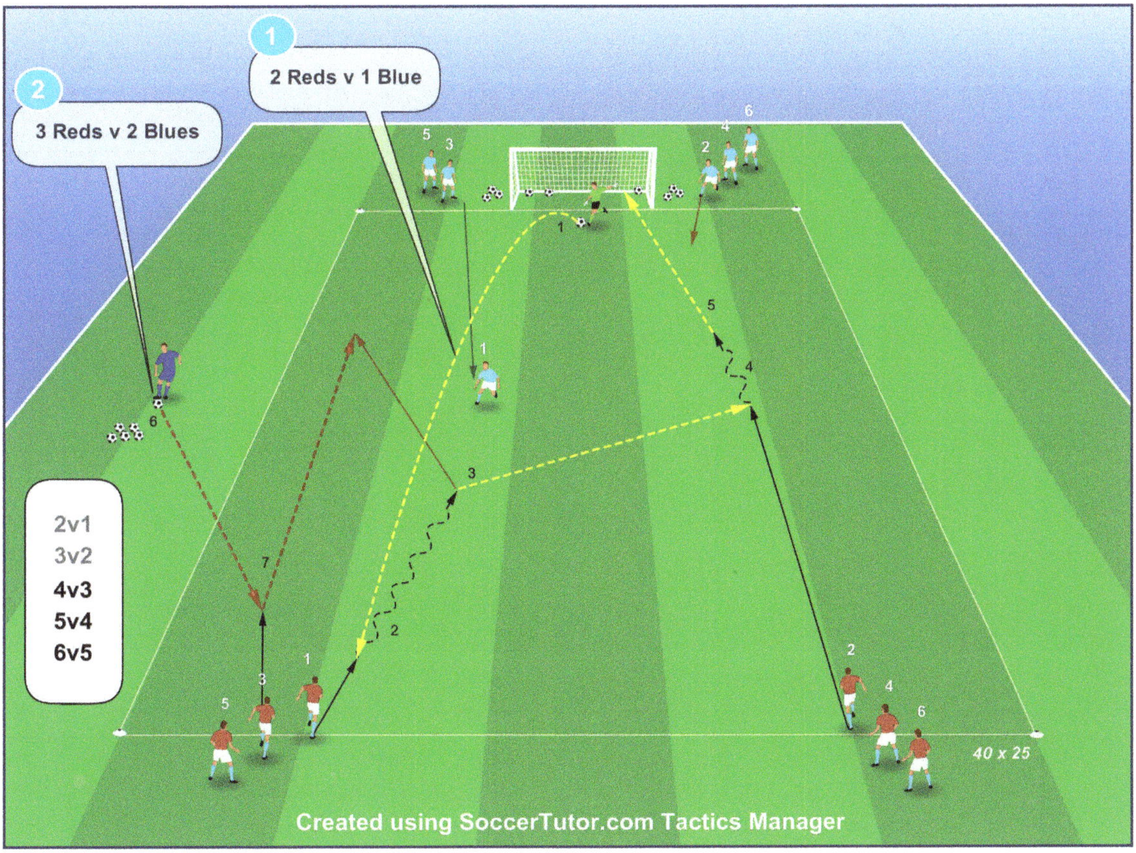

Practice Description

- In a 40 x 25 yard area, we have 2 teams of 6 players and 1 large goal +GK.
- **Ball 1:** The GK starts the game with a pass to a red player (No1 in diagram).
- Red No1 and No2 attack against Blue No1 in a 2v1 situation.
- The reds try to score quickly using their numerical advantage.
- **Ball 2:** As soon as the first phase is over, the Coach passes to the next red player (No3), who enters along with 1 more red defender, for a new 3v2 attack.
- The reds attack every time with the ball fed from the GK or Coach. The practice continues with 4v3, 5v4, and finally 6v5.

Coaching Points

1. Defenders should close down quickly and try to create equal numbers around the ball area.
2. When and how can you win the ball?
3. Communication: When to press and when to drop back.
4. Keep the ball in front of you and protect the depth.

Training Session 13 - Defending in Midfield

4. Defending Potential 3v2 Overloads in a Back to Back Goals 6v6 (+GKs) Small Sided Game

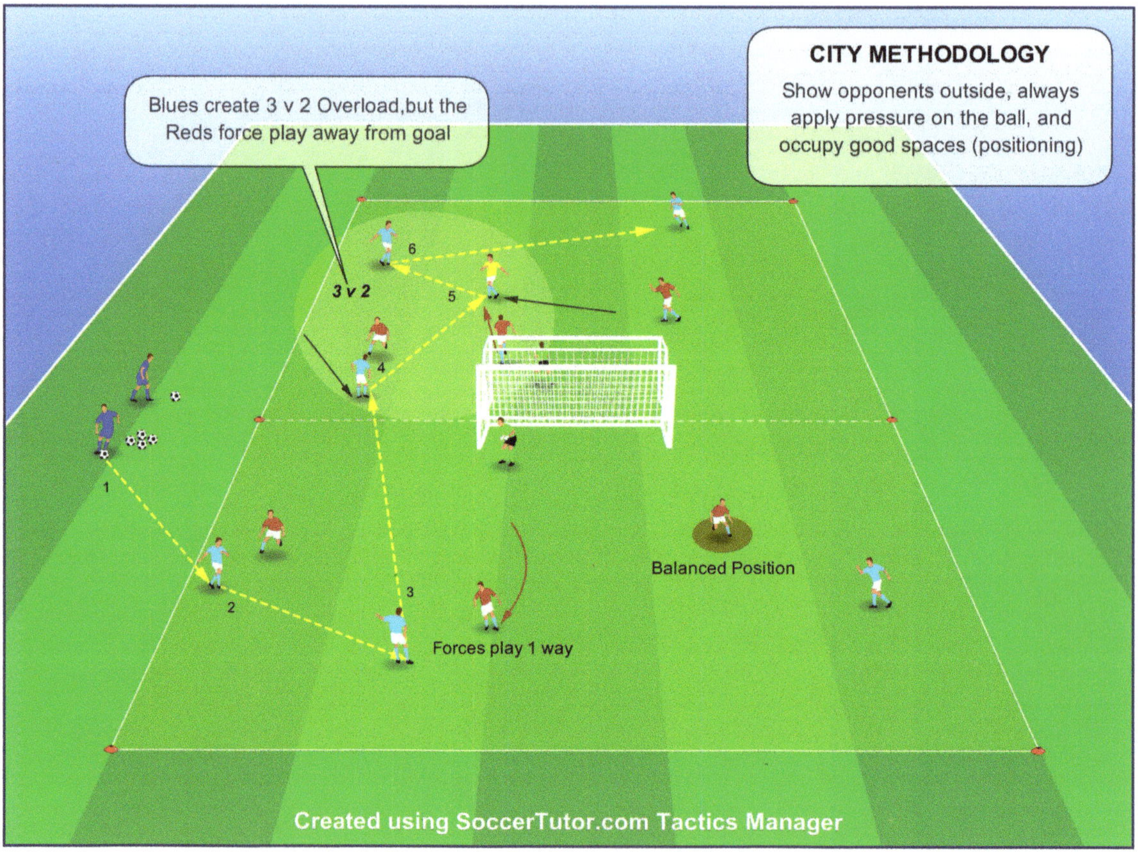

Diagram annotations:
- Blues create 3 v 2 Overload, but the Reds force play away from goal
- **CITY METHODOLOGY:** Show opponents outside, always apply pressure on the ball, and occupy good spaces (positioning)
- 3 v 2
- Balanced Position
- Forces play 1 way

Practice Description

- In a 60 x 40 yard area, we have 2 teams of 6 players (+ 1 Joker) and 2 large goals with GKs positioned back to back in the centre.
- The game starts with the Coach's pass and the team in possession aim to exploit their numerical advantage with the extra Joker to create 3v2 overloads and score.
- The practice and Coach's focus is on the defending team's ability to prevent 3v2 attacking overloads and force the play away from the goal.
- In the diagram example, you can see the defending players working together in their threes to force play one way, using balanced positions to cover players, and protecting the space behind them, etc.

Coaching Points

1. Always be in a position to see the opposition player and the ball.
2. Dictate the game without the ball.
3. Force the ball where we want it to go, win it, and counter to score!
4. Show leadership and communication.

MANCHESTER CITY ACADEMY SESSION 14

Pressing from the Front + Defending in Midfield (1)

Training Session 14 - Pressing from the Front + Defending in Midfield

1. Midfield & Forward Units Attacking Combination Play in Final Third with Free Decision Making

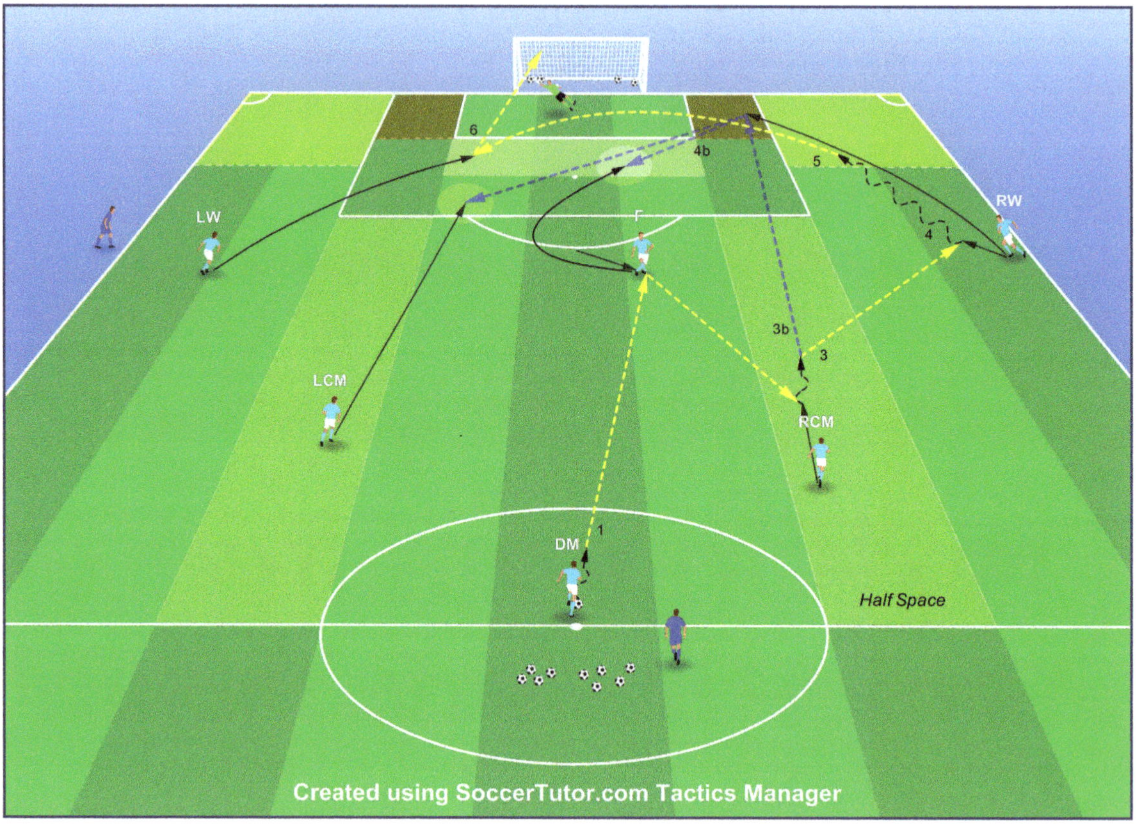

Practice Description

For this practice we work with the midfielders and forwards (3-3 from 4-3-3) and give the players the freedom to use variations of the team's pattern play to result in a cross from either winger.

Throughout the training sessions in the book, you can see the patterns we used at the Manchester City academy.

1-2. In this example, the **defensive midfielder (DM)** passes to the **forward (F)**, who sets the ball back for the oncoming **central midfielder (RCM)**.

3-4. **RCM** takes a touch forward and then plays wide or in behind to the **winger (RW)**, depending on his movement.

5. **RW** delivers a cross into the box for **F**, **LCM**, or the opposite winger **(LW)**.

RULE: *The area the winger receives determines the type of cross.* If the winger dribbles into the wide yellow zone, he crosses to the front or back post. **F** attacks the front post and the opposite winger **LW** attacks the back post. If the winger receives in the small red zone, he cuts the ball back (blue arrows). **LCM** or **RCM** (or both) move for the cut back to the edge of the box.

Training Session 14 - Pressing from the Front + Defending in Midfield

2. Possession Play and Pressing in a 3-Team Transition Game

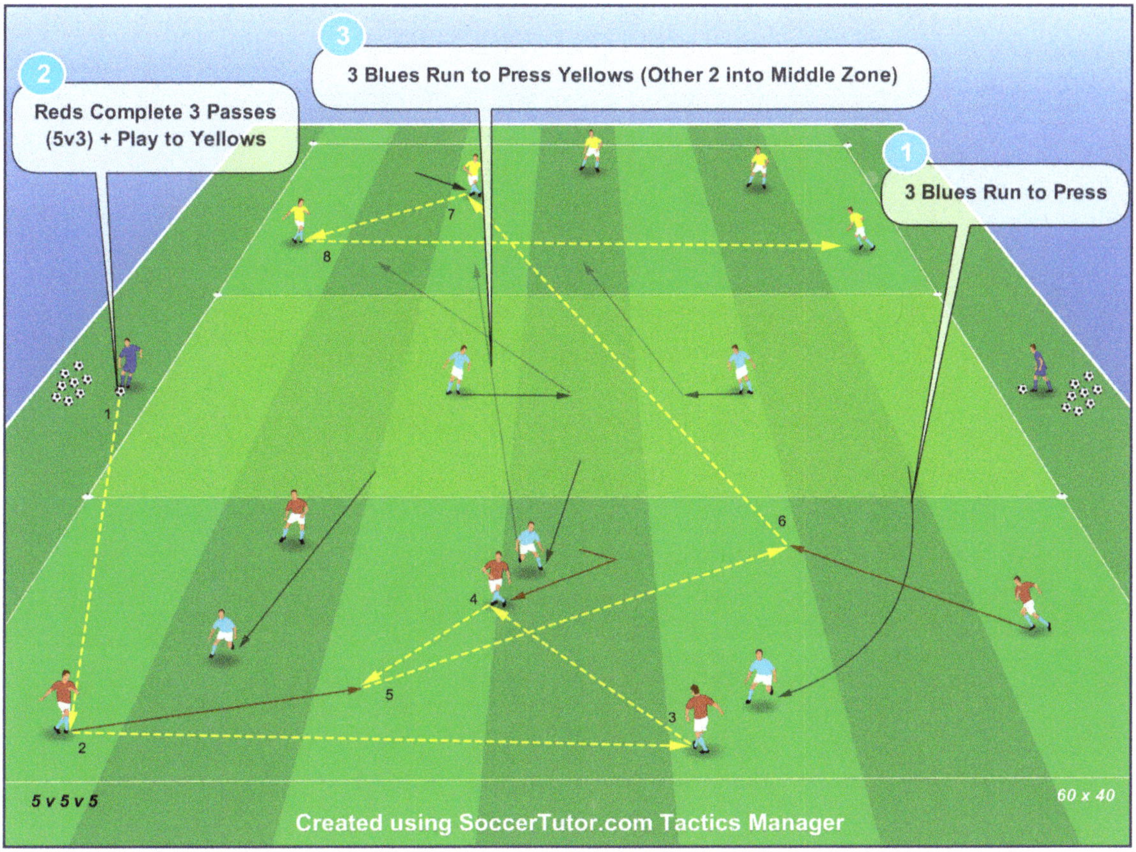

Practice Description

- In a 60 x 40 yard area, each third is 20 yards long. The Coaches stand on each side centrally with balls to start and feed in a new ball if play breaks down, so the game is continuous.
- One team starts in the middle zone (blues), and they will press. The other 2 teams (reds and yellows) start in each end zone.
- Teams need to complete 3 passes before they can transfer the ball to the other team in the opposite end zone.
- The Coach starts by passing into the end zone to the red team and 3 blue players run to press the reds (5v3 situation).
- The reds aim to complete 3 passes and then play to the yellows in the opposite end zone = **1 Point**. The other 2 blue players in the middle zone try to cut out any through passes played. If the blues win the ball, the 2 teams switch roles.
- If the yellows receive, they then have the same aims as the red team with 3 blue players moving across to press.
- You can restrict passes to under head height to play through on ground only.

Training Session 14 - Pressing from the Front + Defending in Midfield

3. Pressing from the Front with Diamond Midfield Shape in a 9v9 (+GKs) Tactical Game

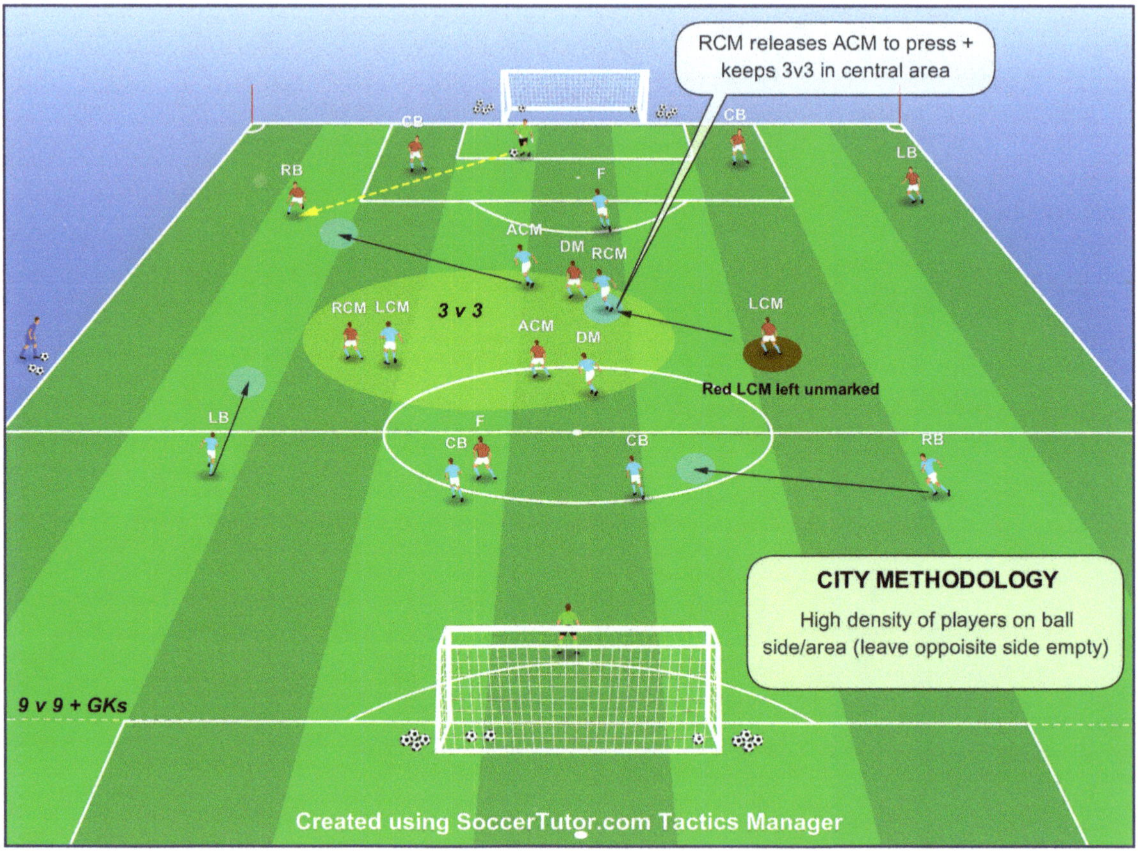

CITY METHODOLOGY

High density of players on ball side/area (leave oppoisite side empty)

Practice Description

- We now play a 9v9 (+GKs) tactical game with 2 large goals. The red team's GK plays out to a defender and the reds build up play with the aim to play through the defending team's pressure and score. The defending team (blues) try to win the ball and then score on the counter attack.

- The blue **forward (F)** forces play to one side. The GK plays to red RB, and the blue right central midfielder **(RCM)** moves to mark the red DM. This releases the blue **ACM** to press the ball, while the 3v3 situation in the central area is retained.

- With a diamond midfield shape, the focus is all about securing the middle part of the pitch when the ball is wide (3v3, or even 4v3).

- The left central midfielder **(LCM)** marks his opponent tightly and the defensive midfielder **(DM)** marks the red ACM. The **left back (LB)** moves forward.

- The red LCM is left unmarked because it's a difficult pass and he can be covered by the blue **DM** anyway, as the ball will take time to travel. The **right back (RB)** moves across and the blues have a 3v1 situation at the back versus the red forward (F).

Training Session 14 - Pressing from the Front + Defending in Midfield

4. Pressing from the Front and Defending Through the Thirds in a Multi-Zone End to End Game

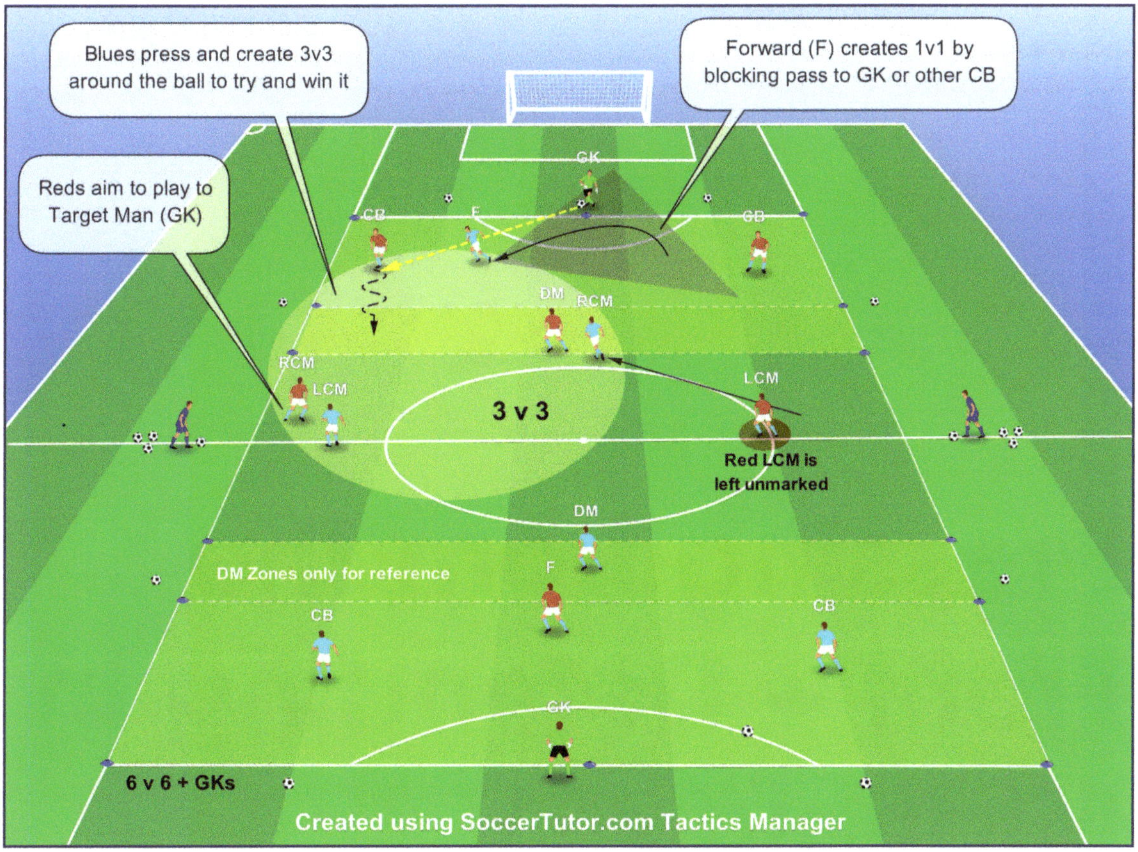

Practice Description

- The end target players can be GKs or Coaches. They feed the ball back in to keep the possession game continuous.

- We start from the GK and a 2v1 situation in the first zone. The **CBs** and **forwards (F)** stay in the end zones, except the CB with the ball can move forward (and F can follow). The middle zone is 3v3 (the DM channels are only there for reference).

- The reds aim to play into the target player (GK). The GK then plays to a blue CB and the team roles are reversed playing in the opposite direction.

- The diagram shows exactly how the Manchester City players were coached to press/defend in this situation. When the red CB receives, the **forward (F)** creates 1v1 by pressing and blocking the pass to the GK or other CB. The **central midfielder (RCM)** moves to press the red DM. This creates a 3v3 situation around the ball area on that side, which makes it likely the blues will win the ball.

- **Coaching Points:** Develop the relationship between the units, defend as a block, delay opponents, deny space, and protect the depth.

MANCHESTER CITY ACADEMY SESSION 15

Pressing from the Front + Defending in Midfield (2)

Training Session 15 - Pressing from the Front + Defending in Midfield

1. Angles of Support and Playing Through the Thirds in a Technical 4-Line Passing Drill

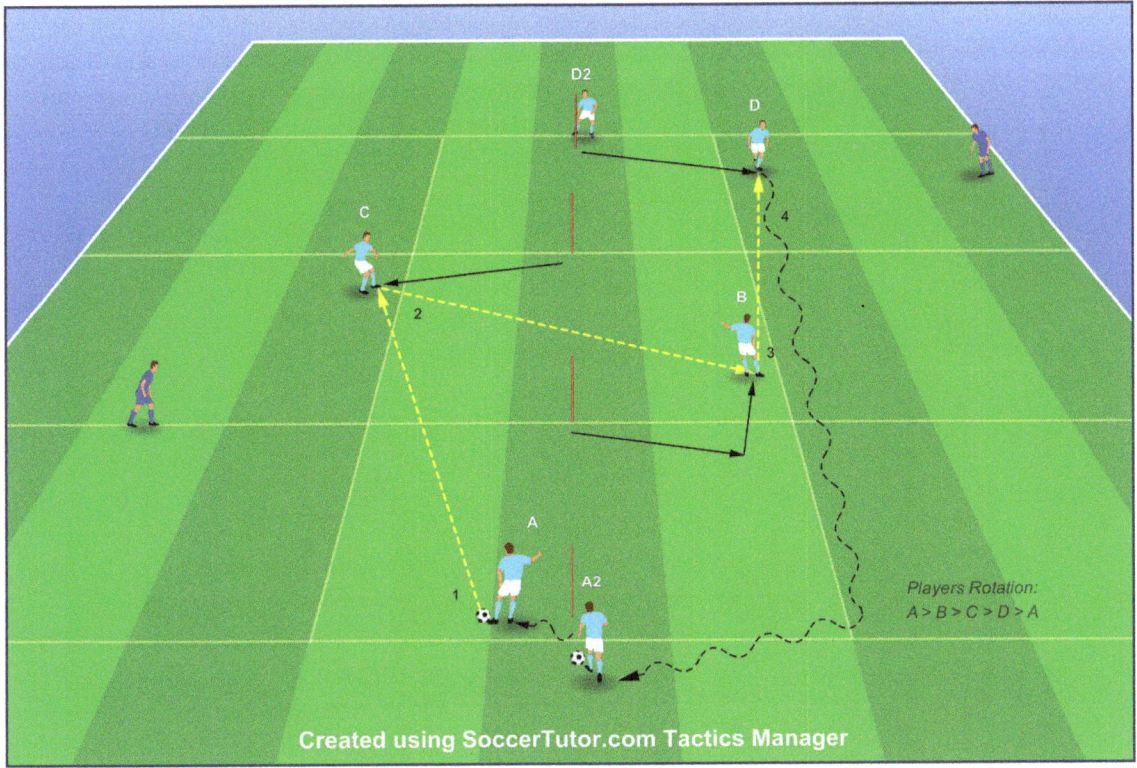

Variation 1 (Diagram Example)

We start with 1 player on each pole + 1 extra player at each end.

The players work in groups of 6 and move the ball through the marked out thirds.

1. **A** passes to **C**, who moves wide to receive.
2. **C** sets the ball back for **B**, who makes a double movement to receive wide on the opposite side.
3. **B** passes forward to **D**, who has moved off the pole at an angle to receive.
4. **D** dribbles the ball forward and around to the starting pole, as shown.

→ All the players rotate to the next position (A → B → C → D2 → D → A2) and **A2** starts the same sequence with a new ball.

Variation 2

A passes to **B**, who sets back to **A**. **A** then passes to **C**, with the rest of the sequence the same as Variation 1.

Coaching Points

1. The important detail is which foot the players pass with and set with (the back foot), which dictates how quickly the players can meet the ball and move it through the thirds.
2. The central players start on the poles, then time their movement away.

Training Session 15 - Pressing from the Front + Defending in Midfield

2. Defensive Organisation and Pressing in a 4v4 (+3) Directional Possession Game

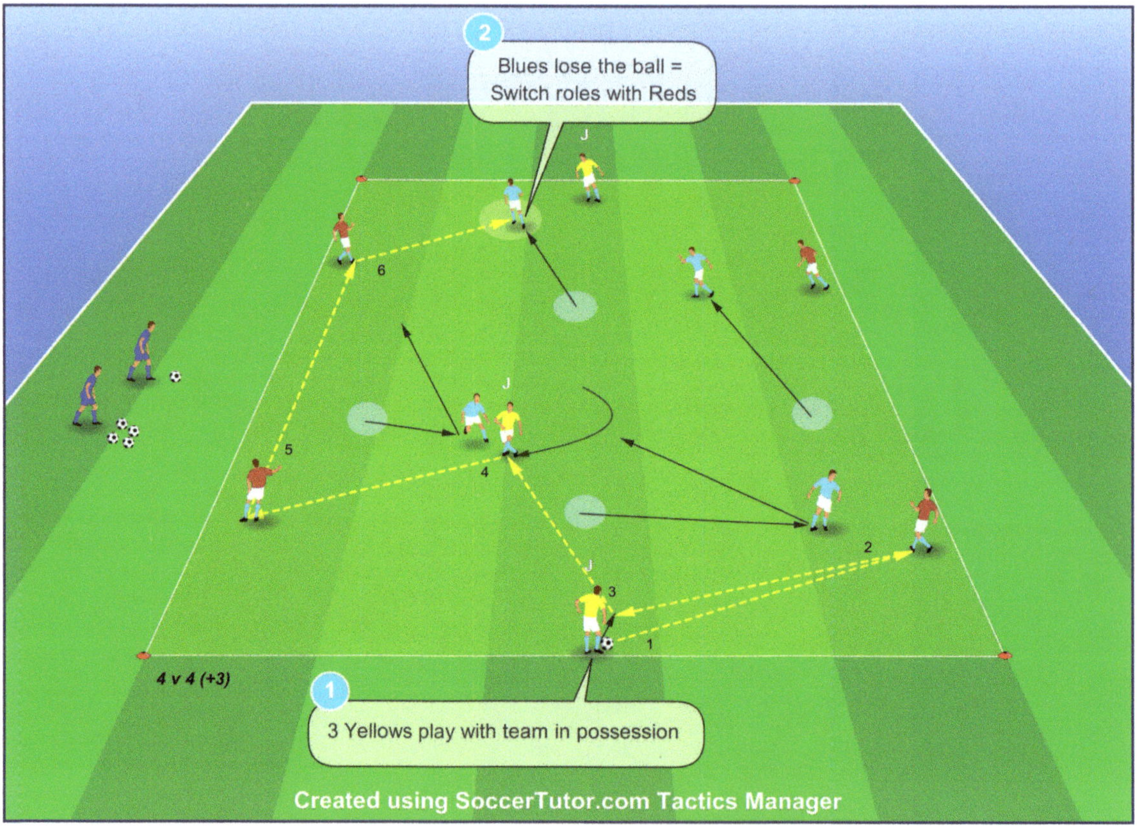

Diagram annotations:
- **2** Blues lose the ball = Switch roles with Reds
- **1** 3 Yellows play with team in possession
- 4 v 4 (+3)
- Created using SoccerTutor.com Tactics Manager

Practice Description

- In a 10 x 15 yard area, we have 2 teams of 4 players (blue and red) + 3 yellow jokers.
- The practice starts with the Coach and the red team try to maintain possession with help from the 3 yellow jokers.
- The blue team work together (pressing) to close off the angles and try to win the ball. If they are able to win the ball, the teams switch roles.
- If you make it position specific, the blue players would be the forward, 2 central midfielders, and 1 defensive midfielder.

Coaching Points

1. The focus is on defensive organisation: How can the 4 defenders stop the 7 playing through and penetrating? Stop the ball being played through the centre.
2. Force the ball down the sides of the defensive diamond to create 1v1 and 2v2 situations
3. Keep the ball in front and protect space in behind. Press quickly as a unit with correct angles and distances.
4. Recognise when to press and when to drop and regroup.

This is a repetition of the practice on Page 112 - it is placed here again as that is how sessions were built at the Manchester City Academy

©SOCCERTUTOR.COM — ELITE ACADEMY COACHING

Training Session 15 - Pressing from the Front + Defending in Midfield

3. Pressing from the Front with Diamond Midfield Shape in a Functional 8v9 (+GK) Practice

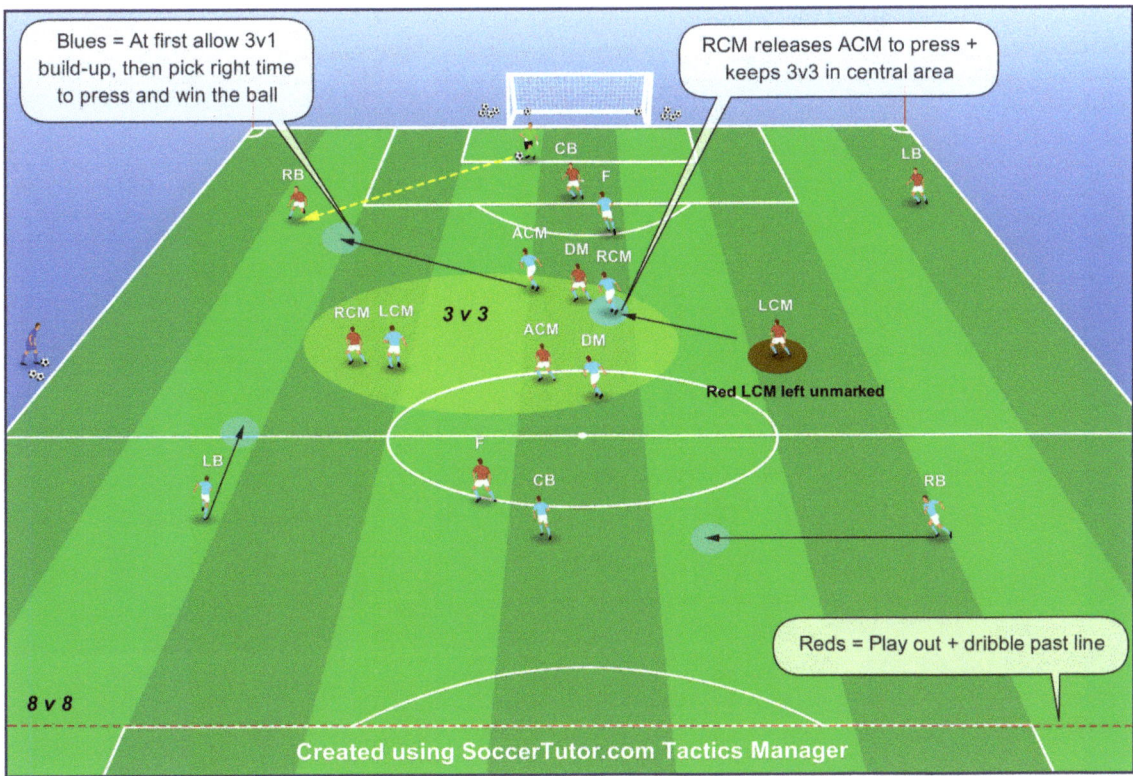

Practice Description

- The red team's GK plays out to a defender and the reds build up play trying to dribble past the red line.

- This blues focus on pressing with a midfield diamond shape (variation). They let the reds have a 3v1 situation to play out, and then it's about the right timing of the press, movements, protecting the depth, and stopping through passes.

- The blue **forward (F)** forces play to one side. The GK plays to red RB, and the blue right central midfielder **(RCM)** moves to mark the red DM. This releases the blue **ACM** to press the ball, while the 3v3 situation in the central area is retained.

- With a diamond midfield shape, the focus is all about securing the middle part of the pitch when the ball is wide (3v3, or even 4v3).

- The left central midfielder **(LCM)** marks his opponent tightly and the defensive midfielder **(DM)** marks the red ACM. The **left back (LB)** moves forward.

- The red LCM is left unmarked because it's a difficult pass and he can be covered by the blue **DM** anyway, as the ball will take time to travel. The **right back (RB)** moves across and the blues leave a 2v1 situation at the back versus the red forward (F).

- The blues try to win the ball and then score on the counter attack.

ELITE ACADEMY COACHING

Training Session 15 - Pressing from the Front + Defending in Midfield

4. Pressing from the Front to "Set the Trap" in a Full Man for Man Pressing Game (10v10 +GK)

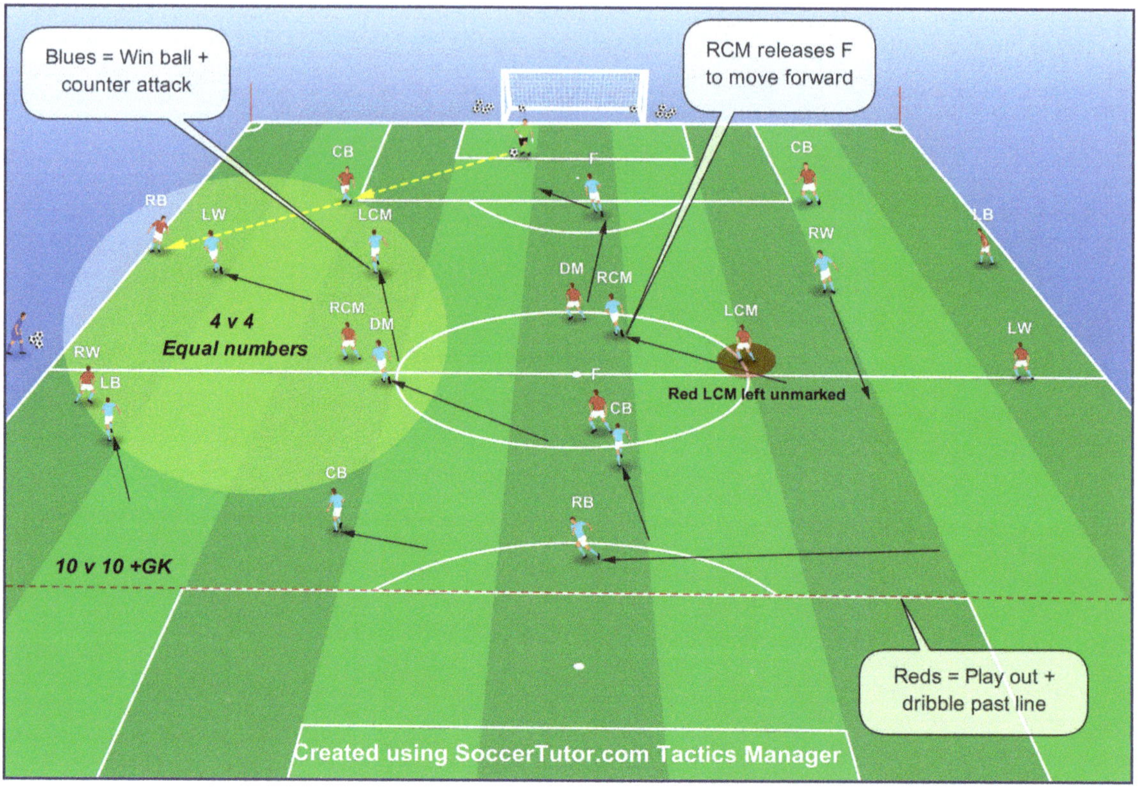

Practice Description

- The red team's GK plays out and the reds build up play trying to play past the red line. The blues try to win the ball and then score on the counter attack.

- The blues implement a full man to man press. The blue **central midfielder (RCM)** moves forward to mark the red DM, which releases the **forward (F)** to be able to press from the front.

- The GK passes to the red CB and the **left central midfielder (LCM)** sprints forward to press the ball. The **defensive midfielder (DM)** moves to mark red RCM.

- This chain reaction is completed with the **centre back (CB)** moving forward to mark the red forward (F).

- The **left winger (LW)** moves to press the red RB once the ball is played to him.

- The blue **left back (LB)** moves forward to mark the red RW. This creates equal numbers (4v4) around the ball area on one side and a good chance for the blues to win the ball.

- The other **centre back (CB)** and the **right back (RB)** shift across to provide balance at the back. The **right winger (RW)** drops back to prevent a switch of play towards the red LW.

This is a repetition of the practice on Page 118 - it is placed here again as that is how sessions were built at the Manchester City Academy

MANCHESTER CITY ACADEMY SESSION 16

Defending Around the Box (1)

Training Session 16 - Defending Around the Box

1. Defending Around the Box and Development of the Defensive Unit Arc when the Ball is Played Wide

Part 1: Pass to the Forward (Close Down and Cover)

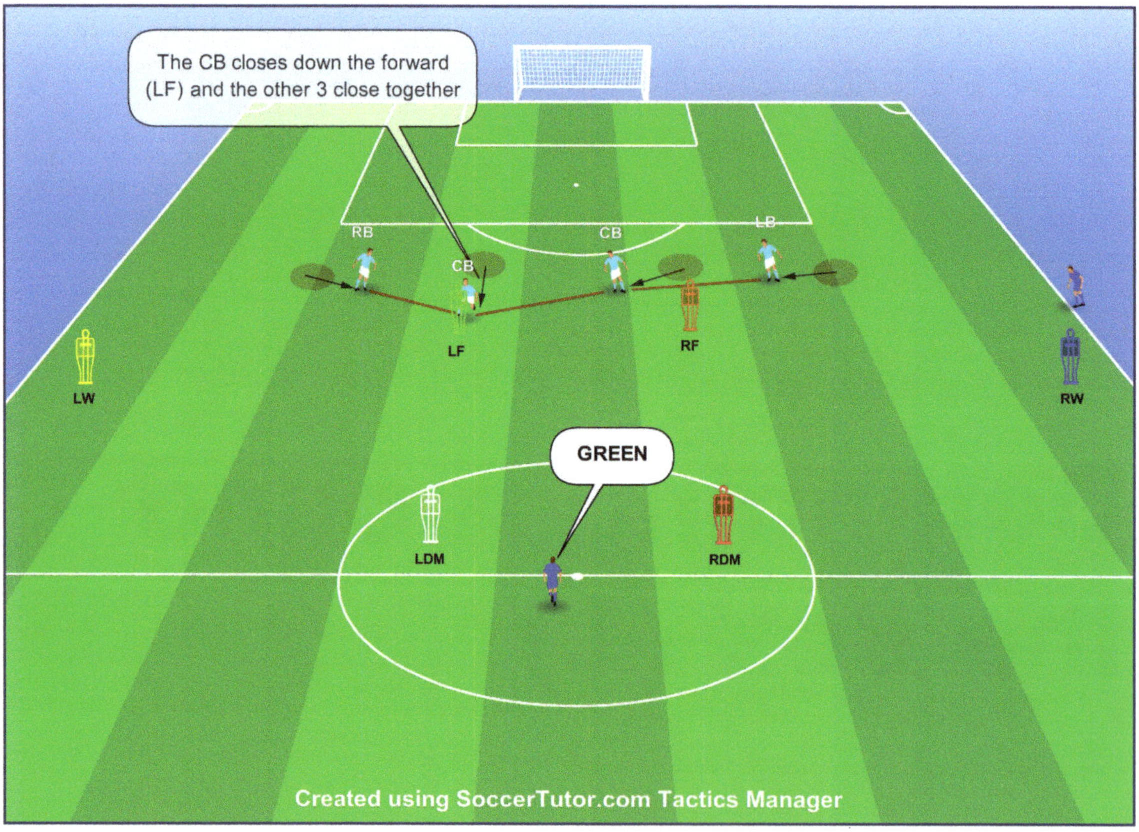

The CB closes down the forward (LF) and the other 3 close together

Practice Description (Part 1)

- Position 6 mannequins in the positions shown which represent the possible positioning of opponents in possession.
- We have the defensive midfielder, who could be on the left or ride side (LDM or RDM), the 2 wingers (LW & RW), and the forward who could be on the left or right side (LF or RF).
- The 4 blue players are organised as a back 4 and start in the positions shown (highlighted circles).
- When the Coach calls out which opposing player the ball has been played to, the back 4 must react collectively in the correct way.
- In Part 1, the Coach calls out **GREEN** relating to the <u>left forward position (LF)</u>.
- The closest blue centre back moves to close down the new ball carrier, and the other 3 defenders move inside to provide cover and defensive solidity/balance.

Training Session 16 - Defending Around the Box

Part 2: Reset and Pass Out Wide to Winger (Defensive Unit Arc)

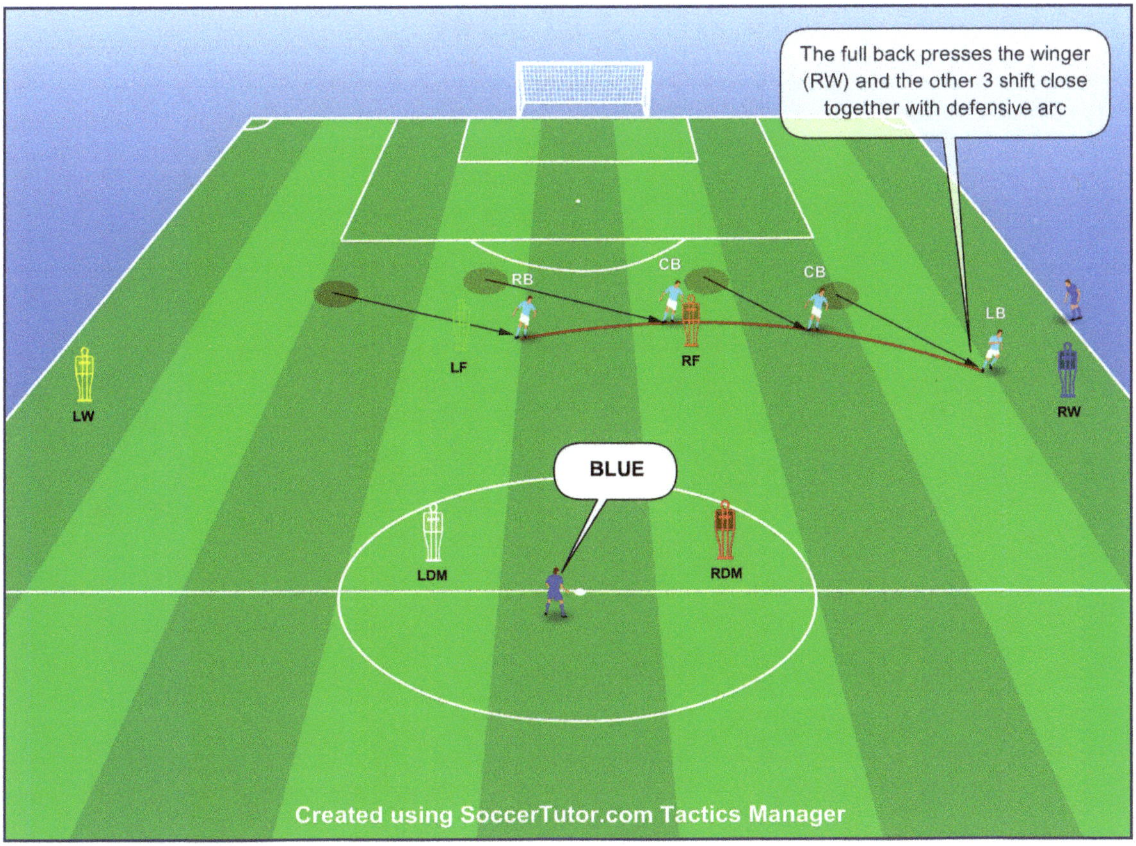

The full back presses the winger (RW) and the other 3 shift close together with defensive arc

Practice Description (Part 2)

- Following on from the previous page, the Coach first calls out **RED** as if the forward has passed the ball back to the **defensive midfielder (RDM)** to reset.

- The Coach then calls out **BLUE** relating to the **right winger position (RW)**, as if the defensive midfielder has played it wide.

- The **left back (LB)** moves to press the new ball carrier and the other 3 defenders shift across together.

- Ideally, you want the players to shift across and form a **Defensive Unit Arc** at the same time, keeping the ball in front by making it as difficult as possible for the opposition to play in behind them.

Coaching Points

1. Keep the correct distances (10-12 yards) and defensive line height relative to whether the ball receiver is in a central or wide position.

2. The defensive unit must travel at the same speed as the ball (as soon as its played / the coach calls out).

3. Body position is important when defending 1v1 and applying pressure to the ball.

4. Also monitor the body positions of the other defenders around and away from the ball.

Training Session 16 - *Defending Around the Box*

2. 8v4 Attacking Overload Non-directional Possession Game with 3 Phases

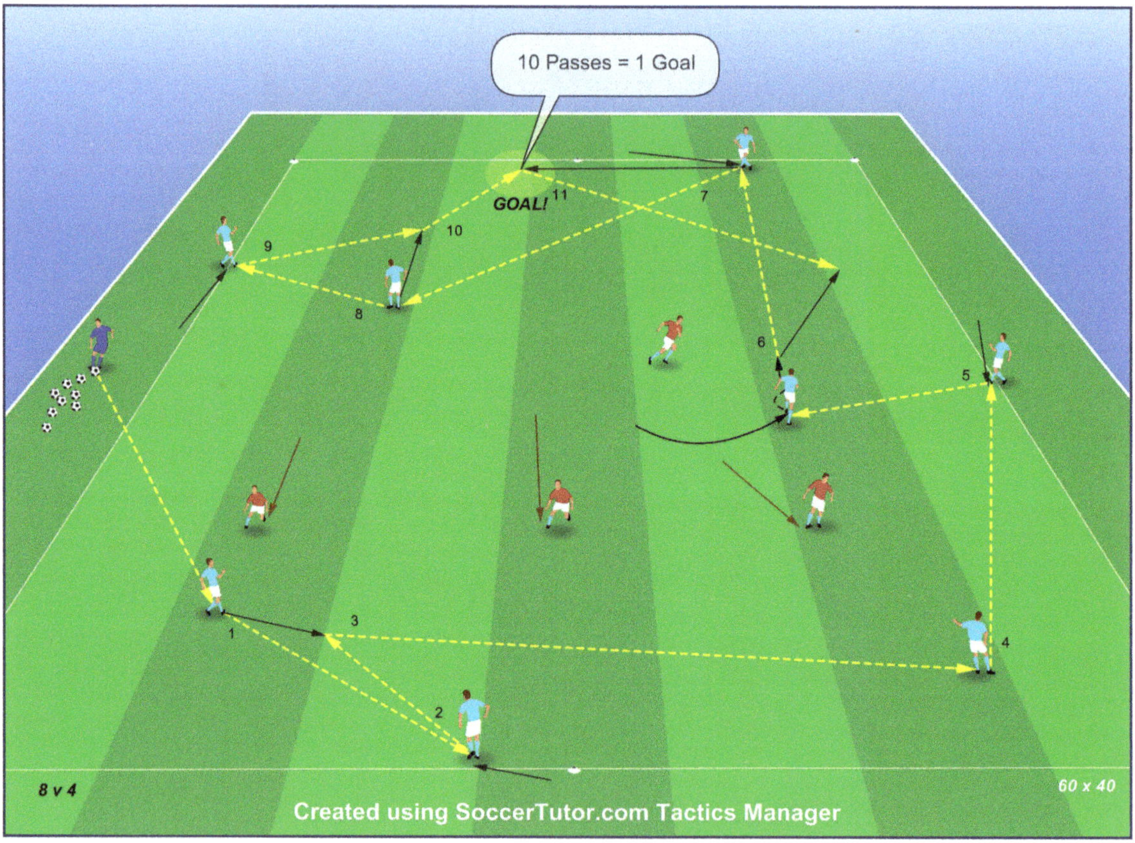

Practice Description

In a 60 x 40 yard area, we play an 8v4 possession game with 3 phases. 10 passes scores <u>1 Point</u>, as does the defending team winning the ball.

Phase 1 (Diagram Example) = 4v4 (+4) possession game with 4 blue players positioned along the 4 sides. The outside players cannot pass to each other, and they cannot move inside the playing area unless the pass is played to them.

Phase 2 = Same as Phase 1 but the inside/outside players rotate after the pass.

Phase 3 = 8v4 with all players inside.

Coaching Points

1. Outside players have 1 touch, so quick support play is needed.
2. In possession, create space. Out of possession, deny space.
3. Possession with a purpose, know when to play round and when to play through.
4. Control the tempo in and out of possession.
5. Shape in and out of possession with good communication.
6. Be ready to attack and defend → Quick reactions to the transition.

Training Session 16 - *Defending Around the Box*

3. Game Related Back 4 Defending Around the Box in a 6v4 (+GK) Phase of Play

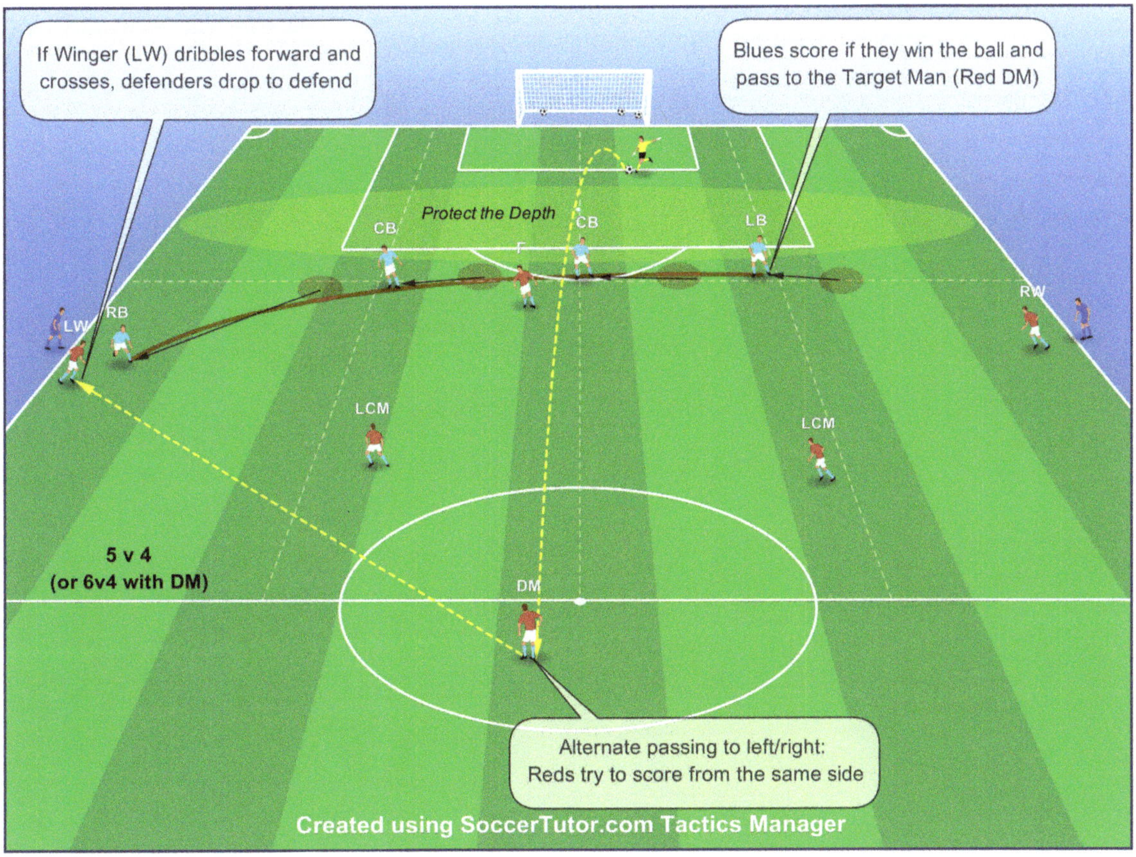

Practice Description

- The GK starts the practice by playing a long pass to the red **defensive midfielder (DM)** on the halfway line, who alternates passing to the left and right sides.

- The red team (either 5 or 6 with DM) try to score playing through the side the ball is played to (left in diagram example).

- The focus of this practice is on the back 4 keeping compact, defending the goal, and trying to win the ball.

- If the blues win the ball, they score by passing to the Target Man (red DM).

Coaching Points

1. Correct angles and distances between the defenders in relation to the width of the pitch and position of the ball.

2. Communication and coordination needed to keep the defensive unit solid.

3. Protect the space in behind and keep the ball in front, utilising the defensive arc shown in the diagram when the ball goes wide.

4. Recognise danger and be ready with the correct body position in relation to the ball.

Training Session 16 - Defending Around the Box

4. Defending Around the Box with Game Principles in an 8v6 (+GK) Position Specific Phase of Play

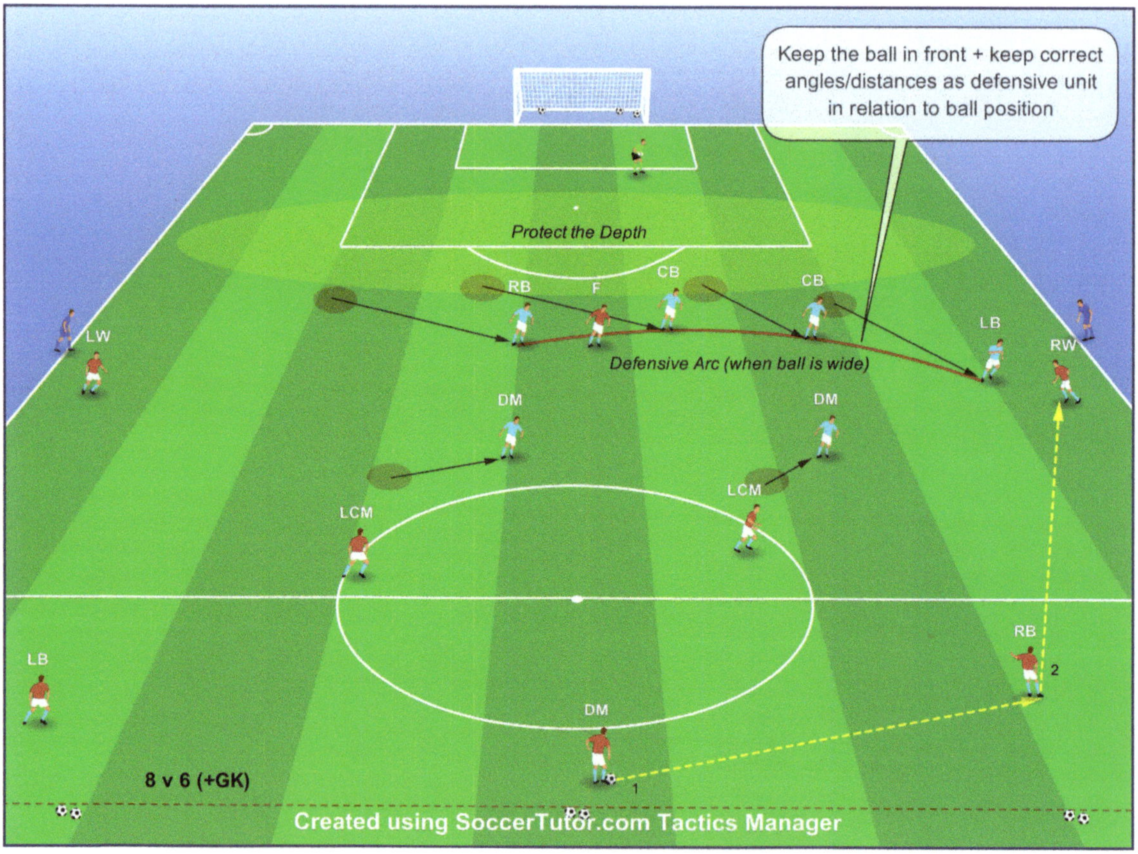

Keep the ball in front + keep correct angles/distances as defensive unit in relation to ball position

Protect the Depth

Defensive Arc (when ball is wide)

8 v 6 (+GK)

Practice Description

- The blues play with their defensive unit (back 4) + 2 defensive midfielders.
- The reds play with their midfield and forward units + 2 full backs.
- The reds build-up play, create attacking overloads and try to score past the GK.
- The blues aim to keep a compact defensive shape with the ball in front of them and use the correct angles and distances in relation to the ball position. If they win the ball, they attempt to dribble over the red line to score 1 Point.

Coaching Points

1. Correct angles and distances between the defensive unit in relation to the ball position.
2. Keep the ball in front and protect the depth.
3. Recognise and communicate when to press and when to drop off.
4. Tight organisation of the defensive unit when the ball is played centrally.
5. Organise the defensive line into a defensive arc when the ball is in an advanced wide area (shown in diagram).

MANCHESTER CITY ACADEMY SESSION 17

Defending Around the Box (2)

Training Session 17 - Defending Around the Box

1. Defending First and Second Phase Long Passes and Crosses Around the Box

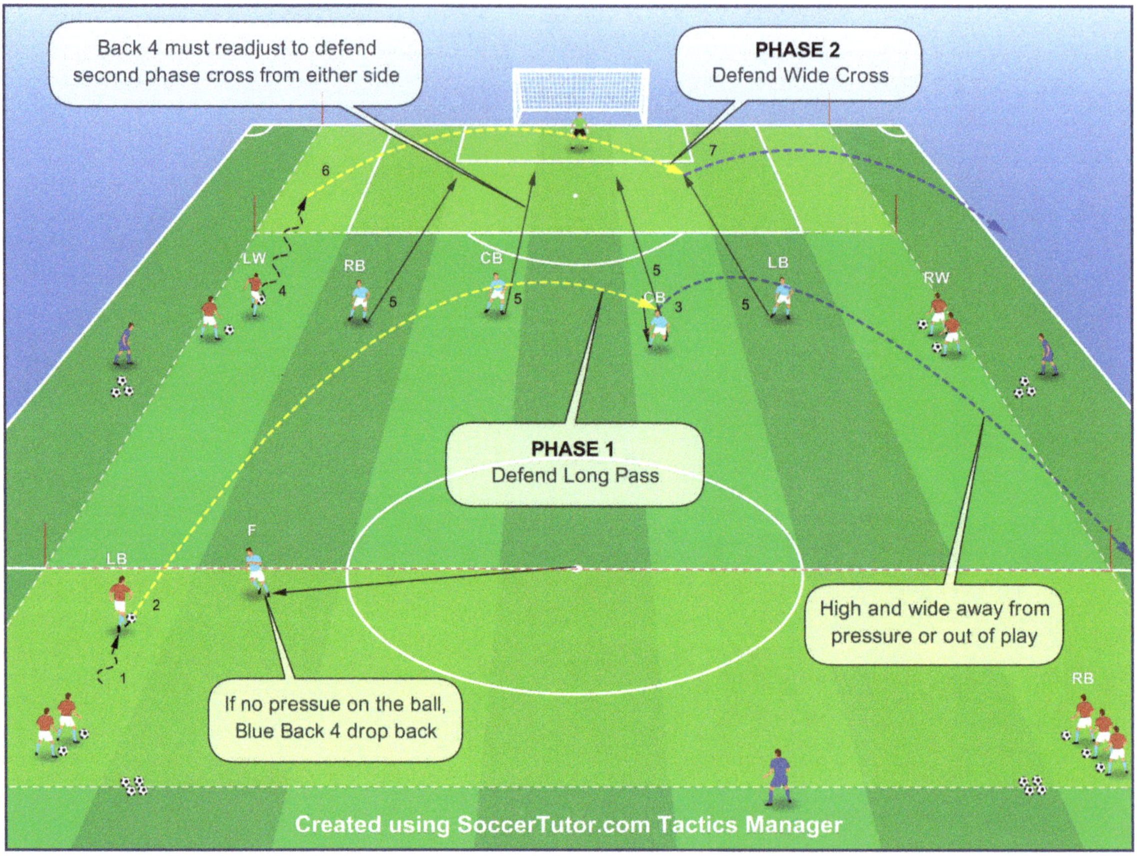

Practice Description

- **NOTE:** For lower age groups/levels, you can use a 60 x 40 yard area.
- The focus of this practice is on the back 4 defending the first and second phases.
- **Phase 1:** A red full back dribbles forward and hits a long pass. The defensive clearance should be high and wide away from pressure, or out of play.
- **Phase 2:** A red winger dribbles forward and delivers a cross into the box. The blue defenders must readjust to defend the second phase cross from either side.

Coaching Points

1. Correct angles and distances between the defenders in relation to the width of the pitch and position of the ball.
2. Defending must be aggressive, decisive, and intelligent.
3. If there is no pressure on the ball, the back 4 drop back a few yards.
4. Should you clear with a header or volley? Should you clear the ball high and wide away from pressure or out of play?
5. The defensive unit must readjust quickly to defend the second phase.

Training Session 17 - Defending Around the Box

2. Game Principles for Defending Around the Box in an 8v8 (+GK) Phase of Play

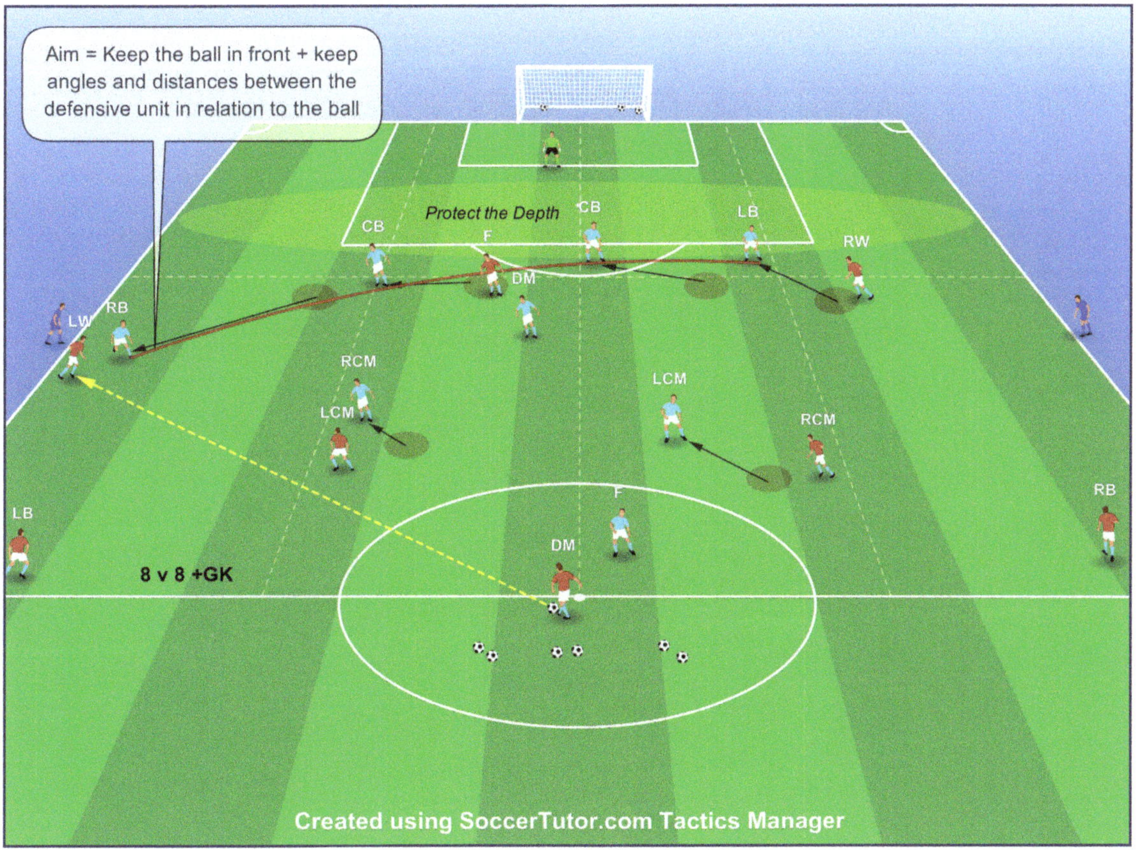

Aim = Keep the ball in front + keep angles and distances between the defensive unit in relation to the ball

Practice Description

- Split the pitch into 4 channels as a reference for the players for their defensive organisation and positioning.
- The practice starts with the red defensive midfielder (DM), who plays to either side. The reds then try to score by attacking through that side (left in diagram).
- The focus of this practice is on the blue team keeping compact, defending the goal, and trying to win the ball.
- If the blues win the ball, they score by passing to the Target Man (red DM).

Coaching Points

1. Correct angles and distances between the defenders in relation to the width of the pitch and position of the ball.
2. Protect the space in behind and keep the ball in front, utilising the defensive arc shown in the diagram when the ball goes wide.
3. Communication for when to drop back and when to press the ball.
4. Make the defensive unit compact when the ball is played central.

Training Session 17 - Defending Around the Box

3. Defending the Box from Crosses in a Functional Practice

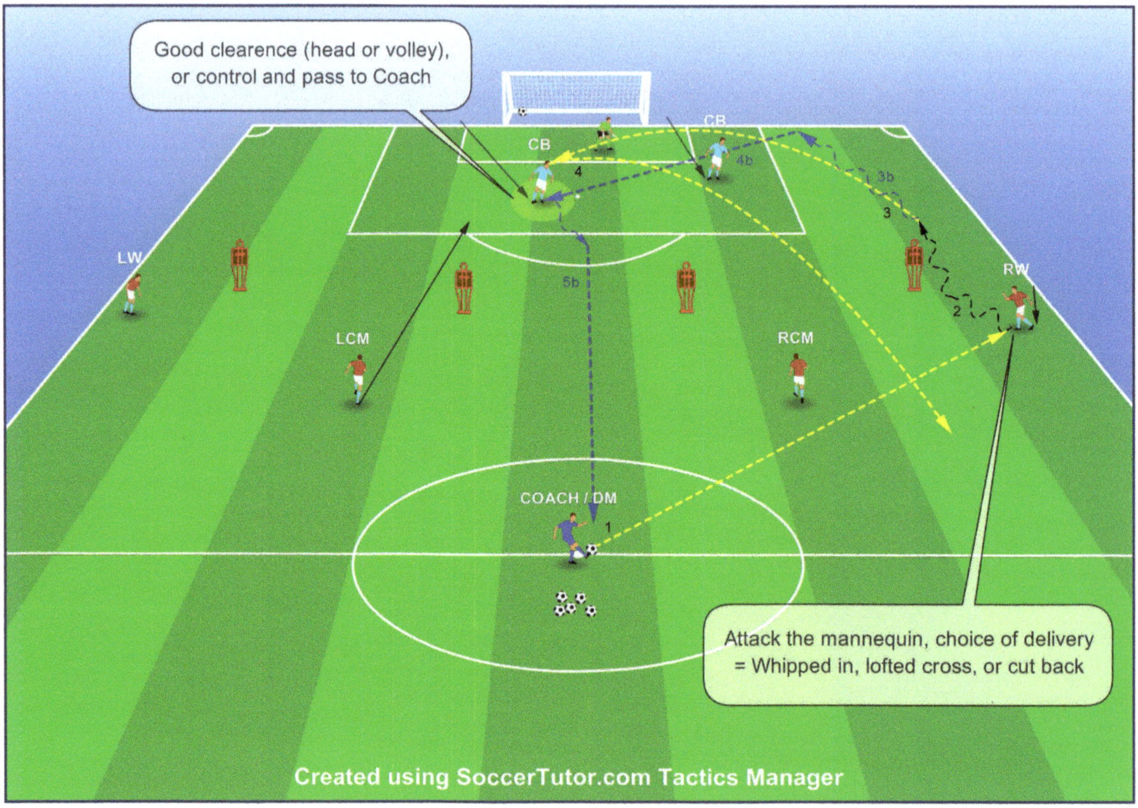

Diagram annotations:
- Good clearance (head or volley), or control and pass to Coach
- Attack the mannequin, choice of delivery = Whipped in, lofted cross, or cut back

Description

- The DM or Coach passes wide to either winger (RW in diagram). The **2 blue centre backs (CB)** enter and take up defensive positions in relation to the ball.

- The red RW attacks the mannequin (opposing full back) at pace and then chooses the best form of delivery: Whipped in, lofted cross, or cut back.

- The blue defenders must be in line with the ball to anticipate the cross and then execute the correct defensive clearance or decision. A good clearance should be with a header or volley back in the direction the ball came from.

- If possible, the defender should try to control and secure possession for his team, starting the build-up phase. You can make the aim to pass to the Coach/DM on the halfway line.

- The GK should also focus on his starting position in relation to the ball, communicate with the defenders, and make the correct decisions in regard to coming to catch the cross or punch, etc.

- If the GK catches the cross, he can also aim to kick or throw the ball to the Coach/DM on the halfway line.

- Make sure to practice defending from a variety of crosses in the defensive third.

Training Session 17 - Defending Around the Box

4. Position Specific Game Related Practice for Zonal 2v3 Defensive Organisation

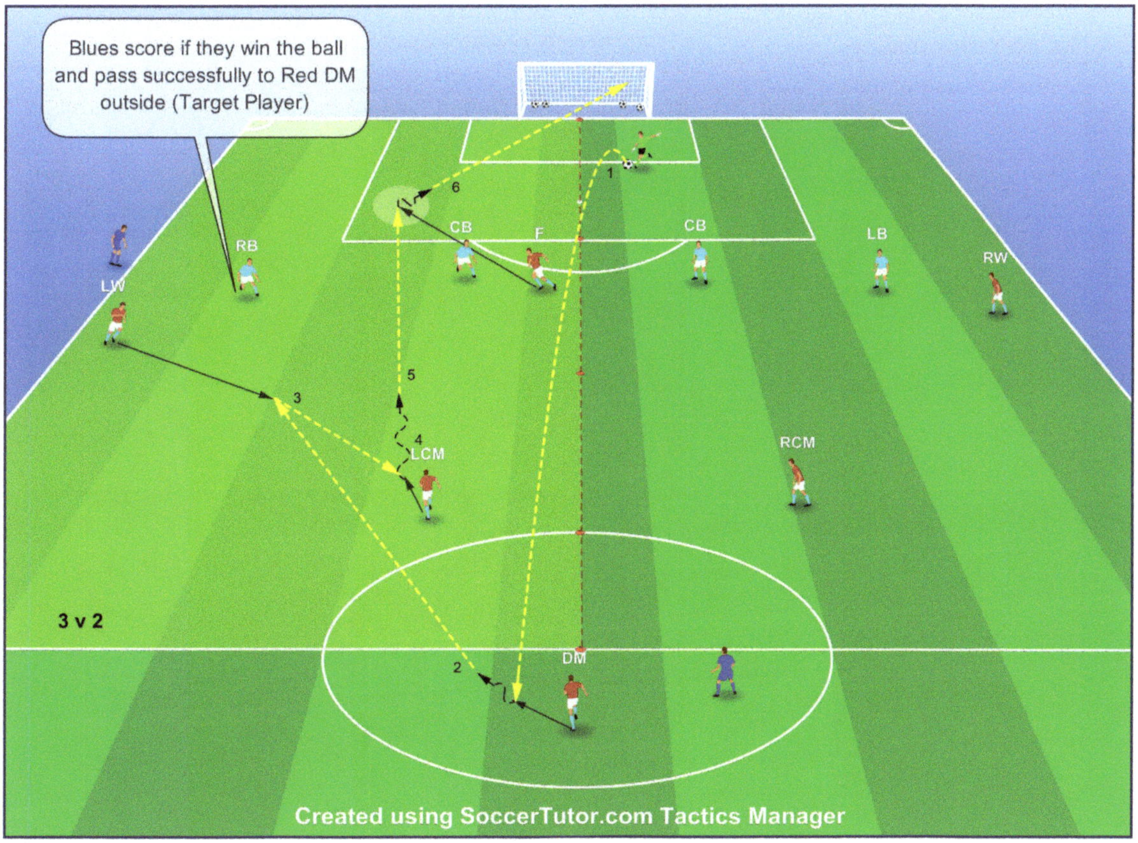

Practice Description

- The GK starts with a long pass to the red defensive midfielder (**DM**). The DM then plays to either side for a 3v2 attack - the forward (F) moves to the relevant side. If the **2 blue defenders (CB & RB)** win the ball, they try to pass to the red DM (target man) = 1 Point.

Progression (Switching Play)

- Once the players feel comfortable, introduce switching play to the other side via the DM. At this point, the half restrictions are removed and the back 4 work together as a unit (6v4 attack).

Coaching Points

1. Stop the ball being played centrally into the forward (F), working as a pair. Be aware of angles and distances in relation to the ball and move with the ball. Keep the ball in front and protect the depth.

2. Force the ball down the sides to create 1v1 and 2v2 situations around the ball.

3. Press quickly as a unit when the angles and distances are correct. Recognise when to press and when to drop off.

4. The deepest defender controls the communication and organisation.

Free Trial

Football Coaching Specialists Since 2001

Tactics Manager
Create your own Practices, Tactics & Plan Sessions!

Tactics Manager App

SoccerTutor.com

Football Coaching Specialists Since 2001

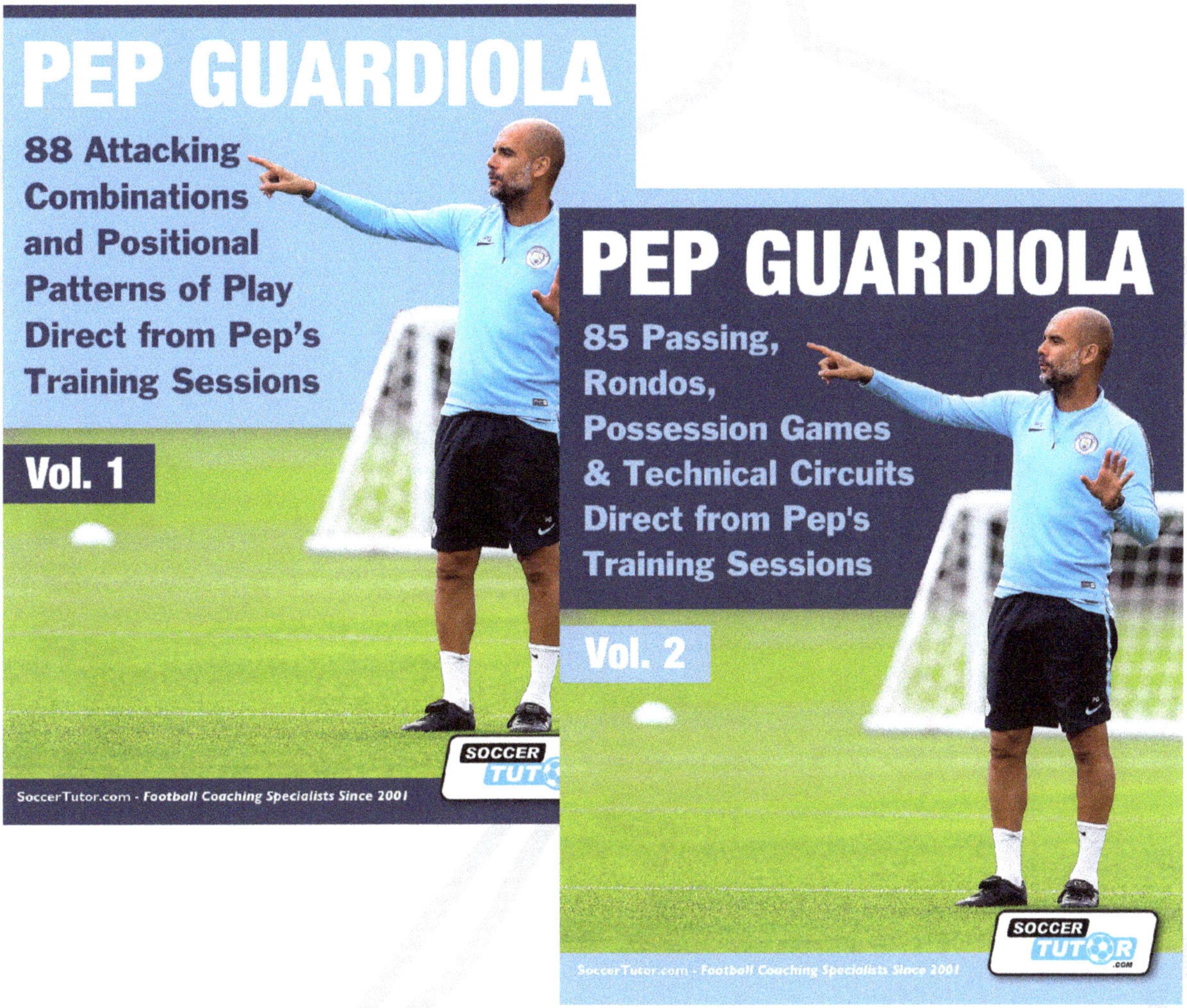

PEP GUARDIOLA
88 Attacking Combinations and Positional Patterns of Play Direct from Pep's Training Sessions
Vol. 1

PEP GUARDIOLA
85 Passing, Rondos, Possession Games & Technical Circuits Direct from Pep's Training Sessions
Vol. 2

Coaching Books Available in Full Colour Print and eBook!
PC | Mac | iPhone | iPad | Android Phone / Tablet | Chromebook

 **FREE** Coach Viewer **APP**

SoccerTutor.com

www.ingramcontent.com/pod-product-compliance
Lightning Source LLC
Chambersburg PA
CBHW040932240426
43673CB00051B/1960